M000280765

HIMALAYA

HIMALAYA

A Literary Homage
to Adventure, Meditation,
and Life on the Roof of the World

EDITED BY

RUSKIN BOND &
NAMITA GOKHALE

SHAMBHALA BOULDER 2018

Shambhala Publications, Inc.
4720 Walnut Street
Boulder, Colorado 80301
www.shambhala.com

9 8 7 6 5 4 3 2

Printed in Canada

♾ This edition is printed on acid-free paper that meets the
American National Standards Institute z39.48 Standard.
♻ This book is printed on 100% postconsumer recycled paper.
For more information please visit www.shambhala.com.
Shambhala Publications is distributed worldwide by Penguin Random House, Inc.,
and its subsidiaries.

Library of Congress Cataloging-in-Publication Data
Names: Bond, Ruskin, editor. | Gokhale, Namita, 1956– editor.
Title: Himalaya: a literary homage to adventure, meditation, and life on the roof of the world/ edited by Ruskin Bond and Namita Gokhale.
Description: First U.S. edition. | Boulder: Shambhala, 2018. | "First published in India by Speaking Tiger Publishing in 2016.: | Includes bibliographical references.
Identifiers: LCCN 2017038612 | ISBN 9781611805901 (pbk.: alk. paper)·
Subjects: LCSH: Himalaya Mountains Region—Description and travel.
Classification: LCCDS485.H6 H5484 2018 | DDC 915.49604—dc23
LC record available at https://lccn.loc.gov/2017038612

In a thousand ages of the gods I could not
tell thee of the glories of the Himalaya . . .

—The Puranas

CONTENTS

MEDITATIONS

LIFE

PREFACE

Some years ago I asked a sailor to describe the most exciting moment of a long sea voyage, and without hesitation he said: "My first sight of land!" And when I asked a landlocked villager from the mountains to describe his most exciting moment, he replied: "The first time I saw the sea."

It is always what lies beyond the horizon that excites us the most, and a seaman has this advantage, that his ship is almost always on the move, from sea to sea, and port to port, while the mountain-dweller is often confined to a particular range or valley. And no matter how beautiful the mountain or the valley, it can grow monotonous after some time. Life in an Indian hill-station is pleasant enough, but two weeks in a remote village at the end of a day-long trek, without electricity or a toilet, and the visitor is soon pining for the fleshpots of the cities.

It isn't surprising, then, that the mountains have been celebrated in prose more often by travelers looking back at a brief adventure than by residents who brave the elements year after year.

The mountainous lands, and the Himalaya in particular, are visited by travelers, explorers, climbers, naturalists, pilgrims. These are people who are evanescent, who come and go and vanish, occasionally giving us their impressions in the books and journals which describe their personal experiences, but they tell us little or nothing about the people who eke out a living on hostile mountain slopes. Only a very few have left enduring and insightful records of their experiences. This is particularly true of those who come in order to "conquer" mountain peaks. In India, Nepal, climbers turn up every year—a handful once, but now in their hundreds—toiling up the slopes of Everest or some other challenging peak and in the process littering the mountain slopes with a trail of garbage as an offering of thanks to the guardian spirits of the Himalaya.

Just occasionally a Frank Smythe comes along, or a Rahul Sankrit-yayan, with a literary bent and a feeling for both mountains and mountain people. The best of them feature in the first two parts of this collection and make for compelling reading.

There is plenty to choose from, as far as accounts of climbing expeditions go. Edmund Hillary has left us a step-by-hazardous-step description of his ascent of Everest; Sven Hedin is more animated in his narrative. Mallory and Younghusband have had their moments and memories. And we have an extraordinary account of a "mutiny" on Kanchenjunga by Aleister Crowley, the self-avowed "wickedest man in the world," who dabbled in black magic and devil worship and became the subject of several sensational biographies such as *The Magical Record of the Great Beast 666*. In his account of an abortive attempt at Kanchenjunga he is at pains to present himself as a nice guy and the ideal leader; even so, he was deserted by most of his companions.

Crowley is, however, genuinely funny at times, especially in his description of the Darjeeling climate; and humor is rare in mountain writing. Climbers are apt to become irritable and quarrelsome when they ascend to great heights, and altitude sickness doesn't help.

The inclusion of an essay by Mark Twain provides welcome relief. He genuinely enjoys his hand-car ride down the railway track from Darjeeling, and he conveys his enjoyment to the reader. The surprise, for many readers in English, will be the Hindi writer Rahul Sankrit-yayan, who writes with a light touch, moving effortlessly from humor to contemplation.

We should remember that mountains are impersonal. You can climb a peak but you can't possess it. It is simply *there*, serene and impervious to your love or hate, and it will be there long after you and I are gone. But sometimes they shift, as we saw last year when an earthquake ran through Nepal, flattening dwellings and causing massive avalanches in the higher reaches of the Himalaya. And in the Indian Himalaya, in Uttarakhand, unseasonal heavy rains and flash floods devastated entire villages and townships, changing the landscape and geography of an entire mountain range. It has happened before; it will happen again.

Yes, the mountains are impersonal, for beauty really exists in the beholder's eye. Once, admiring the view from a fallow field, I commented on the beautiful sunset. My companion, whose crop had been destroyed in a hailstorm, responded: "But you cannot eat sunsets."

The reality of life in the Himalaya has rarely been described as convincingly as in the final part of this volume, which is also my favorite section. Jemima Diki Sherpa, Namita Gokhale, Manjushree Thapa, Bill Aitken, Kirin Narayan, and others bring genuine insight and empathy to their accounts, perhaps because they have lived in the Himalaya themselves. Dom Moraes and Amitav Ghosh prove to be sensitive and intelligent travelers.

Living in the mountains is not a romance for everyone. Wresting a living from the stony, calcified soil does not leave much time for poetry and contemplation. Even so, the mountains have become very personal to me, as they have to other writers who have made their homes here. The changing colors of the hillside, the trees, birds, cicadas, horse-chestnuts, pine cones, cow bells, mule trains, the rain on old tin roofs, the wind in tall deodars, wild flowers in the morning dew—all these things are largely personal, appealing to both the spiritual and sensual in our own natures. If we haven't produced much literature, it is probably because we have still to come to terms with the majesty of these great mountains. Or, perhaps, the Himalaya have taught us humility. We know that just living, and helping our fellow creatures through life, is enough; it is greater than any art.

RUSKIN BOND
Landour, Mussoorie
June 2016

INTRODUCTION

This collection of essays and musings evokes the majesty of the tallest, and youngest, mountains in the world—sky-high peaks that were once the ocean floor.

Variously known as Sagarmatha, Chomolungma, or Everest, the highest peak on our planet stands tall at 8,848 meters. Its neighbors are equally grand: Kanchenjunga (8,598 meters), Makalu (8,481 meters), and Dhaulagiri (8,167 meters). It is but natural that the Himalayan range has inspired awe and wonder since the beginning of mankind. It is Giri-raj, the King of Mountains.

In the opening segment of this collection—"Adventures"—Edmund Hillary tells us of his famous first ascent with Tenzing Norgay in 1953. Hillary recalls,

> But mixed with the relief was a vague sense of astonishment that I should have been the lucky one to attain the ambition of so many brave and determined climbers. It seemed difficult at first to grasp that we'd got there. I was too tired and too conscious of the long way down to safety really to feel any great elation. But as the fact of our success thrust itself more clearly into my mind, I felt a quiet glow of satisfaction spread through my body—a satisfaction less vociferous but more powerful than I had ever felt on a mountaintop before. I turned and looked at Tenzing. Even beneath his oxygen mask and the icicles hanging from his hair, I could see his infectious grin of sheer delight. I held out my hand and in silence we shook in good Anglo-Saxon fashion. But this was not enough for Tenzing and impulsively he threw his arm around my shoulders and we thumped each other on the back in mutual congratulations.

Navigating this remarkable book, the reader gets very different views of the Himalayan massif. The second section, "Meditations," comprises the writings of poets, mystics, and seers, such as Swami Vivekananda, as well excerpts from classics like Peter Matthiessen's *The Snow Leopard* and Andrew Harvey's *A Journey in Ladakh*.

But there are also surprises: the Himalaya alter the souls of even those who do not come to them, or behold them, as seekers. The imperial adventurer Francis Younghusband writes, in "Sunlight on Kinchinjunga":

> A sense of solemn aspiration comes upon us as we view the mountain. We are uplifted. The entire scale of being is raised. Our outlook on life seems all at once to have been heightened. And not only is there this sense of elevation: we seem purified also. Meanness, pettiness, paltriness seem to shrink away abashed at the sight of that radiant purity.

And in the third section, "Life," Bill Aitken describes how he and his companion Prithwi, initially unimpressed by the Valley of Flowers, returned to find unexpected beauty:

> I came across in a protected dell the first outburst of flowers in the form of crocuses. The dew on their golden petals glowed like diamonds in the cold sun and I beckoned Prithwi to descend and see how the valley had won its reputation for beauty. She grumbled at having to lose height but once in the magic dell was bewitched by the tenderness of nature's new leaf. . . . The intensity of the beauty in its uncurled potential seemed more wonderful than the even spread of a thousand species in full blossom.

This final section is more within the immediate range of experience of a native pahari and armchair traveler like myself. The peerless Ruskin Bond, for example, takes us to a village in Garhwal. He sets the scene with a moving description of the Himalayas "striding away into an immensity of sky." He spends many days with the residents of the village, watching how they fashion a life for themselves in the difficult terrain where "pale women plow," laughing at the thunder "as their men go down to the plains for work; for little grows on the beautiful mountains in the north wind."

From his last evening in the village, he brings back this magical memory:

> The moon has not yet risen. Lanterns swing in the dark. The lanterns flit silently over the hillside and go out one by one. This Garhwali day, which is just like any other day in the hills, slips quietly into the silence of the mountains. I stretch myself out on my cot. Outside the small

window the sky is brilliant with stars. As I close my eyes, someone brushes against the lime tree, brushing its leaves; and the fresh fragrance of limes comes to me on the night air, making the moment memorable for all time.

Nostalgia and sepia-tinted views yield to present realities. In a characteristically intense and thoughtful piece, Amitav Ghosh transports us to the troubled vale of Kashmir, where men and mountains meet amidst the toxic "altitude sickness" of warmongers and politics. On the highest battleground on earth, India and Pakistan are locked in tragic, pointless conflict:

It is generally agreed that the [Siachen] glacier has absolutely no strategic, military or economic value whatsoever. It is merely an immense, slowly moving mass of compacted snow and ice, seventy miles long and over a mile deep.

This, then, is the Himalaya, where life unfolds in all its grace and terror, revealing as much as it withholds. This anthology attempts to capture some of its complexity and vastness, traveling through time, place, and altitude. Beauty and melancholy, courage and defeat, philosophy and poetry surprise and illuminate us in these pages. What remains in the end is the sense of intimacy, the exhilaration, and yes, the desolation, of these rugged mountains, the "self-born mockers of man's enterprise."

NAMITA GOKHALE
Nainital
June 2016

ADVENTURES

You don't conquer Everest—you sneak up on it and get the hell outta there.

—ED VIESTURS

THE TRAVELS OF FA-HIEN*

H. A. Giles (Trans.)

Along the route [southwest from Karashar in northwestern China] they found the country uninhabited; the difficulty of crossing rivers was very great; and the hardships they went through were beyond all comparison. After being on the road a month and five days they succeeded in reaching Khotan.

This country is prosperous and happy; its people are well-to-do; they have all received the Faith, and find their amusement in religious music. The priests number several tens of thousands, most of them belonging to the Greater Vehicle. They all obtain their food from a common stock. The people live scattered about; and before the door of every house they build small pagodas, the smallest of which would be about twenty feet in height. They prepare rooms for traveling priests, and place them at the disposal of priests who are their guests, together with anything else they may want. The ruler of the country lodged Fa-Hien and his companions comfortably in a monastery, called Gomati, which belonged to the Greater Vehicle. At the sound of a gong, three thousand priests assemble to eat. When they enter the refectory, their demeanor is grave and ceremonious; they sit down in regular order; they all keep silence; they make no clatter with their bowls, etc.; and for the attendants to serve more food, they do not call out to them, but only make signs with their hands. Hui-ching, Tao-cheng, and Hui-ta, started in advance toward the country of Kashgar; but Fa-Hien and the others, wishing to see the processions of images, stayed on for three months . . .

* Between 399 and 412 C.E., the Chinese Buddhist monk traveled from China to India, Sri Lanka and back. This extract from his travel accounts describes his journey through Buddhist sites and kingdoms in the Hindukush and western Himalaya region.

Seven or eight *li* to the west of the city, there is a monastery called the King's New Monastery. It took eighty years to build and the reigns of three kings before it was completed. It is about two hundred fifty feet in height, ornamentally carved and overlaid with gold and silver, suitably finished with all the seven preciosities. Behind the pagoda there is a Hall of Buddha which is most splendidly decorated. Its beams, pillars, folding doors, and windows are all gilt. Besides this, there are apartments for priests, also beautifully and fitly decorated, beyond expression in words. The kings of the six countries to the east of the Bolor-Tagh range make large offerings of whatsoever most valuable things they may have, keeping few for their own personal use.

The processions of the fourth moon being over, one of the party, Seng-shao, set out with a Tartar Buddhist toward Kashmir, and Fa-Hien and the others went on to Karghalik, which they reached after a journey of twenty-five days. The king of this country is devoted to the Faith; and there are more than one thousand priests, mostly belonging to the Greater Vehicle.

After stopping here for fifteen days, the party went south for four days, and entering upon the Bolor-Tagh range, arrived at the country of Tash-Kurghan, where they went into retreat.

When this retreat was finished, they journeyed on for twenty-five days and reached the country of Kashgar, where they rejoined Hui-ching and his party. The king of this country was holding the *pancha parishad*, which is called in Chinese "the great quinquennial assembly." To this he invites Shamans from all quarters, and these collect together like clouds. The place where the priests are to sit is splendidly adorned beforehand with streaming pennants and canopies of silk; silk, embroidered with lotus flowers in gold and silver, is also laid over the backs of the seats. When all is in order, the king and his ministers make their offerings according to rite. The assembly may last for one, two, or three months, and is generally held in the spring . . .

This country is mountainous and cold; and with the exception of wheat, no grain will grow and ripen. When the priests have received their annual (land) tithes, the mornings forthwith become frosty; therefore the king is always urging the priests to get the wheat ripe before pay-day.

This country has a spittoon which belonged to Buddha; it is made of stone and of the same color as his alms bowl. There is also one of Buddha's teeth, for which the people have raised a pagoda. There are over one thousand priests, all belonging to the Lesser Vehicle. From the hills eastward, the people wear coarse clothes like the Chinese, the only difference being that the former use felt and serge. The observations of the Faith by the Shamans are varied, and too numerous to be recorded here. This country is in the middle of the Bolor-Tagh range; and from this onward all plants, trees, and fruits are different from those of China, with the exception of the bamboo, pomegranate, and sugarcane.

From this point traveling westward toward northern India, the pilgrims after a journey of one month succeeded in crossing the Bolor-Tagh range. On these mountains there is snow in winter and summer alike. There are also venomous dragons, which, if provoked, spit forth poisonous winds, rain, snow, sand, and stones. Of those who encounter these dangers, not one in ten thousand escapes. The people of that part are called men of the Snow Mountains.

On passing this range the travelers were in northern India. Just at the frontier there is a small country, called Darel, where also there are many priests, all of the Lesser Vehicle. In this country there was formerly a Lo-han who, using his divine power, carried a clever artisan up to the Tushita heavens to observe the height, complexion, and features of the Bodhisattva Maitreya, so that when he came down he might carve an image of him in wood. Altogether he made three journeys for observation and afterward executed an image eighty feet in height, the folded legs of which measured eight feet across. On fast-days it always shines with a brilliant light. The kings of near countries vie with one another in their offerings to it. From of old until now, it has been on view in this place.

Keeping to the range, the party journeyed on in a southwesterly direction for fifteen days over a difficult, precipitous, and dangerous road, the side of the mountain being like a stone wall ten thousand feet in height. On nearing the edge, the eye becomes confused; and wishing to advance, the foot finds no resting-place. Below there is a river, named Indus. The men of former times had cut away the rock to make a way down, and had placed ladders on the side of the rock. There are seven hundred rock-steps in all; and when these and the ladders have been negotiated, the river is crossed by a suspension bridge of ropes. The two banks of the river are somewhat less than eighty paces apart. According to the *Records of the Nine Interpreters*, neither Chang Ch'ien nor Kan

Ying of the Han dynasty reached this point. Various priests had asked Fa-Hien if he knew when Buddhism first went eastward, to which Fa-Hien replied, "When I inquired of the people of those parts, they all said that according to an old tradition Shamans from India began to bring the Sutras and Disciplines across this river from the date of setting up the image of Maitreya Bodhisattva." This image was put up about three hundred years after the Nirvana of Buddha, which occurred during the reign of King P'ing of the Chou dynasty (770–719 B.C.E.); hence it was said that the Great Doctrine began to spread abroad from the setting up of the image . . .

Having crossed the river, the pilgrims arrived at the country of Udyana [Swat] which lies due north of India. The language of Central India is universally used here, Central India being what they call the "Middle Kingdom." The clothes and food of the people are also very like those of our Middle Kingdom, and the religion of Buddha is extremely flourishing. They call the places where the priests live or temporarily lodge "Gardens for Assembly" or monasteries. There are altogether five hundred of them, all belonging to the Lesser Vehicle. If any wandering mendicant-priests arrive, they are found in everything for three days, after which they are told to shift for themselves. Tradition says that when Buddha came to Northern India he visited this country, and left behind him a footprint. The footprint appears to be long or short according to the faith in each particular person, and such remains the case up to the present day. The stone too on which Buddha dried his clothes, and the spot where he converted the wicked dragon, may also still be seen. The stone is fourteen feet in height by over twenty in breadth, and one side of it is smooth. Hui-ching, Tao-cheng, and Hui-ta now went on ahead toward "Buddha's Shadow" in the country of Nagarahara [Nangarhar, Afghanistan]. Fa-Hien and the others remained in this country for their summer retreat; and when that was over, they went down southward to the country south of Udyana.

In this country the religion of Buddha is also very flourishing. Of old, Indra, God of Heaven, in order to try the Bodhisattva (as Buddha then was), caused the appearance of a kite pursuing a dove. The Bodhisattva cut off a piece of his flesh to ransom the dove; and when he had perfected his faith and become the Buddha, wandering hither with his disciples, he said, "This is the spot where I cut off my flesh to ransom a dove." Thus the people of the country came to know it, and erected at the place a pagoda ornamented with both gold and silver.

From this point descending eastwards for five days, the pilgrims arrived at the country of Gandhara, which was governed by Fa-i, the son of King Asoka. It was here that Buddha, when a Bodhisattva, sacrificed his eyes for a fellow creature; and it was here too that a pagoda was erected, ornamented with both gold and silver. The people of the country belong mostly to the Lesser Vehicle.

At a distance of seven days' journey eastward from this, there is a country named Takshasila, which in Chinese means "cutting off the head." When Buddha was a Bodhisattva, it was here that he sacrificed his head for a fellow creature; hence the name. After again traveling eastward for two days, the pilgrims arrived at the place where he gave his body to feed a hungry tiger. At both the above spots great pagodas were built, adorned with all the preciosities combined. The kings, ministers, and people of the neighboring countries vie with one another in making offerings, scattering flowers, and lighting lamps, continuously without intermission. Together with the above-mentioned two pagodas, the people of the district call them the Four Great Pagodas.

Traveling from Gandhara southward for seven days, the pilgrims arrived at the country of Peshawur . . .

Buddha's alms bowl being in this country, the king of the Ephthalites formerly got together a large army and attacked, with a view to carrying off the bowl. When he had conquered the country, as he himself was an ardent believer in the religion of Buddha, he wished to take possession of the bowl, and therefore began to make offerings. When he had made his offering to the Precious Trinity, he richly decorated a huge elephant and placed the bowl on its back. Thereupon the elephant promptly collapsed and was unable to move. A four-wheeled cart was then made to convey the bowl, and a team of eight elephants was harnessed to it. When these, too, were unable to stir, the king knew that his hour for possession of the bowl had not yet come. Filled with shame and regret, he built a pagoda on the spot and also a monastery, leaving a garrison to guard the bowl and making all kinds of offerings. There are here perhaps over seven hundred priests; and when it is just on noon, they bring out the bowl and, together with the people, present all kinds of offerings. They then eat their midday meal; and in the evening, at the hour for vespers, they replace the bowl as before. It holds perhaps over two pecks, and is of several colors, chiefly black. The four joinings (of the four bowls fused by Buddha into one) are clearly distinguishable. It is about one-fifth of an inch thick, of transparent brilliancy and of a glossy luster. Poor people throw in a few flowers, and it is full; very rich people wishing to make an offering of a large quantity of flowers, may throw in a hundred or thousand or ten thousand bushels, without ever filling it.

Pao-yun and Seng-ching merely made their offerings and went back home; Hui-ching, Hui-ta, and Tao-cheng had previously gone on to the country of Nagarahara to present offerings before the shadow, tooth, and skull bone of Buddha. Hui-ying now fell ill, and Tao-cheng remained to nurse him; Hui-ta went back alone to Peshawur, where he met the others; and then Hui-ta, Pao-yun, and Seng-ching returned to China. Hui-ying fulfilled his destiny at the Buddha-Bowl Monastery, and Fa-Hien went on alone toward the place of Buddha's skull bone.

Traveling westward sixteen yojanas, Fa-Hien reached the frontier of Nagarahara. In the city of Hiro (= bone; now Hidda) there is a shrine which contains Buddha's skull bone, entirely covered with gold leaf and ornamented with the seven preciosities. The king of the country deeply venerates this skull bone and, fearing lest it should be stolen, has appointed eight men of the leading families in the kingdom to hold each of them a seal, with which to seal and guard the shrine and bone. In the early morning, when the eight have all arrived, and each one has inspected his own seal, they open the door; they next wash their hands in scented water, and then bring out the skull bone which they place on a high altar outside the shrine, resting it on a round block of seven preciosities and covering it with a bell made of brass, both richly studded with pearls and precious stones. The bone is of a yellowish white color, oval in shape, with a length of four inches, and a convex upper side. Every day, when the bone has been brought out, those in charge of the shrine mount to a lofty upper story, beat a big drum, blow a conch, and clash copper cymbals. The king, on hearing the sound, forthwith proceeds to the shrine and makes offerings of flowers and incense, after which he and his attendants in turn bend in adoration and depart, having entered by the east gate and leaving by the west gate. Every morning the king makes offerings and worships in this manner, afterward transacting affairs of state. The elders of the merchant class also first make offerings and then attend to their private affairs. The program is every day the same, without any remissness; and when all the offerings have been made, the skull bone is put back in the shrine, in which there is a pagoda of self-liberation from earthly trammels, which can be opened and closed, made of seven preciosities and over five feet in height, to contain it. In front of the gate to the shrine there will be found, regularly every morning, sellers of flowers and incense, so that all who wish to make offerings may buy of all kinds. The kings of the countries round about also regularly send envoys to make offerings. The shrine stands in a square of forty paces in extent. Though the heavens should quake and the earth gape, this spot would not move.

From this point traveling one yojana to the north, Fa-Hien arrived at the capital of Nagarahara, where (Buddha, then a) Bodhisattva bought with silver money some five-stalked flowers for an offering to Dipankara Buddha (his twenty-fourth predecessor). Here, too, in this city there is a Buddha-Tooth pagoda, offerings being made in the same way as for the skull bone. One yojana to the northeast of the city brought Fa-Hien to the mouth of a valley where there is Buddha's pewter-topped staff; and there too a shrine has been raised at which offerings are presented. The staff is made of sandalwood from the (fabulous) Bull's-head mountain, and is over sixteen or seventeen feet in length. It is kept in a wooden sheath, from which a hundred or thousand men would try to draw it in vain.

Entering the valley and traveling west for four days, Fa-Hien reached a shrine where one of Buddha's robes is the object of worship. When there is a great drought in this country, the officials gather together, bring out the robe, pray, and make offerings; rain then falls in great abundance.

Half a yojana to the south of the capital of Nagarahara, there is a cave. It is on the southwest face of Po mountain. Buddha left his shadow on the rock inside. Looking at it from a distance of ten paces or so, it is like Buddha's actual self, with his golden complexion, his thirty-two greater and eighty lesser characteristic marks, all brightly visible. The nearer one goes, the more indistinct it becomes, appearing as if it were really He. The kings of the various countries round about have sent skillful artists to sketch it, but they have not been able to do so. The people of the country have a tradition which says, "A thousand Buddhas are all to leave their shadows here."

A hundred or so paces to the west of the shadow, Buddha, when here, shaved his head and cut his nails, and with the help of his disciples built a pagoda seventy to eighty feet in height, as a model for pagodas in the future. It exists to this day, and by its side there is a monastery in which there are over seven hundred priests. In this place there is a pagoda in honor of the Lo-han and Buddhist saints, of whom nearly a thousand have dwelt here.

In the second moon of winter, Fa-Hien and his companions, three in all, went southward across the Little Snowy Mountains (Safed Koh), which retain the snow, summer and winter alike. On the northern side, which is in the shade, it is frightfully cold; and when a gale gets up, it makes one shut the mouth and shiver. Hui-ching could go no farther; he foamed at the mouth, and said to Fa-Hien, "I too cannot recover; you had better go on while you can; do not let us all pass away here"; and so he passed. Gently stroking the corpse, Fa-Hien cried out in lamentation, "Our original design cannot be carried out; it is destiny; what is there to be done?"

Then the pilgrims once more struggled forward; and having got across to the south of the range, they arrived at the country where there are approximately three thousand priests belonging to both the Greater and Lesser Vehicles.

Here they kept their summer retreat; and when it was over, they proceeded southward for ten days and reached the country of Falana or Bannu, where also there are over three thousand priests, all belonging to the Lesser Vehicle. From this point they journeyed eastward for three days and again crossed the Indus, on both banks of which the land is flat.

Across the river the pilgrims were in a country called Bhida (in the Punjab), where the Faith is very flourishing under both the Greater and Lesser Vehicles. When the people of the country saw Buddhist priests from China coming among them, they were much affected and said, "How is it possible for foreigners to know that renunciation of family is the essence of our religion, and to travel afar in search of the Faith?" Then they gave to the pilgrims whatsoever they required, and treated them in accordance with the faith.

From this point traveling southeast for somewhat less than eighty yojanas, the pilgrims passed by many monasteries, containing in all nearly ten thousand priests. Having passed by all these, they arrived at a country called Muttra or Mandor, and went along the river Jumna ...

———

AN EMPEROR'S SOJOURN*
Jahangir

The second new year of my auspicious reign began on the twenty-second of Zu-l-ka'da, 1015 A.H. (March 10, 1606 C.E.), and on the seventh of Zu-l-hijja, 1015 A.H. (April 1606 C.E.), I left the fort of Lahore at a prosperous hour, and crossing the Ravi, I alighted at the garden of Dilamez, where I stopped four days ...

On Thursday, the fourteenth, we encamped in the sub-district of Chandwala, and, after one intervening stage, arrived at Hafizabad on Saturday. In two marches more I reached the banks of the Chinab, and on Thursday, the twenty-first of Zu-l-hijja, I crossed the river by a bridge of boats and pitched my tents in the sub-district of Gujarat. When Emperor Akbar was proceeding to Kashmir, he built a fort on the other side of this river, where he settled the Gujars, who had hitherto been devoted to plunder. The place was consequently named Gujarat and formed into a separate sub-district. The Gujars live chiefly upon milk and curds, and seldom cultivate land.

On Friday we arrived at Khawaspur, five leagues from Gujarat, and after two further marches we reached the banks of the Behat, where we pitched our tents. In the night a very strong wind blew, dark clouds obscured the sky, and it rained so heavily that even the oldest persons said they had never seen such floods. The storm ended with showers of hailstones, which were as large as hens' eggs, and the torrent of water,

* An autobiography of Jahangir and a history of his reign, the *Jahangirnama* (1609) is also a vivid record of the many diversions of the royal court. In this short essay, Jahangir describes a jaunt with his entourage.

combined with the wind, broke the bridge. I crossed the river in a boat with the ladies of my harem, and as there were but very few boats for the other men, I ordered them to wait till the bridge was repaired. This was accomplished in a week, after which the whole camp crossed the river without trouble.

The source of the river Behat is a fountain in Kashmir called Virnag, a word which in the Hindi language signifies a snake, since it appears that at one time a very large serpent haunted the spot. I visited this source twice during the lifetime of my father. It is about twenty leagues from the city of Kashmir and rises in an octagonal basin about twenty yards in length by twenty in breadth. The neighborhood contains many vestiges of the abodes of devotees, consisting of numerous caves and chambers made of stone. The water of this spring is so clear that, although its depth is said to be beyond estimation, if a poppy seed be thrown in, it will be visible till it reaches the bottom. There are very fine fish in it. As I was told that the fountain was unfathomably deep, I ordered a stone to be tied to the end of a rope and thrown into it, and thus it was found that its depth did not exceed the height of a man and a half. After my accession to the throne, I ordered its sides to be paved with stones, a garden to be made round it, and the stream which flowed from it to be similarly decorated on both sides. Such elegant chambers and edifices were raised on each side of the basin that there is scarcely anything to equal it throughout the inhabited world.

The river expands much as it approaches the village of Pampur, which lies ten leagues from the city of Kashmir. All the saffron of Kashmir is the product of this village, and perhaps there is no other place in the world where saffron is produced so abundantly. I visited this place once with my father in the season in which the plant blossoms. In all other trees we see, they first get the branches, then the leaves, and last of all the flower. But it is quite otherwise with this plant, for it blossoms when it is only about two inches above the ground. Its flower is of a bluish color, having four leaves and four threads of orange color, like those of safflower, equal in length to one joint of the finger. The fields of saffron are sometimes half a league or a league in length and they look very beautiful at a distance. In the season when it is collected, the saffron has such a strong smell that people get headaches from it, and even though I had taken a glass of wine, yet I myself was affected by it. I asked the Kashmiris who were employed in collecting it whether it had any effect upon them, and was surprised by their reply that "they did not even know what headache was."

. . . On Tuesday, the fourteenth, I marched four leagues and three-quarters to Tillah, which means "a hill" in the Gakkar language. From that place I proceeded to the village of Bhakra, which in the language of the same people is the name of a shrub with odorless white flowers. From Tillah to Bhakra I marched the whole way through the bed of the Kahan, in which water was then flowing, while the oleander bushes were in full bloom and of exquisite color, like peach blossoms. These shrubs grew in special abundance at the sides of this stream, so I ordered my personal attendants, both horse and foot, to bind bunches of the flowers in their turbans and directed that the turbans of those who would not decorate themselves in this fashion should be taken off their heads. I thus got up a beautiful garden.

On Thursday, the sixth, the campground was Hatya, so called from its founder, a Gakkar named Hati. On this march a great many dhak trees were found in blossom. This shrub has no fragrance in its flowers, which are of a fiery orange color and the size of a red rose, or even bigger. It was such a sight that it was impossible to take one's eyes off it. As the air was very charming, and as there was a slight shower in consequence of a veil of clouds which obscured the light of the sun, I indulged myself in drinking wine. In short, I enjoyed myself amazingly on this march.

SLIPPING INTO TIBET*

Sarat Chandra Das

November 23.—Our way led along an extensive moraine, the huge reddish boulders of which were covered with creeping tamarisks and dwarf

* Explorer, scholar, and spy, Sarat Chandra Das made three trips into Tibet, a forbidden land, between 1879 and 1884, each time returning with Tibetan and Sanskrit texts. He went on to become a noted expert on Tibetan language, culture, and politics. His adventures are recorded in *Journey to Lhasa and Central Tibet* (1902).

junipers. After about a mile we reached Manda-phug, a hollow between two gigantic boulders, the one inclined toward the other; and here we took our breakfast of rice and buttered tea. The vegetation improved as we neared Manda-la, and the sight of thick forest growth in the deep glens refreshed our eyes, so long tired with looking on barren rocks. From Tama-la, where we saw some shepherds tending their flocks and some yaks, one descends the Yamatari valley, the top of the slope being held sacred to the dreaded Mamo goddesses; on the rhododendron bushes were white and red flags offered to them by wayfarers. From this point I obtained a good view of the Kangpa-chan valley.

Finding that I was greatly exhausted, Dao Namgyal, Phurchung's brother-in-law, took me on his back and carried me till we reached the northwest flank of the Tama-la. Soon after this we came to a flat, grass-covered valley with tall rhododendrons and ferns growing about. Phurchung held this spot to have been a singularly lucky one for him, for it was here that his parents had met [Joseph Dalton] Hooker some thirty-five years ago, while the great botanist was exploring Nepal. Phurchung's father, suffering from snow-blindness, was led by his wife to the Doctor, who not only gave him excellent medicine, but presented her with a pretty coin to hang about the neck of her child, Phurchung, then a baby in the arms.

At about 2:00 p.m. we reached the Yamata-ri, formed by the streams which issue from Kanchanjinga. The gorge in which this river flows is singularly beautiful. Above the steep crags on either side were blue glaciers, and at their feet forests of native firs and larches, covered with pendant mosses waving like feathers in the breeze. Just before reaching Kangpa-chan (Gyunsar) village, the Yamata-ri river is crossed by a little bridge, and then the village with its wooden huts comes in view. Some of the houses were empty; a few old hags with goiter sat on their thresholds basking in the sun and spinning.

Phurchung had reached this, his native village, ahead of us, and he now came, much the worse for drink, to greet us, and led us into his mother's house, where a fire of rhododendron boughs and aromatic firs blazed in the middle of the room. Chang was ready in wooden bottles, and his mother poured some boiling water into them as soon as we were seated on the cushions placed for us. Some dry junipers and pines were burnt as incense, and two joss sticks smoked before us. Then two brass plates full of boiled, red-skinned potatoes were offered us, followed by rice and boiled mutton, the rice being served wrapped up in the broad leaves of some kind of hill plant. When night came on we sat around the fire, each with a bottle of murwa before him; but drowsiness soon overtook me, and I fell asleep.

November 24.—The village of Kangpa-chan is built on several terraces facing the southwest, the houses enclosed in low stone walls. Several small streams empty into the Kangchan below the village, and mountains covered with snow and ice rise precipitously on either side of it, their lower slopes clad with thick forest growth of moss-covered silver firs, deodars, and larches. Juniper and rhododendron bushes surround the village. Round about it are patches of barley, from one to the other of which flew flocks of wild pigeons.

Coming back from a stroll, I found two men waiting to invite me to drink chang at their houses; and having accepted their invitation, I went first to that of a man called Jorgya. Taking my seat on a thick mattress-like seat covered with a piece of Khamba carpet, a bamboo bottle filled with murwa, with a little piece of butter placed on top of it, was set before us. Tea was first drunk, the housewife serving mine in a china cup, a form of Tibetan politeness shown only to persons of superior social standing, those of equal or inferior rank to the host using the wooden bowls each one carries about in the breast of his gown. After this, a brass plate filled with potatoes was placed before us on a little table, together with parched Indian corn, milk, and butter, all of which we ate heartily.

Our host advised me not to attempt to go by Wallung, as I would be sure to meet with much difficulty, but rather to enter Tibet by Yangma and the Kangla-chen pass, which was still possible, he said, even at this advanced season of the year.

I next went to the house of Pemazang, Phurchung's uncle, which I found well plastered and with a tastefully painted chapel. His son and wife received me at the head of the ladder and led me into the house; Pemazang had long, thick, and tangled hair. He wore gold earrings in the shape of magnolia flowers, and his looks and talk were grave and serious. He often sits in deep meditation for the purpose of arresting hail or other storms by the potency of the charms he is able to pronounce.

Leaving Pemazang, we crossed the river and paid a visit to the Tashi-chos ding monastery, which we found nearly deserted, one or two old women here and there turning the prayer wheels outside the temple. Ascending two flights of ladder stairs, we entered the lama's house. He and his ani received us most kindly, and the latter asked me for some medicines for the old gentleman, who was suffering with dyspepsia.

Returning to our lodgings, we found that the lock of the bag in which I kept my money had been tampered with, but I did not open it, as six other persons were living in the room we occupied, and I feared lest they might see the contents. Whatever the loss might be, I made up my mind to bear it silently, and keep my suspicions to myself.

November 25.—Phurchung's brother, Dao Namgyal, brought me a quantity of presents—potatoes, murwa, millet, butter, and last, but not least, a kid, for which I gave him a return present of five rupees. The poor people of the village all followed with various presents—not that they had any great respect for me, but solely with an eye to return presents, which they hoped would be greater than the value of theirs. Fortunately there were but few people in the village, otherwise they would have drained me of all my cash.

By noon Phurchung had sufficiently slept off his drunkenness to procure for me several pairs of kyar, or snowshoes, from the people of the village. I had learnt from a newly engaged coolie that he had lately crossed the Kangla pass on kyar, and had reached Jongri, where he had met Captain Harman, who had been much struck by the great usefulness of this rude contrivance.

In the evening the men killed two kids; the blood was poured into the intestines, which had been washed and cleaned, barley flour (tsamba) being mixed with it. These blood puddings were boiled and packed away with the tripe in a small wicker basket for my use on the journey ...

November 26.—We left Kangpa-chan, our party now comprising four coolies. Phurchung marched along with my gun as a sign of his importance, but its red cloth cover, its principal beauty, had been stolen the night before; his younger brother, Sonam-dorj, carried his pack. Ugyen gyatso and *I* rode ponies, hired for eight annas each, to take us halfway up the Nango-la. The old women of the village waited our approach at the east end of the bridge to give us the stirrup cup (a custom invariably observed in Tibet at the parting of friends setting out on a long journey), with bowls of wine in their right hand, and plates full of parched barley flour in their left. Each of the old women poured a little wine into a china cup, to which a pinch of flour was added, and we were asked to take a sip, with the wish of "May we offer you the like on your return." We thanked them for their kindness, and put a couple of rupees in one of their plates, to be divided amongst them.

We rode slowly on by the bounding river, into which a number of little rills empty, flowing down from behind the monastery, and over which were several prayer wheels turned by the water. Our way lay amidst thick woods up to Daba ngonpo, where the natives used to get blue clay to make images. This clay they held to be exceptionally good, as it came from the summit of a holy mountain. From this point we followed up the bed of a former glacier, passing Kamai phugpa, and reaching, at Khama kang tung, the timber line. A mile beyond the latter place we came to the end of the pasture-lands on this side of the Nango-la, not far from which we saw a flock of spotted birds, called sregpa, which Ugyen tried, without success, to shoot.

The ascent of the Nango-la now began over deep snow, in some places its surface frozen, in others so soft that we sunk knee-deep in it. I soon became so exhausted that I had to get one of the coolies to carry me on his back, and so we reached the summit of the pass.

Two miles to the west of the pass is Sayong-kong, a plateau whence there is a direct road leading to Yangma. A mile below this place is Sayong-hok, where vegetation begins again, and gradually increases as one advances along the Lungkyong-chu. We camped on the river bank under a great boulder, spreading our rugs on beds of long dry grass, which covered, but very imperfectly, the rough, stony soil.

November 27.—We followed down the Lungkyong-chu (the only way of communication between Kangpa-chan, Yangma, and Wallung), the mountains on our left nearly hidden in the morning mists. For part of the way our road led along a steep path through thick woods of firs, feathery larches, and deodars, amidst which I saw many pheasants and other kinds of birds, and the coolies told me that musk deer and wild sheep were also found there.

About two miles above the junction of the Yangma with the Lungkyong, we crossed the former stream by a wooden bridge, and finally arrived at the village of Tingugma, where we rested a while and ate a light meal.

Shortly after starting again we met a party of Yangma natives driving before them a few sheep and a dozen yaks laden with blankets, yak hides, barley, and salt. They were going to a village called Chaini, in the Tambur valley, to exchange their goods for rice and Indian corn. Phurchung asked them if the Kangla-chen pass was still open. Some said we could easily cross it; others expressed doubts about it, for they said three feet of snow had fallen on it a few days previously.

Passing by Maya-phug (a cavern sacred to the goddess Mamo), we crossed a little juniper-covered plateau called Shugpa-thang ("Juniper plain"), and after a short but steep climb reached the summit of the pass, from whence I had a most extended and beautiful view of the surrounding country—behind me great reddish granite rocks, looking like the ruins of gigantic ramparts; before me a plain some two miles long, the bed of a former glacier, encircled by snowy mountains rising the one above the other; while to the southeast was the Nango-la, and behind it the plain of Sumdongma. Crossing the Djari-thang, or "Plain of Gravel," and the Do-la, or "Rocky pass" (round the base of which the Yangma flows), I reached by dusk the monastery of Yangma, or Manding gomba, situated on a broad, shrub-covered terrace some forty to fifty feet above the stream, where Phurchung found me lodgings in a wretched cell, where I settled myself as best I could for the night. He obtained a few eggs and some milk from the lamas; and while one of the nuns (*ani*) helped Dao Namgyal to cook the food, another blew the bellows. The lamas were engaged in their annual reading of the Kahgyur, which occupied them daily from in the morning to 7:30 p.m., when they retired to their respective cells. There were fifteen monks and seven ani in the lamasery.

Ugyen had been suffering most of the day with violent pains in the bowel; he now wrapped himself in all the blankets I could spare, and lay groaning and crying, "*Achi-che apa-ouh!*" so that I felt grave apprehensions for him, and feared that his illness might oblige us to stop over in this wretched place.

November 28.—Phurchung had been away on a drunken bout all night, and I arose full of fear lest he might have disclosed our plans to his companions, and Ugyen shared my alarm. After a while Phurchung and Phuntso appeared, and with much salaaming and lolling of the tongue asked me to wait here a day, the latter assuring me that he hoped to obtain, without much difficulty or the payment of custom duty (called *chua* in this part of Nepal), permission for us to proceed on our journey. Shortly after the elders arrived, the richest man among them recognizable by his tamaski hat, a long earring, and a deep red serge robe of purug. He had come from the village of Yangma riding a half-breed yak (*jo*), which, with the saddle still on its back, stood tied at the gate of the monastery. I anxiously awaited the result of their conference with my men, and in great anxiety prayed to the Supreme Dispenser of our destinies that nothing might happen unfavorable to ourselves and our enterprise.

The Manding gomba, or Nub Man-ding gomba, "The Western Flying-Medicine Monastery," owes its name to the fact that lama Lha-tsun once lived for three years in a cave close by called the Zim-phug, to discover medicines of wonderful potency, and that he there obtained three wonderful pills. One came to him through the air, falling on the spot where the lamasery now stands. The second pill fell a little above the monastery, where the people of the village now burn their dead; and the third alighted on the spot where the great chorten now stands.

Manding gomba is held in great sanctity, for it is one of the first cis-Himalayan lamaseries founded by the great red-hat Lama Lha-tsun; but Wallung ranks first, and Kangpa-chan second, in point of wealth and power. Manding possesses a fine copy of the Kahgyur in 125 volumes.

The *Lhakhang*, or temple, has massive and neatly painted walls and doors, after the manner of the Sikkim *donpa*. The huts or cells of the monks in its immediate vicinity, all painted red with clay obtained from the adjacent mountains, are of irregular and ugly style, the doors, windows, and cornices being roughly made; each house has around it a low stone wall, inside of which the sheep and yak find shelter.

After a little while Phurchung and Phuntso came back to me in high spirits over the result of their conference with the village elders. They had told them that I was only a pilgrim who spoke Tibetan and dressed in Tibetan fashion. The head lama said that he knew of no order from the Nepalese government for stopping pilgrims on their way to Tibet, and that he would certainly not prevent me from doing so, as I spoke Tibetan with greater fluency and accuracy than many Nepalese. The headman asked that Phurchung should give bond, holding himself personally responsible for my character as a traveler, and a custom duty of eight annas a head was levied on our party. Phurchung also told me that the headman and head lama were coming to bid me farewell, and that I must not forget, after exchanging compliments with them, to say "sangpoi ja chog," "May we meet again next year."

In a little while the big men arrived. The headman, conspicuous by his earring, boots, and red serge robe, nodded to me slightly, and took off his hat. He asked me why I had chosen such a bad season for going to Tibet. I told him that I did so in obedience to the command of our holy and learned chief lama, and not by my own wish. His object in coming to see me was to find out if I spoke Tibetan and understood the Buddhist religion. My fluency in Tibetan, and the citing of one or two proverbial sayings in course of conversation, made him form a high opinion of my knowledge of the sacred texts and histories, as well as of my character and holiness. "Laso, laso" (yes, yes), he said, and then he apologized for not having brought me some presents; but I answered him that our acquaintance was only just begun, and there would be time in the future to cultivate it, and, handing him a scarf (khatag), I expressed the hope that we might meet the next year (sangpoi ja chog). Many of the bystanders made wishes for our welfare, but someone in the crowd said that I was certainly not a Tibetan. Then another swore I was an Indian; and a third said that they would soon have news of me: "That Hindu will surely die in the snows, and his servants will soon return here with the news of his death."

It was past noon when the coolies picked up their loads, and I set out in excellent spirits, having now escaped the much-feared obstruction from the Yangma people, on whose mercy and goodwill our success entirely depended.

We passed by some mendong and chorten at the entrance to the convent, and then followed up the course of the Yangma, passing by a pretty lakelet, the Miza, or "man eating," now filled with ice, and seeing on the way some very high chorten, known as thongwa kundol, "bringing deliverance when seen," which had a few years previously been repaired by the head lama of Wallung. Near these we saw a half-dozen wild sheep, but we gave up all ideas of shooting them when told that the Yangma people think the gods of the land and mountains would be deeply offended if anyone molested them.

By 3:00 p.m. we got sight of the village of Yangma, whose houses could only be distinguished from the boulders everywhere strewing the ground by the smoke issuing from the roofs. There were not more than a hundred houses in the village, and the fields round about were enclosed within low stone walls. Buckwheat, barley, turnips, radishes, and potatoes are grown here, and rice brought from Yang-ku tang and other villages in the warmer valleys is procurable. The village was founded by Tibetans from Tashi-rabka, one of them having discovered the valley and its comparative fertility while hunting for a lost yak calf. The name Yangma was given it on account of the breadth of the valley.

The male part of the population is idle in the extreme, but the women are correspondingly busy; some I saw were threshing corn, some gathering fuel, others engaged in various kinds of household work.

By 5:00 p.m. we got off from this wretched valley, where Phurchung and the coolies, by the way, were most desirous to remain to continue drinking chang, though Phurchung showed unmistakable signs of having already imbibed too much. After an hour's march we reached Kiphug, where we found, under an overhanging rock, a bit of ground free from snow on which to camp; but Phurchung remained behind in Yangma, in a helplessly drunken condition.

November 29.—The way lay along the Yangma, which was scarcely visible, snow and ice covering entirely its bed. There was nothing to give life to the scenery; the river flowed in a deep gorge, or else opened out into lake-like expanses; on either side the mountains seemed to reach to the sky; not a bird, not even a cloud in the heaven, not a sound save that of our feet crushing the light dry snow. It was 11:00 a.m. when we came to an unfrozen pool, by which we ate our breakfast of tea and meal. This place, which is in a broad portion of the valley, is a favorite summer pasture-ground for the Pokpas, who, from July to September, bring their herds of yaks here.

Po-phug was reached after a march of three miles through the snow, then the ascent became steeper and freer from snow, and we came to Luma goma, "Fountain head," the source of the Yangma river; and after an easy ascent of half an hour we arrived at Tsa-tsam, the limit of vegetation.

Here we began climbing a huge glacier, a quarter of a mile wide and more than three miles long, the Chyang-chub gya-lam, or "Highway to Holiness," over which I was carried on Phurchung's back wherever the snow lay deep. Then we climbed a huge mass of bare black rocks, and darkness had overtaken us before we reached the "White Cavern," where we proposed passing the night. The fog added to the obscurity of the night, our feet were benumbed by the cold, and we frequently slipped into crevasses or between the clefts of rocks. Finding it impossible to reach the cavern, we scraped away the snow from between some rocks, and there I sat, my knees drawn up, hugging myself during the long night.

How exhausted we were with the fatigue of the day's journey, how overcome by the rarefication of the air, the intensity of the cold, and how completely prostrated by hunger and thirst, is not easy to describe. The very remembrance of the sufferings of that dreadful night makes me shudder even now, but I quickly recover under the inexpressible delight I feel at the consciousness of my great success. This was the most trying night I ever passed in my life. There was a light breeze blowing, attended with sleet, which fortunately weighed my blankets down and made them cover me closer than they otherwise would have done. And so with neither food nor drink, placed as if in the grim jaws of death in the bleak and dreary regions of snow, where death alone dwells, we spent this most dismal night.

November 30.—The coolies once more picked up their loads, and our guide began in his gravest tones to recite his "Pema-jung-ne samha doha" and other mantras. The morning was gloriously radiant, and the great Kangla-chen glittered before us, bathed in a glory of golden light. Fortunately for us, there was no fresh snow on the ground; for, had there been any, we could not possibly have advanced. We found that we had stopped not more than a furlong from the Phugpa karpo, which, by the way, is not a cave at all, but only a crevasse between two detached rocks. Our guide, leaving his load in the charge of his brother, took the lead, driving his long stick into the snow at each step, and digging footholds in the soft snow. From the White Cavern the top of the pass bore due east, and was distant about two miles. Just at the base of the final ascent there is a little sandy plain, in the middle of which is a huge boulder: this is the "Place of Salvation," thus called because, when once this point is reached, travelers may be confident of attaining the summit of the pass.

I steadily followed in the footsteps of the guide, and would not let him take me on his back; for if I succeeded in ascending to the highest summit of Kangla-chen without any help, I could look to the achievement with greater pride. Ugyen here gave out, and it was with difficulty that I persuaded Phurchung to carry him on his back, for they were far from being on the best of terms. An hour's hard climbing brought us to the summit of the pass. The sky was cloudless and of the deepest blue; against it a snow-clad world of mountains stood out in bold relief. Far beyond the maze of snow-clad peaks we saw in the northwest the mountains of Pherug, in Tibet, while those of Shar Khambu stood gloriously out to the west.

The summit of Kangla-chen is a plateau, some two miles from east to west, and one mile and a quarter from northwest to northeast; it inclines toward the west, while to the northwest it is bounded by a mountain of considerable height. Our snowshoes now stood us in good need; unfortunately we had but three pairs, so Phurchung and I had to wade through the deep snow in the footsteps of the others, with many slips and more than one narrow escape from falling into the deep crevasses. On all sides there was nothing visible but an ocean of snow. Innumerable snowy peaks touched with their white heads the pale leaden skies, where stars were shining. The rattling roar of distant avalanches was frequently heard; but, after having succeeded in crossing the loftiest of snowy passes, I felt too transported with joy to be frightened by their thunder.

These splendid scenes of wonderland, the grandest, the most sublime my eyes have ever beheld, which bewildered me so that even now my pen finds no words to describe them, inspired me with feelings of deep gratitude to Heaven, by whose mercy my life had been spared thus far.

We camped on a rock bare of snow, and passed another miserable night with nothing to drink, and but a couple of dry biscuits to stave off our hunger. To add to my misery, Ugyen was still suffering, and I had to give him half my covering, for he had none of his own; and so, with not even enough room to lie down, we passed the night huddled together, the loads placed on the lower side of the rock so as to prevent our falling off in our sleep.

December 1.—'Twas not yet dawn when all were on foot and busy packing up. The track was hardly visible; below our path lay the great glacier, extending for miles, which feeds the Tashi-rabka river. The snowy sides of the mountains beyond this were furrowed by glacial streams, very noticeable in their varied shades of blue and green, and on the surface of the glacier itself rose huge rounded surfaces, or hummocks, evidently produced by boulders concealed under the ice.

Following carefully in the footsteps of Phurchung, we crossed some six spurs of the Dorjetagh range, and then came to an easy path down the central moraine of a former glacier, now only a huge heap of boulders and debris. The mountains lost, as we advanced, the whitish color peculiar to the Indian ranges, and assumed the blackish or ocher color distinctive of the Tibetan region. It was with a feeling of intense relief that we finally discerned vegetation and heard the babbling of a little brook, near which flew birds feeding on rhododendron and juniper berries, and a little way off we saw some herds of yaks grazing, and smoke rising from a campfire; here we stopped at the foot of a great rock, and enjoyed, after our long fast of two days, a meal of rice and buttered tea.

We continued down the course of the stream, passing with some apprehension near a huge bull-yak or *shalu*, though low stone walls separated us from him and kept him away from the she-yaks (*di*) in the adjacent pasturage. This part of the valley is frequently visited by packs of wolves, which kill large numbers of yaks, but the bulls are able to drive them off with their long sharp horns.

At 3:00 p.m. we passed Dsongo, the extreme border of the district of Tashi-rabka, and where are the ruins of a stone house built on a huge boulder. This was formerly a stage-house used by the Sikkim Raja's people, when the Yangma and Wallung districts still belonged to him, when going to or returning from Tibet. A little way beyond this point we met some herdsmen, who made inquiries as to whence we came and where we were going. Near by were their tents, where I noticed two swarthy women and a fierce Tibetan mastiff. Phurchung entered one of the tents, sat down to chat and drink a cup of tara, a sort of thin curd.

Ugyen was much preoccupied about our getting by Tashi-rabka and escaping its headman. At about six o'clock we were close to the village, and so we hid till dusk in a gully, where we boiled our tea and ate some tsamba. The moon shone out brightly when we resumed our march and passed along a portion of a high stone wall, erected by the Tibetans during the Nepalese war, when, it is said, they put up five miles of it in a day under orders of their general, the Shape Shata. This wall is carried across the river on a bridge, where it has eight small watchtowers. It crosses the whole valley, its ends being high up on the sides of the mountains. On the farther side of the wall is the village. Ugyen and Phurchung stood trembling, not knowing whether to turn back toward the Kangla-chen pass or to proceed onward toward the chorten, near which the headman resides. Phuntso alone was equal to the occasion. "If the guards are awake, we will sing some of our national walking songs, and pass ourselves off for Wallungpa." After a few words of encouragement to the others, we set out. Before we had reached the chorten, a voice from a yak-hair tent cried out, "Whence are you, and where are you going?" To which Phuntso replied that we were Wallungpa going to Shigatse, and asked them where they were going, and without waiting for a reply we hurried on and passed by the dreaded headman's house without awakening anyone, not even the fierce mastiffs tied up in front of the dwelling.

About thirty yards beyond the house we came to the bridge, a rough structure of logs and stone slabs. The Tashi-rabka river was partly frozen, and its swift current was sweeping down blocks of ice. We crossed over unnoticed, and I then broke the silence with thanks to merciful God who had enabled us to overcome this the most dreaded of all difficulties, one which had frightened my staunch friend Phurchung, that the snows of the Kangla-chen had not daunted.

—=•◦•=—

REPORT OF A ROUTE-SURVEY

MADE BY PUNDIT [NAIN SINGH] FROM NEPAL TO LHASA*

The route between Kathmandu and Kumaon taken by the Pundit is the worst part of the whole of his route. It crosses the Himalayas twice, and also several high passes, and the road on the cis-Himalayan side is particularly rough and rocky, with great ascents and descents. It was consequently to be expected that his pace would be somewhat shorter

* This essay is part of a report read to the Royal Geographic Society, London, on March 23, 1868, by Captain T. E. Montgomerie, in-charge of the Trans-Himalayan Survey Parties. Pundit Nain Singh and his brother were employed by the British to conduct a secret survey of Tibet, a mission of great secrecy and high risk. At the time of the writing of this report they were still employed on explorations and could not be named in it.

than on the route between Tadum and Gyangze, which runs the whole distance by the easiest slopes possible, without crossing a single steep pass . . .

. . . Between the Mansarowar lake and Lhasa the Pundit traveled by the great road called the Jong-lam (or Whor-lam), by means of which the Chinese officials keep up their communications for 800 miles along the top of the Himalayan range from Lhasa, north of Assam, to Gartokh, northeast of Simla. A separate memorandum is given hereafter as to the stages, etcetera, on this extraordinary road. Starting from Gartokh on the Indus, at 15,500 feet above the sea, the road crosses the Kailas range by a very high pass, descends to about 15,000 feet in Nari Khorsum, the upper basin of the Sutlej, and then coasting along the Eakas Tal, the Mansarowar, and another long lake, rises gradually to the Mariham-la pass, the watershed between the Sutlej and Brahmaputra, 15,500 feet above the sea. From the Mariham-la the road descends gradually, following close to the north of the main source of the Brahmaputra, and within sight of the gigantic glaciers, which give rise to that great river. At about 50 miles from its source the road is for the first time actually on the river, but from that point to Tadum it adheres very closely to the left bank. Just before reaching Tadum the road crosses a great tributary, little inferior to the main river itself. The Tadum monastery is about 14,200 feet above the sea.

From Tadum, the road follows down the Brahmaputra, sometimes close to it, sometimes several miles from it, but at 80 miles east of Tadum the road leaves the river, and crossing some higher ground, descends into the valley of the Baka Sangpo river, which is a great tributary of the Brahmaputra; leaving the Eakas valley, the road crosses over the mountains, and again reaches the Brahmaputra at about 180 miles below Tadum. About 10 miles lower the road changes from the left bank to the right bank, travelers having to cross the great river by ferry-boats near the town of Janglache. Below Janglache, the road follows the river closely to a little below its junction with the Baka Sangpo. From that point the road runs some 10 miles south of the river, crossing the mountains to the large town of Shigatze, 11,800 feet above the sea. From Shigatze the road runs considerably south of the river, ascends the Penanangchu river, and, crossing the Kharola pass, 17,000 feet above the sea, descends into the basin of the Yamdokcho lake. For two long stages the road runs along this great lake, which is 13,700 feet above the sea, then rising sharply, crosses the lofty Khamba-la pass, and descends to the Brahmaputra again, now only 11,400 feet above the sea. Following the great river for one stage more, the road (which has hitherto been running from west to east) here leaves the Brahmaputra, and ascends its tributary, the Kichu Sangpo, in a northeasterly direction for three stages more to Lhasa, which is 11,700 feet above the sea. The total distance is about 800 miles from Gartokh to Lhasa.

This long line of road is generally well-defined, though it is not a made road, in the European sense of the word. The natural slopes over which the road is carried are however wonderfully easy. The Tibetans have, as a rule, simply had to clear away the loose stones, and only in three or four places, for a few miles, has anything in the way of making a road been necessary.

In many parts there appears to have been considerable danger of losing the road in the open stretches of the table-land, the whole surface looking very much like a road; but this danger is guarded against by the frequent erection of piles of stones, surmounted with flags on sticks, etcetera. These piles, called lapcha by the Tibetans, were found exceedingly handy for the survey; the quick eye of the Pundit generally caught the forward pile, and even if he did not, he was sure to see the one behind, and in this way generally secured a capital object on which to take his compass bearings. The Tibetans look upon these piles partly as guide posts, and partly as objects of veneration; travelers generally contribute a stone to them as they pass, or if very devout and generous, add a piece of rag; consequently, on a well-used road, these piles grow to a great size, and form conspicuous objects in the landscape. Over the table-land the road is broad and wide enough to allow several travelers to go abreast; in the rougher portions the road generally consists of two or three narrow paths, the width worn by horses, yaks, men, etcetera, following one another. In two or three places these dwindle down to a single track, but are always passable by a horseman, and, indeed, only in one place, near Phuncholing, is there any difficulty about laden animals. A man on horseback need never dismount between Lhasa and Gartokh, except to cross the rivers.

The road is, in fact, a wonderfully well-maintained one, considering the very elevated and desolate mountains over which it is carried. Between Lhasa and Gartokh there are twenty-two staging places, called

Tarjums, where the baggage animals are changed. These Tarjums are from 20 to 70 miles apart; at each, shelter is to be had, and efficient arrangements are organized for forwarding officials and messengers. The Tarjums generally consist of a house, or houses, made with sun-dried bricks. The larger Tarjums are capable of holding 150 to 200 men at a time, but some of the smaller can hold only a dozen people; in the latter case, further accommodation is provided by tents. At six Tarjums tents only are forthcoming. Each Tarjum is in charge of an official, called Tarjumpa, who is obliged to have horses, yaks, and coolies in attendance whenever notice is received of the approach of a Lhasa official. From ten to fifteen horses, and as many men, are always in attendance night and day. Horses and beasts of burden (yaks in the higher ground, donkeys in the lower) are forthcoming in great numbers when required; they are supplied by the nomadic tribes, whose camps are pitched near the halting houses.

Though the iron rule of the Lhasa authorities keeps this high road in order, the difficulties and hardships of the Pundit's march along it cannot be fully realized, without bearing in mind the great elevation at which the road is carried. Between the Mansarowar lake and the Tadum monastery the average height of the road above the sea must be over 15,000 feet, or about the height of Mont Blanc. Between Tadum and Lhasa its average height is 13,500 feet; and only for one stage does the road descend so low as 11,000 feet, whilst on several passes it rises to more than 16,000 feet above the sea. Ordinary travelers with laden animals make two to five marches between the staging-houses, and only special messengers go from one staging-house to another without halting. Between the staging-houses the Pundit had to sleep in a rude tent that freely admitted the biting Tibetan wind, and on some occasions be had to sleep in the open air.

Bearing in mind that the greater part of this march was made in mid-winter, it will be allowed that the Pundit has performed a feat of which a native of Hindustan, or of any other country, may well be proud. Notwithstanding the desolate track they crossed, the camp was not altogether without creature comforts. The yaks and donkeys carried a good supply of ordinary necessaries, such as grain, barley meal, tea, butter, etcetera, and sheep and goats were generally procurable at the halting places. A never-failing supply of fuel, though not of the pleasantest kind, was generally forthcoming from the argols or dried dung of the baggage animals, each camp being supposed to leave behind at least as many argols as it burns. At most of the halting places there is generally a very large accumulation.

Between the Mansarowar and Sarkajong nothing in the shape of spirits was to be had, but to the eastward of the latter place a liquor made from barley could generally be got in every village. This liquor, called chung, varies in strength, according to the season of the year, being in summer something like sour beer, and in the winter approximating closely in taste and strength to the strongest of smoked whiskey. The good-natured Tibetans are constantly brewing chung, and they never begrudge anyone a drink. Thirsty travelers, on reaching a village, soon find out where a fresh brew has been made; their drinking cups are always handy in their belts, and they seldom fail to get them filled at least once. The Pundit stoutly denied that this custom tended to drunkenness among his Tibetan friends; and it must be allowed that in Ladak, where the same custom prevails, the people never appeared to be much the worse for it; guides had, however, to be rather closely watched, if the march took them through many villages, as they seldom failed to pull out their cup at each one.

A good deal of fruit is said to be produced on the banks of the Brahmaputra, between Shigatze and Chushul. The Pundit only saw it in a dried state.

When marching along the great road, the Pundit and his companions rose very early; before starting they sometimes made a brew* of tea, and another brew was always made about the middle of the march, or a mess of stirabout (*suttoo*)[†] was made in their cups, with barley meal and water. On arriving at the end of a march they generally had some more tea at once, to stave off the cravings of hunger, until something more substantial was got ready, in the shape of cakes and meat, if the latter was available. Their marches generally occupied them from dawn till 2:00 or 3:00 p.m., but sometimes they did not reach their camping ground till quite late in the evening. On the march they were often passed and met by special messengers, riding along as hard as they could go. The Pundit said these men always looked haggard and worn. They have to ride the whole distance continuously, without stopping

* The Tibetans stew their tea with water, meal, and butter; the tea leaves are always eaten.
† A Tibetan always carries meal with him, and makes suttoo whenever he feels hungry.

either by night or day, except to eat food and change horses. In order to make sure that they never take off their clothes, the breast fastening of their overcoat is sealed, and no one is allowed to break the seal, except the official to whom the messenger is sent. The Pundit says he saw several of the messengers arrive at the end of their 800-mile ride. Their faces were cracked, their eyes bloodshot and sunken, and their bodies eaten by lice into large raws, the latter of which they attributed to not being allowed to take off their clothes.

It is difficult to imagine why the Lhasa authorities are so very particular as to the rapid transmission of official messages, but it seems to be a principle that is acted upon throughout the Chinese empire, as one of the means of government. Ordinary letters have a feather attached to them, and this simple addition is sufficient to carry a letter from Lhasa to Gartokh, 800 miles, in little over thirty days. A messenger arriving at a village with such a letter is at once relieved by another, who takes it on to the next village. This system was frequently made use of by the Surveyors in Ladak and Little Tibet, and it generally answered well.

If any very special message is in preparation, and if time permits, an ordinary messenger is sent ahead to give notice. Food is then kept ready, and the special messenger only remains at the staging-house long enough to eat his food, and then starts again on a fresh horse. He rides on day and night, as fast as the horses can carry him. The road throughout can be ridden over at night; if there is no moon the bright starlight* of Tibet gives sufficient light. Tibet is rarely troubled by dark nights; but, in case it should be cloudy, or that a horse should break down, two mounted men always accompany the messenger. These men are changed at every stage, and are thoroughly acquainted with their own piece of road. Each of these two men has, at least, two spare horses attached behind the horse he is mounted on. If any horse gets tired it is changed at once, and left on the road, to be picked up on the return of the men to their own homes. By this means the messenger makes great progress where the road is good, and is never stopped altogether, even in the rougher portion. A special messenger does the 800 miles in twenty-two days on average, occasionally in two or three days less, but only on very urgent occasions.

* The starlight in Tibet, as in all very elevated regions, is particularly bright.

The Pundit made fifty-one marches between Lhasa and the Mansarowar lake, and his brother makes out the remaining distance to Gartokh seven marches more, or, in all, fifty-eight marches. The Pundit found very few of the marches short, while a great many were very long and tedious . . .

. . . From the Mansarowar lake to Tadtim (140 miles) glaciers seem always to have been visible to the south, but nothing very high was seen to the north; for the next 70 miles the mountains north and south seem to have been lower, but further eastward a very high snowy range was visible to the north,* running for 120 miles parallel to the Raka Sangpo River. From Janglache to Gyangze the Pundit seems to have seen nothing high, but he notices a very large glacier between the Penanang valley and the Yamdokcho lake.

From the lofty Khamba-la pass the Pundit got a capital view. Looking south he could see over the island in the Yamdokcho lake, and made out a very high range to the south of the lake; the mountains to the east of the lake did not appear to be quite so high. Looking north the Pundit had a clear view over the Brahmaputra, but all the mountains in that direction were, comparatively speaking, low, and in no way remarkable.

About Lhasa no very high mountains were seen, and those visible appeared to be all about the same altitude. Hardly any snow was visible from the city, even in winter. From the Mansarowar to Ralung, 400 miles, there were no villages, and no cultivation of any kind. The mountains had a very desolate appearance, but still numerous large camps of black tents, and thousands of sheep, goats, and yaks were seen—the fact being that the mountain sides, though looking so arid and brown, do produce a very nourishing coarse grass.

East of Ralung, cultivation and trees were seen every day near the villages. Near the Yamdokcho lake the lower mountains seem to have had a better covering of grass. The Pundit mentions the island in the Yamdokcho as being very well grassed up to the summit, which must be 16,000 or 17,000 feet above the sea. This extra amount of grass may be due to a larger fall of rain, as the Pundit was informed that the rains were heavy during July and August.

As a rule, the Pundit's view from the road does not seem to have

* With a very high peak at its western extremity, called Harkiang. A very high peak was also noticed to the south between the Raka and Brahmaputra valleys.

been very extensive, for although the mountains on either side were comparatively low, they generally hid the distant ranges.

The only geological fact elicited is that the low range to the east of the Lhasa River was composed of sandstone. According to the Pundit, this sandstone was very like that of the Siwalik range at the southern foot of the Himalayas.

The probability of this is perhaps increased by the fact that fossil bones are plentiful in the Lhasa district. They are supposed to possess great healing properties when applied to wounds, etcetera, in a powdered state. The Pundit saw quantities of fossils exposed for sale in the Lhasa bazaar. The people there call them Dug-rupa, or lightning bones. One fossil particularly struck the Pundit; it consisted of a skull which was about two and a half feet long, and one and a half feet broad. The jaws were elongated, but the points had been broken off. The mountains crossed were generally rounded with easy slopes. The roundness of those on the Yamdokcho Island seems to have been very remarkable; this general roundness and easiness of slope probably points to former glacier or ice action.

Besides the Yamdokcho, a good many smaller lakes were seen, and two much larger ones were heard of. Those seen by the Pundit were all at about 14,000 feet above the sea. There are hardly any lakes in the lower Himalayas, the few that exist being all at or below 6,000 feet, but from about 14,000 to 15,000 feet, lakes and tarns are particularly numerous.* This may be another evidence of former ice action.

Whilst the Pundit was at Shigatze and Lhasa, he took a series of thermometer observations to determine the temperature of the air. During November, at Shigatze, the thermometer always fell during the night below the freezing point, even inside a house. The lowest temperature recorded was 25°F, and during the day the temperature hardly ever rose to 50°F. At Lhasa, in February, the thermometer generally fell below 32°F during the night, and the lowest observed temperature was 26°F; during the day it seldom rose to 45°F. During the whole time the Pundit was in the Lhasa territory, from September to the end of June, it never rained, and snow only fell once whilst he was on the march, and twice whilst in Lhasa.

* There are no lakes known in the Himalayas higher than 16,000 feet, but possibly one of those heard of by the Pundit may turn out to be a little higher.

The snowfall at Shigatze was said to be never more than 12 inches; but the cold in the open air must have been intense, as the water of running streams freezes if the current is not very strong.

BETWEEN WOLVES AND SHIPWRECK*

Sven Hedin

The 24th of September [1906 was a] memorable day—my sails on Tibetan lakes, curiously enough, almost always ended in adventures. Of my Ladakis five had been in the service of Deasy and Rawling, and two of them affirmed that a shiny spot east-southeast was the spring where Captain Deasy had encamped for ten days in July 1896, and which he names in his narrative "Fever Camp." Their indication agreed with Deasy's map; so Muhamed Isa was ordered to lead the caravan thither, light a large beacon fire on the nearest point of the shore as soon as darkness set in, and keep two horses in readiness.

Our plan was to sail in an east-northeasterly direction for the northern shore, and thence southward again to the signal fire. Rehim Ali was on this occasion assisted by Robert, who subsequently developed into an excellent boatman. The lake was nearly quite calm; its water, owing to its small depth, is greener, but quite as clear as that of its western neighbor. It is so salty that everything that touches it—hands, boat, oars, etcetera—glitters with crystals of salt. The shore and bottom of the lake consist chiefly of clay cemented together by crystallized salt into slabs and blocks as hard as stone, so that great care must be exercised when the boat is pushed into the water, for these slabs have edges and corners as sharp as knives. The lake is a salt basin of approximately elliptical outline with very low banks; nowhere do mountains descend

* Between the end of the nineteenth century and the turn of the twentieth, the explorer Sven Hedin mounted four expeditions to Central Asia, particularly the Trans-Himalayan region, and was instrumental in making it known to the Western world.

to the strand. The three-foot line runs about 100 yards from the shore; but even 650 yards out the depth is only 15 feet. We executed our first line of soundings across the lake in the most delightful calm, and I steered the boat toward the point I had fixed by observations. At one o'clock the temperature was 49°F in the water, and 50½° in the air. The depth increased very regularly, the maximum of 52.8 feet occurring not far from the northern shore. Robert was much delighted with the sail, and begged that I would always take him with me in future, which I the more readily granted since he was always cheerful and lively, and he gave me valuable help in all observations. A little bay on the north shore served us as a landing-place. We surveyed the neighborhood, and then hurriedly ate our breakfast, consisting of bread, marmalade, *pâté de foie*, and water. My companions had brought sugar, a teapot, and enamelled bowls, but left the tea behind; but this forgetfulness only raised our spirits.

Then we put off again to make for the spring to the southeast. A row of stone blocks and lumps of salt ran out from the landing-place east-southeastward, and the water here was so shallow that we had to propel our boat with great care. Just as we had passed the last rock, of which I took a specimen, the west wind got up, the surface of the lake became agitated, and a couple of minutes later white horses appeared on the salt waves.

"Up with the sail and down with the leeboards."

The lake before us is tinted with shades of reddish purple, a reflection from the clayey bottom; there it must be very shallow, but we shall soon pass it.

"Do you see the small white swirls in the southwest? Those are the forerunners of the storm, which stirs up the salt particles," I said.

"If the storm is bad, the boat will be broken on the sharp ledges of the bottom before we can reach land," remarked Robert.

"That is not clouds of salt," said Rehim Ali; "that is the smoke of fires."

"But Muhamed Isa should be camping at Sahib Deasy's source; that lies towards the southwest."

"There is no smoke there," replied Robert, who had the field glass; "perhaps they have not been able to cross the salt flats on the south of the lake."

"Then it is their beacon fires which we see; but we cannot cross over in this boat in a storm."

"Master," suggested Robert, who always addressed me thus, "would it not be more prudent to land again before the storm reaches its height? We should be safe behind the stones, and we can gather a quantity of fuel before sunset."

"Yes, that will perhaps be best; this lake is much more dangerous in a storm than Lake Lighten. We have, indeed, no furs, but we shall manage. Take in the sail and row behind the boulders. What are you gazing at?"

"Master, I see two large wolves, and we have no guns."

He was right; two light, almost white, Isegrims were pacing the shore. They were so placed that they must be able to scent us in the boat; the odor of fresh live meat tickled their noses. When we stopped they stopped too, and when we began to move they went on close to the margin of the water. "Sooner or later you must come on shore, and then it will be our turn," perhaps they thought. Rehim Ali opined that they were scouts of a whole troop, and said it was dangerous to expose ourselves to an attack in the night. He had only a clasp-knife with him, and Robert and I only penknives in our pockets; we had, therefore, little chance of defending ourselves successfully. Robert, for his part, preferred the lake in a storm to the wolves. I had so often slept out of doors unarmed, that I no longer troubled myself about them. But in the midst of our consultation we were suddenly compelled to think of something else. The storm came whistling over the lake.

Fortunately, the sail was still standing and the centerboards were down; the wind caught the canvas, the water began to rush under the stern, and we shot smoothly southward with a side wind. Robert gave vent to a sigh of relief. "Anything but wolves," he said. I made Robert and Rehim Ali row to save time, and soon the two beasts were out of sight. "They will certainly gallop round the lake, as they know quite well that we must land somewhere," said Robert. He was quite right—the situation was exceedingly unpleasant; we had only a choice between the storm and the wolves. We could not depend on our people; they were evidently cut off from us by salt morasses, which it was dangerous to venture into. We would therefore try to reach a suitable point on the south shore before dark.

The hours fled past, and the sun sank in glowing yellow behind the mountains. For two hours we held on our course toward Deasy's camp, but when the beacon fires became more distinct in the gathering twilight we changed our direction and steered southward to reach our people. The distance, however, was hopelessly long, and just from that direction the storm blew, and in the broken, freakish light of the moon the waves looked as weird as playing dolphins. Sometimes I was able to take some rapid soundings; they gave depths of 32 and 36 feet. Our fate was just as uncertain as on the former occasion on Lake Lighten; we steered for the shore, but did not know how far off it was. Rehim Ali judged from the length of the path of moonlight on the water that it was a long distance. Two more hours passed. I gave my orders to the oarsmen in English and Turki. We had now the waves on our quarter, and if we did not parry their rolling, foaming crests, they would fill the boat and sink it; so we had to sail straight against them.

The situation was not a little exciting, but good luck attended us. The boat cut the waves cleanly, and we got only small splashes now and then. The spray trickled down our necks, was pleasantly cool, and had a saline taste. I again took soundings, and Robert read the line: 33 feet, then 25, and lastly 20.

"Now the southern shore cannot be very far," I said; but my companions remained still and listened. "What is it?" I asked.

"A heavy storm from the west," answered Rehim Ali, letting his oar fall.

A regular humming noise was heard in the distance, which came nearer and nearer. It was the storm, which swept over the lake with redoubled violence and lashed up foam from the waves.

"We shall not reach the shore before it overtakes us. It will be here in a minute. Master, we shall capsize if the waves become twice as high as they are now."

The waves swelled with incredible rapidity, the curves in the streak of moonlight became greater and greater, and we rocked as in a huge hammock. The sounding line had just marked 20 feet. How long would it be before the boat would ground on the hard, salt bottom, if it found itself in a trough between two waves? The leeboards beat against the sides, the boat pitches and rolls, and anyone who does not sit firmly and stiffen himself with his feet must go overboard. A terrible wave, like an all-devouring monster, comes down upon us, but the boat glides smoothly over it, and the next moment we are down in a trough so deep that all the horizon is concealed by the succeeding crest. We were not quick enough in negotiating this new wave; it ran along the gunwale and gave us a good footbath.

"Master, it looks dangerous."

"Yes, it is not exactly pleasant, but keep quiet. We cannot land in such a sea. We must turn and make for the open lake. About midnight the storm may abate, and then we can land."

"If we can only keep on rowing so long."

"We will help ourselves with the sail."

"I am not tired yet."

To land on the southern shore would be certain shipwreck; we should all be drenched to the skin, and that is dangerous on this night when we cannot reckon on the slightest help from the caravan. We shall be frozen before the dawn. To look for fuel before the sun sets is not to be thought of, for the saline plains in the south are absolutely barren. No, we will turn.

At the same moment we felt a violent blow, which made the boat tremble. The larboard oar, which Rehim Ali worked, had struck against the ground and started loose from the screw which fastened it to the gunwale. Rehim Ali managed to catch hold of it just in time, while he shouted, "It is only a stone's throw to the land."

"Why, how is this?—here the lake is quite smooth."

"A promontory juts out into the lake. Master, here we shall find shelter."

"All right, then we are saved; row slowly till the boat takes ground." That soon happened; the sail was furled, the mast unshipped. We took off our boots and stockings, stepped into the water, and drew the boat on to dry land. My feet were so numbed in the briny water, cooled down to 41°F, that I could not stand, and had to sit down and wrap my feet in my ulster. We found a patch of lumps of salt—thoroughly moist, indeed, though drier than elsewhere, and the best spot to be had; for water lay all around us, and the bank was extremely low. How far it was to really dry ground we could not ascertain; the moon threw a faintly shining strip of light for a considerable distance farther toward the land.

While I endeavored to restore life to my feet by friction, the others carried our belongings to our wretched salt island. Then the boat was taken to pieces, and the two halves were set up as shelters. At nine o'clock we noted 31°F on the thermometer, and at midnight 17½°F; yet it was warmer now than on the previous days, for the water of the lake retains some of the heat of the summer air. Muhamed Isa had made a new roller for the sounding line, with frame and handle, out of an empty box; it was of course immediately utilized as fuel.

The provision bags and the water cans were brought out again, and we drank one cup of hot sugar-and-water after another, and tried to imagine it was tea. As long as the fire lasted we should not freeze—but then, what a night! Toward ten o'clock the wind abated—now came the night frost. We lay down on the life buoys to avoid direct contact with the briny soil; Robert had the fur coat, I the ulster, and Rehim Ali wrapped himself in the sail. He slept huddled up with his forehead on the ground, as is the Mohammedan custom, and he did really sleep. Robert and I rolled ourselves together in a bunch, but of what use was it? One cannot sleep just before freezing. My feet were, indeed, past feeling, but this consolation was a sorry one. I stood up and stamped on the salt patch, and tried to walk without moving, for the space was very limited. I sang and whistled; I hummed a song, and imitated the howl of the wolves to see if they would reply. But the silence was unbroken. I told anecdotes to Robert, but he was not amused by them. I related adventures I had had before with wolves and storms, but they had little encouraging effect in our present position. We looked in vain for a fire; there was nothing to be seen in any direction. The moon slowly approached the horizon. The wind had sunk entirely. Little by little the salt waves, splashing melodiously against the shore, also sank to rest—an awful silence reigned around. We were too cold to think much of the wolves. Twice we raised a wild scream, but the sound of our voices died away suddenly without awaking the slightest echo; how could it reach the campground?

"Now it is midnight, Robert; in four hours it will be day."

"Master, I have never been so starved in my life. If I get back to India alive, I shall never forget this dreadful night on Yeshil-kul and the hungry wolves on the shore, though I live to a hundred."

"Oh, nonsense. You will think of it with longing, and be glad that you were here."

"It is all very fine to look back on, but at present I should be delighted to have my warm bed in the tent and a fire."

"Life in Tibet is too monotonous without adventures; one day's journey is like another, and we want a little change occasionally to wake us up. But we will take tea and firewood with us next time."

"Shall you have more of such lake voyages, Master?"

"Certainly, if there is an opportunity; but I fear that the winter cold will soon make them impossible."

"Will it, then, be still colder than now?"

"Yes, this is nothing to what the cold will be in two months."

"What time is it, Master?"

"Two o'clock; we shall soon have been lying six hours on the morass."

We nodded a little once more, but did not really sleep for a minute; from time to time Robert told me how badly his feet were frozen. At three o'clock he exclaimed, after a long silence: "Now I have no more feeling in any of my toes."

"The sun will soon come." At a quarter past four begins a faint glimmer of dawn. We are so chilled through that we can hardly stand up. But at length we pull ourselves up and stamp on the ground. Then we cower again over the cold ashes of our fire. We constantly look to the east and watch the new day, which slowly peeps over the mountains as though it would look about before it ventures out. At five o'clock the highest peaks receive a purple tinge, and we cast a faint shadow on the bottom of the boat, and then the sun rises, cold and bright yellow, over the crest to the east. Now the springs of life revive. Rehim Ali has disappeared for an hour, and now we see him tramping through the swamp with a large bundle of wood, and soon we have kindled a sparkling, crackling fire. We undress to get rid of our wet and cold clothes, and warm our bodies at the flames, and soon our limbs are supple again.

———◦———

THE TRAIN TO DARJEELING *

Mark Twain

Some time during the forenoon, approaching the mountains, we changed from the regular train to one composed of little canvas-sheltered cars that skimmed along within a foot of the ground and seemed to be going

* Mark Twain traveled to India, and Darjeeling, as part of his circumnavigation of the globe, which he recorded in *Following the Equator: A Journey Round the World* (1897).

fifty miles an hour when they were really making about twenty. Each car had seating capacity for half a dozen persons; and when the curtains were up one was substantially out of doors, and could see everywhere, and get all the breeze, and be luxuriously comfortable. It was not a pleasure excursion in name only, but in fact.

After a while we stopped at a little wooden coop of a station just within the curtain of the somber jungle, a place with a deep and dense forest of great trees and scrub and vines all about it. The royal Bengal tiger is in great force there, and is very bold and unconventional. From this lonely little station a message once went to the railway manager in Calcutta: "Tiger eating stationmaster on front porch; telegraph instructions."

It was there that I had my first tiger hunt. I killed thirteen. We were presently away again, and the train began to climb the mountains. In one place seven wild elephants crossed the track, but two of them got away before I could overtake them. The railway journey up the mountain is forty miles, and it takes eight hours to make it. It is so wild and interesting and exciting and enchanting that it ought to take a week. As for the vegetation, it is a museum. The jungle seemed to contain samples of every rare and curious tree and bush that we had ever seen or heard of. It is from that museum, I think, that the globe must have been supplied with the trees and vines and shrubs that it holds precious.

The road is infinitely and charmingly crooked. It goes winding in and out under lofty cliffs that are smothered in vines and foliage, and around the edges of bottomless chasms; and all the way one glides by files of picturesque natives, some carrying burdens up, others going down from their work in the tea gardens; and once there was a gaudy wedding procession, all bright tinsel and color, and a bride, comely and girlish, who peeped out from the curtains of her palanquin, exposing her face with that pure delight which the young and happy take in sin for sin's own sake.

By and by we were well up in the region of the clouds, and from that breezy height we looked down and afar over a wonderful picture—the Plains of India, stretching to the horizon, soft and fair, level as a floor, shimmering with heat, mottled with cloud-shadows, and cloven with shining rivers. Immediately below us, and receding down, down, down, toward the valley, was a shaven confusion of hilltops, with ribbony roads and paths squirming and snaking cream-yellow all over them and about them, every curve and twist sharply distinct.

At an elevation of 6,000 feet we entered a thick cloud, and it shut out the world and kept it shut out. We climbed 1,000 feet higher, then began to descend, and presently got down to Darjeeling, which is 6,000 feet above the level of the Plains.

We had passed many a mountain village on the way up, and seen some new kinds of natives, among them many samples of the fighting Ghurkas. They are not large men, but they are strong and resolute. There are no better soldiers among Britain's native troops. And we had passed shoals of their women climbing the forty miles of steep road from the valley to their mountain homes, with tall baskets on their backs hitched to their foreheads by a band, and containing a freightage weighing—I will not say how many hundreds of pounds, for the sum is unbelievable. These were young women, and they strode smartly along under these astonishing burdens with the air of people out for a holiday. I was told that a woman will carry a piano on her back all the way up the mountain; and that more than once a woman had done it. If these were old women I should regard the Ghurkas as no more civilized than the Europeans. At the railway station at Darjeeling you find plenty of cab substitutes—open coffins, in which you sit, and are then borne on men's shoulders up the steep roads into the town.

Up there we found a fairly comfortable hotel, the property of an indiscriminate and incoherent landlord, who looks after nothing, but leaves everything to his army of Indian servants. No, he does look after the bill—to be just to him—and the tourist cannot do better than follow his example. I was told by a resident that the summit of Kinchinjunga is often hidden in the clouds, and that sometimes a tourist has waited twenty-two days and then been obliged to go away without a sight of it. And yet went not disappointed; for when he got his hotel bill he recognized that he was now seeing the highest thing in the Himalayas. But this is probably a lie.

After lecturing I went to the Club that night, and that was a comfortable place. It is loftily situated, and looks out over a vast spread of scenery; from it you can see where the boundaries of three countries come together, some thirty miles away; Thibet is one of them, Nepaul another, and I think Herzegovina was the other. Apparently, in every town and city in India the gentlemen of the British civil and military service have a club; sometimes it is a palatial one, always it is pleasant and homelike. The hotels are not always as good as they might be, and the stranger who has access to the Club is grateful for his privilege and knows how to value it.

Next day was Sunday. Friends came in the gray dawn with horses, and my party rode away to a distant point where Kinchinjunga and Mount Everest show up best, but I stayed at home for a private view; for it was very cold, and I was not acquainted with the horses anyway. I got a pipe and a few blankets and sat for two hours at the window, and saw the sun drive away the veiling gray and touch up the snow peaks one after another with pale pink splashes and delicate washes of gold, and finally flood the whole mighty convulsion of snow mountains with a deluge of rich splendors.

Kinchinjunga's peak was but fitfully visible, but in the between times it was vividly clear against the sky—away up there in the blue dome more than 28,000 feet above sea level—the loftiest land I had ever seen, by 12,000 feet or more. It was forty-five miles away. Mount Everest is a thousand feet higher, but it was not a part of that sea of mountains piled up there before me, so I did not see it; but I did not care, because I think that mountains that are as high as that are disagreeable. I changed from the back to the front of the house and spent the rest of the morning there, watching the swarthy strange tribes flock by from their far homes in the Himalayas. All ages and both sexes were represented, and the breeds were quite new to me, though the costumes of the Thibetans made them look a good deal like Chinamen. The prayer wheel was a frequent feature. It brought me near to these people, and made them seem kinfolk of mine. Through our preacher we do much of our praying by proxy. We do not whirl him around a stick, as they do, but that is merely a detail.

The swarm swung briskly by, hour after hour, a strange and striking pageant. It was wasted there, and it seemed a pity. It should have been sent streaming through the cities of Europe or America, to refresh eyes weary of the pale monotonies of the circus pageant. These people were bound for the bazaar, with things to sell. We went down there, later, and saw that novel congress of the wild peoples, and plowed here and there through it, and concluded that it would be worth coming from Calcutta to see, even if there were no Kinchinjunga and Everest.

There are two times in a man's life when he should not speculate: when he can't afford it, and when he can.

—Pudd'nhead Wilson's New Calendar

On Monday and Tuesday at sunrise we again had fair-to-middling views of the stupendous mountains; then, being well cooled off and refreshed, we were ready to chance the weather of the lower world once more.

We traveled up hill by the regular train five miles to the summit, then changed to a little canvas-canopied handcar for the thirty-five-mile descent. It was the size of a sleigh, it had six seats and was so low that it seemed to rest on the ground. It had no engine or other propelling power, and needed none to help it fly down those steep inclines. It only needed a strong brake, to modify its flight, and it had that. There was a story of a disastrous trip made down the mountain once in this little car by the lieutenant governor of Bengal, when the car jumped the track and threw its passengers over a precipice. It was not true, but the story had value for me, for it made me nervous, and nervousness wakes a person up and makes him alive and alert, and heightens the thrill of a new and doubtful experience. The car could really jump the track, of course; a pebble on the track, placed there by either accident or malice, at a sharp curve where one might strike it before the eye could discover it, could derail the car and fling it down into India; and the fact that the lieutenant governor had escaped was no proof that I would have the same luck. And standing there, looking down upon the Indian Empire from the airy altitude of 7,000 feet, it seemed unpleasantly far, dangerously far, to be flung from a handcar.

But after all, there was but small danger—for me. What there was, was for Mr. Pugh, inspector of a division of the Indian police, in whose company and protection we had come from Calcutta. He had seen long service as an artillery officer, was less nervous than I was, and so he was to go ahead of us in a pilot handcar, with a Ghurka and another native; and the plan was that when we should see his car jump over a precipice we must put on our (brake) and send for another pilot. It was a good arrangement. Also Mr. Barnard, chief engineer of the mountain division of the road, was to take personal charge of our car, and he had been down the mountain in it many a time.

Everything looked safe. Indeed, there was but one questionable detail left: the regular train was to follow us as soon as we should start, and it might run over us. Privately, I thought it would. The road fell sharply down in front of us and went corkscrewing in and out around the crags and precipices, down, down, forever down, suggesting nothing so exactly or so uncomfortably as a crooked toboggan slide with no end to it. Mr. Pugh waved his flag and started, like an arrow from a bow, and before I could get out of the car we were gone too. I had previously had but one sensation like the shock of that departure, and that was the gaspy shock that took my breath away the first time that I was discharged from the summit of a toboggan slide. But in both instances the sensation was pleasurable—intensely so; it was a sudden and immense exaltation, a mixed ecstasy of deadly fright and unimaginable joy. I believe that this combination makes the perfection of human delight.

The pilot car's flight down the mountain suggested the swoop of a swallow that is skimming the ground, so swiftly and smoothly and gracefully it swept down the long straight reaches and soared in and out of the bends and around the corners. We raced after it, and seemed to flash by the capes and crags with the speed of light; and now and then we almost overtook it—and had hopes; but it was only playing with us; when we got near, it released its brake, made a spring around a corner, and the next time it spun into view, a few seconds later, it looked as small as a wheelbarrow, it was so far away. We played with the train in the same way. We often got out to gather flowers or sit on a precipice and look at the scenery, then presently we would hear a dull and growing roar, and the long coils of the train would come into sight behind and above us; but we did not need to start till the locomotive was close down upon us—then we soon left it far behind. It had to stop at every station, therefore it was not an embarrassment to us. Our brake was a good piece of machinery; it could bring the car to a standstill on a slope as steep as a house roof.

The scenery was grand and varied and beautiful, and there was no hurry; we could always stop and examine it. There was abundance of time. We did not need to hamper the train; if it wanted the road, we could switch off and let it go by, then overtake it and pass it later. We stopped at one place to see the Gladstone Cliff, a great crag which the ages and the weather have sculptured into a recognizable portrait of the venerable statesman. Mr. Gladstone is a stockholder in the road, and Nature began this portrait ten thousand years ago, with the idea of having the compliment ready in time for the event.

We saw a banyan tree which sent down supporting stems from branches which were sixty feet above the ground. That is, I suppose it was a banyan; its bark resembled that of the great banyan in the botanical gardens at Calcutta, that spider-legged thing with its wilderness of vegetable columns. And there were frequent glimpses of a totally leafless tree upon whose innumerable twigs and branches a cloud of crimson butterflies had lighted—apparently. In fact these brilliant red butterflies were flowers, but the illusion was good. Afterward in South Africa, I saw another splendid effect made by red flowers. This flower was probably called the torch-plant—should have been so named, anyway. It had a slender stem several feet high, and from its top stood up a single tongue of flame, an intensely red flower of the size and shape of a small corncob. The stems stood three or four feet apart all over a great hill-slope that was a mile long, and make one think of what the Place de la Concorde would be if its myriad lights were red instead of white and yellow.

A few miles down the mountain we stopped half an hour to see a Thibetan dramatic performance. It was in the open air on the hillside. The audience was composed of Thibetans, Ghurkas, and other unusual people. The costumes of the actors were in the last degree outlandish, and the performance was in keeping with the clothes. To an accompaniment of barbarous noises the actors stepped out one after another and began to spin around with immense swiftness and vigor and violence, chanting the while, and soon the whole troupe would be spinning and chanting and raising the dust. They were performing an ancient and celebrated historical play, and a Chinaman explained it to me in pidjin English as it went along. The play was obscure enough without the explanation; with the explanation added, it was (opaque). As a drama this ancient historical work of art was defective, I thought, but as a wild and barbarous spectacle the representation was beyond criticism. Far down the mountain we got out to look at a piece of remarkable loop engineering—a spiral where the road curves upon itself with such abruptness that when the regular train came down and entered the loop, we stood over it and saw the locomotive disappear under our bridge, then in a few moments appear again, chasing its own tail; and we saw it gain on it, overtake it, draw ahead past the rear cars, and run a race with that end of the train. It was like a snake swallowing itself. Halfway down the mountain we stopped about an hour at Mr. Barnard's house for refreshments, and while we were sitting on the veranda looking at the distant panorama of hills through a gap in the forest, we came very near to seeing a leopard kill a calf.—(It killed it the day before.)—It is a wild place and lovely. From the woods all about came the songs of birds—among them the contributions of a couple of birds which I was not then acquainted with: the brain-fever bird and the coppersmith. The song of the brain-fever demon starts on a low but steadily rising key, and is a spiral twist which augments in intensity and severity with each added spiral, growing sharper and sharper, and more and more painful, more and more agonizing, more and more maddening, intolerable, unendurable, as it bores deeper and deeper and deeper into the listener's brain, until at last the brain fever comes as a relief and the man dies. I am bringing some of these birds home to America. They will be a great curiosity there, and it is believed that in our climate they will multiply like rabbits.

The coppersmith bird's note at a certain distance away has the ring of a sledge on granite; at a certain other distance the hammering has a more metallic ring, and you might think that the bird was mending a copper kettle; at another distance it has a more woodeny thump, but it is a thump that is full of energy, and sounds just like starting a bung. So he is a hard bird to name with a single name; he is a stone-breaker, coppersmith, and bung-starter, and even then he is not completely named, for when he is close by you find that there is a soft, deep, melodious quality in his thump, and for that no satisfying name occurs to you. You will not mind his other notes, but when he camps near enough for you to hear that one, you presently find that his measured and monotonous repetition of it is beginning to disturb you; next it will weary you, soon it will distress you, and before long each thump will hurt your head; if this goes on, you will lose your mind with the pain and misery of it, and go crazy. I am bringing some of these birds home to America. There is nothing like them there. They will be a great surprise, and it is said that in a climate like ours they will surpass expectation for fecundity.

I am bringing some nightingales, too, and some cue-owls. I got them in Italy. The song of the nightingale is the deadliest known to ornithology. That demoniacal shriek can kill at thirty yards. The note of the cue-owl is infinitely soft and sweet—soft and sweet as the whisper of a flute. But penetrating—oh, beyond belief; it can bore through boiler-iron. It is a lingering note, and comes in triplets, on the one unchanging key: hoo-o-o, hoo-o-o, hoo-o-o; then a silence of fifteen seconds, then the triplet again; and so on, all night. At first it is divine; then less so; then trying; then distressing; then excruciating; then agonizing, and at the end of two hours the listener is a maniac.

And so, presently we took to the handcar and went flying down the mountain again, flying and stopping, flying and stopping, till at last we were in the plain once more and stowed for Calcutta in the regular train. That was the most enjoyable day I have spent in the earth. For rousing, tingling, rapturous pleasure there is no holiday trip that approaches the bird-flight down the Himalayas in a handcar. It has no fault, no blemish, no lack, except that there are only thirty-five miles of it instead of five hundred.

THE ABOMINABLE SNOWMAN*

Frank S. Smythe

On July 16 I left the base camp, taking with me Wangdi, Pasang, and Nurbu with light equipment and provisions for five days. The past week had seen many more flowers come into bloom, prominent among which was the *pedicularis*. This plant goes by the unpleasant popular name of lousewort, from the Latin *pediculus*, a louse, as one of the species, *Pedicularis palustris*, was said to infect sheep with a lousy disease; but it

* Frank Smythe is credited with having popularized the Valley of Flowers, now part of the Nanda Devi Biosphere Reserve in the western Himalaya, after he spent a few weeks in the valley in 1937, where he trekked and climbed—and nearly met the Yeti. He wrote about his time there in *The Valley of Flowers* (1949).

would be difficult to associate the beautiful *pedicularis* of the Bhyundar Valley with any disease, particularly the *Pedicularis siphonantfia* with its light purple blooms.

There were also many dwarf geraniums and the *saussurea*, which grows in an astonishing variety of forms, varying from wide-spreading, flattish leaves with purple cornflower-like blooms rising almost stalk-less in the center, to curious balloon-shaped plants and little balls of silver-gray wool that grow high up above the snow line.

Gentians, formerly conspicuous by their absence, with the exception of the ubiquitous *Gentiana aprica*, were also in bloom, and I came across a plant (*G. venusta*) like a small edition of that well-known denizen of the Alps, *G. acaulis*. It seems very shy of opening its petals and its little flower is almost stalkless. There was also growing in moist mossy places among the rocks *Primula reptans*, which rivals the *Primula minutissima* in delicacy. With so much beauty and interest attached to the ascent I scarcely noticed that I was walking uphill.

As we passed near some boulders, there was a sudden startled squawking and half a dozen or more young pheasants flew out from a small cave. Wangdi was greatly excited at this, and said that the birds would return to roost. I must confess that my mouth watered so much at the thought of roast pheasant as a change from sheep and goat that then and there I consented to a most nefarious expedition, which was planned to take place after dark.

In order to shorten the morrow's march we camped several hundred feet above our former camping place by the edge of a snowdrift amidst hundreds of *Primula denticulata*, many of which were still in bud. As I had found the same species of primula in seed five weeks previously, this struck me as remarkable. As late as October 7 I found flowering plants in ground where avalanche snow had recently melted. It would be interesting to know what process takes place in a plant that is covered for a year or more by avalanche snow, as must often occur in this country. Does it continue to live? Presumably it does, as even compacted avalanche snow contains an appreciable quantity of air. Small wonder that in England gardeners experience difficulty in growing a high Alpine or Himalayan plant, for these supposedly hardy plants are not really as hardy as plants that grow at much lower elevations, which are exposed to climatic conditions all the year round. It is nothing short of miraculous that a plant which lies dormant, protected by a covering of snow for six months of the year, should deign to grow in our bewildering climate.

It was almost completely dark when Wangdi poked his head in at the door of my tent and with a wicked grin announced himself as ready for the murder of the innocents. Together with Nurbu and Pasang, who were armed with blankets, we descended the boulder-clad hillside. A few yards from the cave Wangdi whispered to me to wait, then he and the other two conspirators crept forward as softly as cats. The next moment there was a concerted rush and both entrances to the cave were stopped by blankets. There was no answering scurry of startled birds, so Wangdi crawled under one of the blankets and groped about inside. There were no pheasants roosting there, and he retired into the open, saying things in Tibetan which doubtless exercised the nuances of that language, but at the meaning of which I could only guess. For a few moments I was as disappointed as he, then the humor of our attempted murder struck us both simultaneously and we burst into a roar of laughter.

Next morning we were away in excellent weather. Being lightly laden, I was well ahead of the men. On approaching the pass, I was surprised to notice some tracks in the snow, which I first took to be those of a man, though we had seen no traces of shepherds. But when I came up to the tracks I saw the imprint of a huge naked foot, apparently of a biped, and in stride closely resembling my own tracks. What was it? I was very interested, and at once proceeded to take some photographs. I was engaged in this work when the porters joined me. It was at once evident when they saw the tracks that they were frightened. Wangdi was the first to speak:

"Ban Manshi!" he said, and then "Mirka!" And in case I still did not understand, "Kang Admi (Snowman)."

I had already anticipated such a reply, and to reassure him and the other two, for I had no wish for my expedition to end prematurely, I said it must be a bear or snow leopard. But Wangdi would have none of this and explained at length how the tracks could not possibly be those of a bear, snow leopard, wolf, or any other animal. Had he not seen many such tracks in the past? It was the Snowman, and he looked uneasily about him.

I am not superstitious. The number thirteen even in conjunction with a Friday means nothing to me. I do not hesitate to walk under a ladder unless there is the danger of a paint pot falling on my head.

Crossed knives, spilt salt, sailors drowning when glasses are made to ring, black coats, new moons seen through glass, chimney sweeps, and such-like manifestations leave me unmoved. But there was something queer, and I must admit that Wangdi's argument and fear was not without its effect. The matter must be investigated. So I got out of my rucksack a copy of the *Spectator* and with a pencil proceeded to mark the size and stride of the track, while the men huddled together, a prey to that curious sullenness which in the Tibetan means fear.

About four inches of snow had fallen recently, and it was obvious that the tracks had been made the previous evening after the sun had lost its power and had frozen during the night, for they were perfect impressions distinct in every detail. On the level the footmarks were as much as 13 inches in length and 6 inches in breadth, but uphill they averaged only 8 inches in length, though the breadth was the same. The stride was from 18 inches to 2 feet on the level, but considerably less uphill, and the footmarks were turned outward at about the same angle as a man's. There were the well-defined imprints of five toes, 1½ inch to 1¾ inches long and ¾ inch broad, which, unlike human toes, were arranged symmetrically. Lastly there was at first sight what appeared to be the impression of a heel, with two curious toe-like impressions on either side.

Presently the men plucked up courage and assisted me. They were unanimous that the Snowman walked with his toes behind him and that the impressions at the heel were in reality the front toes. I was soon able to disprove this to my own satisfaction by discovering a place where the beast had jumped down from some rocks, making deep impressions where he had landed, and slithering a little in the snow. Superstition, however, knows no logic, and my explanation produced no effect whatever on Wangdi. At length, having taken all the photographs I wanted on the pass, I asked the men to accompany me and follow up the tracks. They were very averse to this at first, but eventually agreed, as they said, following their own "logic," that the Snowman had come from, not gone, in that direction. From the pass the tracks followed a broad, slightly ascending snow ridge and, except for one divergence, took an almost straight line. After some 300 yards they turned off the ridge and descended a steep rock face fully 1,000 feet high and seamed with snow gullies. Through my monocular glass I was able to follow them down to a small but considerably crevassed glacier, descending toward the Bhyundar Valley, and down this to the lowermost limit of the new snow. I was much impressed by the difficulties overcome and the intelligence displayed in overcoming them. In order to descend the face, the beast had made a series of intricate traverses and had zigzagged down a series of ridges and gullies. His track down the glacier was masterly, and from our perch I could see every detail and how cunningly he had avoided concealed snow-covered crevasses. An expert mountaineer could not have made a better route, and to have accomplished it without an ice ax would have been both difficult and dangerous, whilst the unroped descent of a crevassed snow-covered glacier must be accounted as unjustifiable. Obviously the "Snowman" was well qualified for membership of the Himalayan Club.

My examination in this direction completed, we returned to the pass, and I decided to follow the track in the reverse direction. The man, however, said that this was the direction in which the Snowman was going, and if we overtook him, and even so much as set eyes upon him, we should all drop dead in our tracks, or come to an otherwise bad end. They were so scared at the prospect that I felt it was unfair to force them to accompany me, though I believe that Wangdi, at least, would have done so had I asked him.

The tracks, to begin with, traversed along the side of a rough rock ridge below the minor point we had ascended when we first visited the pass. I followed them for a short distance along the snow to one side of the rocks, then they turned upward into the mouth of a small cave under some slabs. I was puzzled to account for the fact that, whereas tracks appeared to come out of the cave, there were none going into it. I had already proved to my own satisfaction the absurdity of the porters' contention that the Snowman walked with his toes behind him; still, I was now alone and cut off from sight of the porters by a mist that had suddenly formed, and I could not altogether repress a ridiculous feeling that perhaps they were right after all; such is the power of superstition high up in the lonely Himalayas. I am ashamed to admit that I stood at a distance from the cave and threw a lump of rock into it before venturing further. Nothing happened, so I went up to the mouth of the cave and looked inside; naturally there was nothing there. I then saw that the single track was explained by the beast having climbed down a steep rock and jumped into the snow at the mouth of the cave. I lost the track among the rocks, so I climbed up to the little summit we had previously visited. The mist was now dense and I waited fully a quarter of an hour for it to clear. It was a curious experience seated there with no other human being within sight and some queer thoughts passed through my mind. Was there really a Snowman? If so, would I encounter him? If I did an ice ax would be a poor substitute for a rifle, but Wangdi had said that even to see a Snowman was to die. Evidently he killed you by some miraculous hypnotism, then presumably gobbled you up. It was a fairy tale come to life.

Then, at last, the mists blew aside. At first I could see no tracks coming off the rock island on which I was seated, and this was not only puzzling but disturbing, as it implied that the beast might be lurking in the rear vicinity. Then I saw that the tracks traversed a narrow and almost concealed ridge to another rock point, and beyond this descended a glacier to the east of our ascending route to the pass. Whatever it was, it lived in the Bhyundar Valley; but why had it left this pleasant valley for these inhospitable altitudes, which involved difficult and dangerous climbing, and an ascent of many thousands of feet?

Meditating on this strange affair, I returned to the porters, who were unfeignedly glad to see me, for they had assumed that I was walking to my death.

I must now refer to the subsequent history of this business.

On returning to the base camp some days later, the porters made a statement. It was witnessed by Oliver and runs as follows:

We, Wangdi Nurbu, Nurbu Bhotia, and Pasang Urgen, porters employed by Mr. F. S. Smythe, were accompanying Mr. Smythe on July 17 over a glacier pass north of the Bhyundar Valley when we saw on the pass tracks which we knew to be those of a Mirka or Jungli Admi (wild man). We have often seen bear, snow leopard, and other animal tracks, but we swear that these tracks were none of these, but were the tracks of a Mirka.

We told Mr. Smythe that these were the tracks of a Mirka and we saw him take photographs and make measurements. We have never seen a Mirka because anyone who sees one dies or is killed, but there are pictures of the tracks, which are the same as we have seen, in Tibetan monasteries.

My photographs were developed by Kodak Ltd. of Bombay under conditions that precluded any subsequent accusation of faking and, together with my measurements and observations, were sent to my literary agent, Mr. Leonard P. Moore, who was instrumental in having them examined by Professor Julian Huxley, Secretary of the Zoological Society, Mr. Martin A. C. Hinton, Keeper of Zoology at the Natural History Museum, and Mr. R. I. Pocock. The conclusion reached by these experts was that the tracks were made by a bear. At first, due to a misunderstanding as to the exact locality in which the tracks had been seen, the bear was said to be *Ursus arctos pruinosus*, but subsequently it was decided that it was *Ursus arctos isabellinus*, which is distributed throughout the western and central Himalayas. The tracks agreed in size and character with that animal and there is no reason to suppose that they could have been made by anything else. This bear sometimes grows as large, or larger, than a grizzly, and there is a well-grown specimen in the Natural History Museum. It also varies in color from brown to silver-gray.

The fact that the tracks appeared to have been made by a biped is explained by the bear, like all bears, putting its rear foot at the rear end of the impression left by its front foot. Only the side toes would show, and this explains the Tibetans' belief that the curious indentations, in reality superimposed by the rear foot, are the front toes of a Snowman who walks with his toes behind him. This also explains the size of the spoor, which when melted out by the sun would appear enormous. Mr. Eric Shipton describes some tracks he saw near the peak of Nanda Ghunti in Garhwal as resembling those of a young elephant. So also would the tracks I saw when the sun had melted them away at the edges.

How did the legend originate? It is known over a considerable portion of Tibet, in Sikkim and parts of Nepal, including the Sola Khombu Valley, the home of the Sherpas on the south side of the Himalayas. The reason for this probably lies in the comparative ease of communication on the Tibetan plateau, as compared with that in the more mountainous regions south of the Himalayan watershed, where it is known only to peoples of Buddhist faith, such as the Sherpas of Nepal and the Lepchas of Sikkim. The Snowman is reputed to be large, fierce, and carnivorous; the large ones eat yaks and the small ones men. He is sometimes white, and sometimes black or brown. About the female, the most definite account I have heard is that she is only less fierce than the male, but is hampered in her movements by exceptionally large pendulous breasts, which she must perforce sling over her shoulders when walking or running.

Of recent years considerable force has been lent to the legend by Europeans having seen strange tracks in the snow, sometimes far above the permanent snow line, apparently of a biped. Such tracks had in all cases been spoiled or partially spoiled by the sun, but if such tracks were made by bears, then it is obvious that bears very seldom wander on to the upper snows, otherwise fresh tracks unmelted by the sun would have been observed by travelers. The movements of animals are incalculable, and there seems no logical explanation as to why a bear should venture far from its haunts of woodland and pasture. There is one point in connection with this which may have an important bearing on the tracks we saw, which I have omitted previously in order to bring it in at this juncture. On the way up the Bhyundar Valley from the base camp, I saw a bear about 200 yards distant on the northern slopes of the valley. It bolted immediately, and so quickly that I did not catch more than a glimpse of it, and disappeared into a small cave under an overhanging crag. When the men, who were behind, came up with me, I suggested that we should try to coax it into the open, in order that I could photograph it, so the men threw stones into the cave while I stood by with my camera. But the bear was not to be scared out so easily, and as I had no rifle it was not advisable to approach too near to the cave. It is possible that we so scared this bear that the same evening it made up the hillside some 4,000 feet to the pass. There are two objections to this theory: firstly, that it appeared to be the ordinary small black bear, and too small to make tracks of the size we saw and, secondly, that the tracks ascended the glacier fully a mile to the east of the point where we saw the bear. We may, however, have unwittingly disturbed another and larger bear during our ascent to our camp. At all events, it is logical to assume that an animal would not venture so far from its native haunts without some strong motive to impel it. One last and very interesting point—the Sikh surveyor whom I had met in the Bhyundar Valley was reported by the postmaster of Joshimath as having seen a huge white bear in the neighborhood of the Bhyundar Valley.

It seems possible that the Snowman legend originated through certain traders who saw bears when crossing the passes over the Himalayas and carried their stories into Tibet, where they became magnified and distorted by the people of that superstitious country which, though Buddhist in theory, has never emancipated itself from ancient nature and devil worship. Whether or not bears exist on the Tibetan side of the Himalayas I cannot say. It is probable that they do in comparatively low and densely forested valleys such as the Kharta and Kharma Valleys east of Mount Everest, and it may be that they are distributed more widely than is at present known.

After my return to England I wrote an article, which was published by *The Times*, in which I narrated my experiences and put forward my conclusions, which were based, of course, on the identifications of the zoological experts.

I must confess that this article was provocative, not to say dogmatic, but until it was published I had no idea that the Abominable Snowman, as he is popularly known, is as much beloved by the great British public as the sea-serpent and the Loch Ness Monster. Indeed, in debunking what had become an institution, I roused a hornet's nest about my ears. It was even proposed by one gentleman in a letter to *The Times* that the Royal Geographical Society and the Alpine Club should send a joint expedition to the Himalayas in an attempt to prove or disprove my observations and conclusions. It was obvious that the writer hoped that this expedition, if it took place, would not only disprove them, but would prove the existence of the Abominable Snowman. I can only say in extenuation of my crime that I hope there is an Abominable Snowman. The tracks I saw were undoubtedly made by a bear, but what if other tracks seen by other people were made by Abominable Snowmen? I hope they were. In this murky age of materialism, human beings have to struggle hard to find the romantic, and what could be more romantic than an Abominable Snowman, together with an Abominable Snow-woman, and, not least of all, an Abominable Snow-baby?

MUTINY ON KANGCHENJUNGA*

Aleister Crowley

Darjeeling is a standing or rather steaming example of official ineptitude. Sir Joseph Hooker, one of the few men of brains who have

* The British occultist Aleister Crowley was, among many other things, a mountaineer who headed the first-ever attempt to climb Kanchenjunga. The mission, which ended in disaster, is chronicled in his "autohagiography," *The Confessions of Aleister Crowley* (1929).

explored these parts, made an extended survey of the district and recommended Chumbi as a hill station. "Oh well," they say, "Darjeeling is forty miles nearer than Chumbi. It will do rather better." So Darjeeling it was. The difference happens to be that Chumbi has a rainfall of some forty inches a year; Darjeeling some two hundred odd. The town is perched on so steep a ridge that there is practically no level road anywhere and one gets from one house to another by staircases as steep as ladders.

The whole town stinks of mildew. One's room is covered with mildew afresh every morning.

India being the last hope of the unmarriageable shabby-genteel, Darjeeling is lousy with young ladies whose only idea of getting a husband is to practice the piano. In such a climate it is of course impossible to keep a piano in tune for five minutes, even if one could get it into that condition. The food itself is as mildewed as the maidens. The hotels extort outrageous rates which they attempt to justify by describing the meals in bad French. To be reminded of Paillard is adding insult to injury, for what the dishes are made of I never did discover. Almost the whole time I was there I was suffering from sore throat, arthritis, every plague that pertains to chronic soddenness. Do I like Darjeeling? I do not!

On the other hand, I hound the heaven-born and the army as full of cordiality and comradeship as ever. As luck would have it, a new worshipful master was to be installed at the Lodge of Freemasons, so I went to the Jadugar-Khana and received a most brotherly welcome to the ceremony and banquet. There I met Sir Andrew Fraser, the lieutenant governor, the commissioner, the deputy commissioner, the Maharaja of Kuch Behar, and all sorts of delightful people. Everyone was only too willing to help in every way.

I wanted to start for the mountain as early in the season as possible. We had reliable information as to what the weather on the higher peaks was likely to be. We had no Zojila to cross, no forty marches to the foot of the peak but twelve or fifteen at the outside. If we found it continuously bad, one could retreat into the valley and recuperate almost as one can in the Alps, for Tsetam is only about twelve thousand feet.

I had reconnoitered Kangchenjunga from England, thanks to the admirable photographs of every side of the mountain taken by Signor Vittorio Sella, who accompanied some man named Freshfield in a sort of old-world tour around the mountain. I had also a map by Professor Garwood, the only trouble with which was that, not having been up the Yalung glacier himself, he had had to fill in the details from what he himself calls the unintelligible hieroglyphics of a native surveyor, who had not been there either.

It did not matter; but I was very much puzzled by the appearance of a peak where no peak should have been, according to the map.

The bandobast for this expedition was very different from that necessary for Chogo Ri, if one takes Darjeeling as the analogy to Srinigar, for there are no villages and supplies of men and food to be had anywhere on the way. I had to send on eight thousand pounds of food for the coolies to a depot as near the Yalung glacier as possible. The government transport officer, Major White, very kindly undertook to oversee this part of the transport and I left it entirely in his hands. Unfortunately, things did not go as well as could be desired. The coolies in this part of India compare very unfavorably with the Baltis and the Kashmiris. They are Tibetan Buddhists with an elaborate priestcraft and system of atonement which persuaded early Jesuit travelers that Satan had perpetrated—in advance!—a blasphemous parody on Christianity; for they found only trivial, formal distinctions between the religions of Lhasa and Rome. They are therefore accessible to emotion and acquire a sentimental devotion to people for whom they take a fancy. But they have no notion of self-respect, no loyalty, no honesty, and no courage. Many of Major White's men deserted, either dumping their loads anywhere on the way or stealing them; and there was no means of controlling their actions. I prepared to expect trouble and was very glad that I had sent to Kashmir for three of our best men of 1902—Salama, Subhana, and Ramzana.

My throat gave me such trouble that I decided to go to Calcutta for a few days—from July 13 to 20. I had in any case to purchase a number of additional stores, as Guillarmod had "economized." The bandobast went on in charge of the manager of the Drum Druid Hotel, to which I had moved shortly after my arrival. He was an Italian named Righi. He offered to join the expedition as transport officer and I, relying on his knowledge of the language and the natives, thought it best to accept him, though his character was mean and suspicious and his sense of inferiority to white men manifested itself as a mixture of servility and insolence to them and of swaggering and bullying to the natives. These traits did not seem so important in Darjeeling, but I must blame myself for not foreseeing that his pin-brain would entirely give way as soon as he got out of the world of waiters.

I was quite happy about the mountain. On July 9, only twenty-six days after my arrival in Darjeeling, the rain stopped for a few minutes and I was able to get a good view of the mountain through my glasses. It entirely confirmed my theoretical conclusions; the highest peak was almost certainly easy to reach from the col to the west of it, and there could be no doubt that it was an easy walk up to that col by a couloir of sorts which I called Jacob's Rake (a "portmanteau" of Jacob's Ladder and Lord's Rake). The word couloir does not quite describe it; the word "rake" does, but I can't define "rake." Anyone who wants to know what I mean must go to Cumberland.

The foot of this rake is in a broad snow basin and the only possible question was whether that snow basin was reachable from the Yalung glacier. I have told already of my ability to describe accurately parts of a mountain which I cannot see. I judged the snow basin accessible. My clairvoyance turned out to be exactly correct.

But more promising even than the feasibility of the route was the appearance of the mountain. Despite the perpetual bad weather at Darjeeling, which made me feel absolutely hopeless, there was no new snow at all on the mountain. Only forty-five miles away, it had been continuous fine weather. I went down to Calcutta with a light heart. I had had good news too from Tartarin. He had persuaded a Swiss Army officer, Alexis Pache, to join us. The other man of the party was named Remond, who had had a fair amount of guideless experience on the Alps.

On the fifteenth I had a telegram from the doctor that he had been shipwrecked in the Red Sea. I might have known it! The three Swiss arrived on July 31. I had got everything into such a forward state of preparation that we were able to start of August 8. There was nothing to be done but to pack the baggage which the doctor seemed to have brought out, in the units which I had got ready for him. The doctor seemed to be suffering from ill health from various trifling causes. He seemed a shade irritable and fussy. I suspect the cause was partly physical. His sense of his own importance was hurting him. Reymond I liked well enough—a quiet if rather dour man, who seemed to have a steady mind and common sense. But Pache won my heart from the moment I met him—a simple, unaffected, unassuming gentleman. He was perfectly aware of his own inexperience on mountains, and therefore in a state to acquire information by the use of his eyes rather than of his ears.

Everything went off without a hitch, except the affair of the depot. We learnt on August 6 that the coolies had dumped the food at Chabanjong, scarcely eighteen miles northwest of Darjeeling, instead of at Jongri, thirty miles due north. This fact, among others, led to my deciding to approach Kangchenjunga by way of the ridge which leads from Ghum practically directly to the head of a side valley through which a tributary of the Yalung Chu descends from the Kang La.

Our party consisted of five Europeans, three Kashmiris, the sirdar of the coolies, six personal servants, and seventy-nine regular coolies. We left Darjeeling at ten sixteen on Tuesday, August 8. The expedition had begun.

⌇

One can certainly reach the neighborhood of Kangchenjunga with delightful comfort. Though the mountain is only forty-five miles from Darjeeling, as the crow flies, the way is round about. The stages from Ghum are Jorpakri 8½, Tongly 18½, Sandakphu 33, Falut 45, Chabanjong 51. Up to this point there is an excellent riding path, while the first four stages have well-furnished dak baghlas.

Unpleasant features of the journey are two: one, the rain, and the other the leeches. I thought I knew a bit about rain—I didn't. At Akyab one puts one's head under water in the hope of getting out of the wet; at Darjeeling one's head is under water all the time. But on that ghastly ridge, I met a quality and quantity of bad weather that I had never dreamt of in my wildest nightmares. What follows sounds exaggerated. On getting into a dak baghla and standing stripped in front of a roaring fire, one expects to get dry. But no! the dampness seems to be metaphysical rather than physical. The mere removal of the manifestations of the elements of water do not leave one dry. But one used to obtain a sort of approximation to dryness by dint of fires; and of course we were provided with waterproofs specially constructed for that abominable climate. One morning I timed myself; after taking every precaution, it was eight and one half minutes from the door of the baghla before I was dripping wet. When I say "dripping wet," I mean that the water was coursing freely inside my clothes. In most parts of the world rain falls, but on that accursed ridge it rises. It is blown up in sheets from the valley. It splashes on the rocks so as to give the effect of waterfalls upside down.

On the thirteenth, fourteenth, and fifteenth, there were short spells of respite; otherwise, from the eighth to the twentieth it never slackened and outside the dak baghlas I was not dry, even partially, for a single second.

The leeches of the district are a most peculiar tribe. For some reason, they can only live within a very well-defined belt. Thus, I never saw a leech at Darjeeling, while at Lebong, some five hundred feet lower, they are a pest. The Terai is the haunt of some of the most tenacious of animals, but the leech has cleared them out completely. A single leech will kill a pony. It works its way up into the nostril and the pony simply bleeds to death. Hence the Anglo-Indian proverb "A jok's a jok, but a jok up your nose is no jok."

I witnessed a remarkable sight on the road to Chabanjong, which was here a *paka rasta* (that is, a road made by engineers as opposed to *kacha rasta*, a track made by habit or at most by very primitive methods) wide enough for carts to pass. I had squatted near the middle of the road as being the least damp and leech-infested spot available and got a pipe going by keeping the bowl under my waterproof. I lazily watched a leech wriggling up a blade of tall grass about fifteen inches high and smiled superiorily at its fatuity—though when I come to think of it, my own expedition was morally parallel—but the leech was not such a fool as I thought. Arrived at the top, it began to set the stalk swinging to and fro; after a few seconds it suddenly let go and flew clean across the road. The intelligence of and ingenuity of the creature struck me as astonishing. (Legless animals are practically helpless on open ground. One can walk up to a king cobra on a smooth road and set one's heel on its head, as prophesied in Genesis, without much danger of being struck, and though it sees you coming, it is quite unable to escape. But give the same snake a little grass to flagellate and the eye can hardly follow its motion. It goes like a snipe.)

Coming back over the same ridge, I was on an open hillside running fast. It was raining downward instead of upward for once, and that but slightly. I heard a little noise, as if something had fallen on my hat, and took no notice. A few moments later I found that my hand was wet with blood, running fast, and looking down I saw a leech on the back of it. How it managed to fall from the sky I don't know. I have seen leeches up to seven inches long; and there seems hardly any limit to the amount of blood they can assimilate. I heard of a gorged leech weighing nearly two pounds and I believe it without effort.

Another strange sight in these parts is the sheep. Tartarin, still proud of his haggis, invented wonderful theories to explain the fact that they are muzzled. However, they are not *mountons enragés*; the muzzle is to prevent them from poisoning themselves with wild aconite.

The scenery along the while of his ridge is extraordinarily grand, so far as the mist permits one to see anything. Some of the Himalayan trees are superb. But the prevailing vegetation is the rhododendron, a plant which has little in common with its English cousin. It grows to a height of fifteen feet or more and the stems are often as thick as a man's thigh. It grows in unbroken forests and the worst Mexican chaparral I ever saw was not worse to have to cut one's way through.

At Chabanjong the road stops and I sent back my horse. Thence a shepherd's track leads along the ridge. On the whole it was very good walking.

We had already found trouble with our own coolies. To begin with, the police had caught me up at Jorpakri and arrested one of them for some petty offense—he joined us for more reasons than one. Six of the men deserted in the early part of the march. I was a small percentage and they had evidently never had any intention of earning their advances. Later, when I had to go on ahead, five men deserted Pache, whom I had to leave in charge. They were probably scared by superstitious fears. Pache could not talk to them and did not know how to encourage them.

After leaving Chabanjong it was impossible to tell exactly where one was on the ridge. The *paros* have names, but I could never discover that they applied to anything; it was all rain and rhododendra. There is a place called Nego Cave which I hoped was a cave where I could shelter from the rain for a few hours, but nobody seemed to know here it was and I never found out. I had actually to rest a day in this abominable place, as the official permit for our party to enter Nepal had not arrived; but it did so during the day and on the eighteenth came a very long march of something like eight hours of actual going. During the latter part of the march the path dips suddenly and one descends some three thousand feet into a valley.

Well do I remember this camp Gamotang! Apart from the flora and fauna, the last two days might have been spent on the Welsh mountains, but the descent to Gamotang was like stepping into fairyland. There are certain places—Sonamarg in Kashmir is one of them—which possess the quality of soft brilliance quite unearthly. There is really nothing to distinguish them from a hundred other spots in the neighborhood, yet they stand out, as a genius does from a hundred other men in evening dress. I find these phenomena quite as real as any others and I feel impelled to seek an explanation.

Assuming the existence of inhabitants imperceptible by our grosser senses, the problem presents no difficulty. One of a row of similar houses is often quite different from its neighbors, perhaps on account of the loving care and pride of its chatelaine. When I see an analogous phenomenon in scenery, I cannot blame myself if a similar explanation comes to my mind.

The weather was already noticeably better than at Darjeeling. It did not begin to rain till eight or ten in the morning every day.

The partial failure of the bandobast kept us a day at Gamotang. There was in any case no great hurry. I was glad of every opportunity to acquire the affection of the men. I was careful not to overwork them. I gave a prize to the first three men to come into camp every day and those who had come in first three times had their pay permanently raised. I made friends with them, too, by sitting with them round the campfire and exchanging songs and stories. On the other hand, I made it clear that I would tolerate no nonsense. They responded for the most part very well—I never had any trouble in all my wanderings with natives, servants, dogs, and women. The secret is that I am really unconscious of superiority and treat all alike with absolute respect and affection; at the same time I maintain the practical relations between myself and others very strictly indeed.

It is the fable of the belly and the members. It is absurd for one speck of protoplasm to insist on its social superiority to another speck, but equally absurd for one cell to want to do the work of another. There is another point, admirably stated by Wilkie Collins. Count Fosco says that the way to manage women is "never to accept a provocation from a woman's hands." It holds with animals, it holds with children, and it holds with women, who are nothing but children grown up. Quiet resolution is the one quality the animals, the children, and the women all fail in. If they can once shake this superior quality in their master, they get the better of HIM. If they can never succeed in disturbing it, he gets the better of THEM.

I make it an absolute rule to be imperturbable, to impress people with the idea that it is impossible to avoid doing what I have done. I never try to arouse enthusiasm. I never bribe, I never threaten, but I identify my purpose with destiny and I administer reward and punishment unsparingly and impersonally.

The coolies began to be very fond of me, not only because of my good comradeship and my cheerful calm and confidence, but because they were subconsciously relieved by my conduct from their personal demons of fear, jealousy, desire, and the like. They became unconsciously aware that they were parts of a machine. As long as they did their duty, there was absolutely nothing to worry about. Most people suffer all their lives from subconscious irritation, due to what the Hindus call Ahamkara, the ego-making faculty. The idea of self is a continual torment and though I was still far from having got rid of this idea completely, I was pretty free of it in practice in matters where my responsibility was extensive. I had begun to understand how to work "without lust of result."

Unfortunately, Tartarin and Righi were undoing my web as fast as I wove it. Righi was a low-class Italian, who ran his hotel by hectoring the men under him. Finding himself for the first time in his life in a position of real responsibility, and without the background of an external authority to which he could appeal to enforce his orders, he was utterly at sea. On one occasion he actually threatened a disobedient coolie with his kukri and revolver, and the man, knowing he would not dare to use them, laughed in his face. The natives despised him as a weak man, which is the worst thing that can befall anyone that has anything to do with them.

Tartarin too, though cheerful and genial . . . was fussy and helpless. On one occasion he actually tried to bribe a man with boots and claws to do his ordinary duty. As long as I was with the main body, these things didn't matter. Nobody dared to disobey the Bara Sahib. A moment's hesitation in complying with any order of mine and they saw a look in my eyes which removed the inhibition. They knew that I would not scold or wheedle, but had a strong suspicion that I might strike a man dead without warning; at the same time they knew that I would never give an unreasonable order and that my active sympathy with the slightest discomfort of any one of them was as quick as my insight to detect and deal with malingering or any other attempt to pull my leg.

From Gamotang one has to climb to the Chumbab La—about four hours' march. Then one skirts the slopes of the Kang La and descends to the branch valley of the Yalung Chu. I found a great block of quartz three and one half hours beyond the pass and pitched camp. The doctor arrived late—eight thirty. He had had some trouble with the coolies, but they were safely camped some short distance above.

The next day was fearfully wet. There is another little pass to cross, an hour beyond the quartz block; two and a half hours more took me down the valley to a camp near Tseram, which is a group of huts on the main stream a couple of miles below the snout of the Yalung glacier. I avoided camping in Teseram itself, on the general principle of having nothing to do with natives. The Dewan of Nepal was sending an officer to superintend our journey. I should perhaps have mentioned before that England has a special treaty with Nepal, one of its terms to the effect that no foreigners are to enter the dewan's dominions. He knew that the most harmless of Europeans is the herald of disaster to any independent country. Where the white man sets his foot, the grass of freedom and the flower of good faith are trampled into the mire of vice and commercialism.

But in the present instance our route touched only this one tiny out-lying hamlet of Tseram and permission had been obtained without difficulty for us to pass. At the same time, the Dewan was going to have a man on the spot to see that we did not maltreat and corrupt the natives as we have done in every other part of the globe in which our impulses of greed and tyranny have seen a possibility of satisfaction.

I saw no reason for waiting for the arrival of the Dewan's "guide" and, leaving a man with a message for him, continued the advance.

I took only a very small party and left Pache in command. He was to wait until the arrival of the main body of the coolies, while I went on the glacier to reconnoiter. I wanted to establish the main camp as high as possible, but of course I did not know whether I might not have to retrace my steps. The glacier stream might prove uncrossable. I would make sure that the whole party could reach the glacier without difficulty.

I left the camp at 6:00 a.m. on the twenty-first. I was now in really mountainous country. The valley was gorgeously wild—it glowed with rich bright grass and masses of marvelous flowers. There was an admirable track. The day was fine and I had views of both Little and Big Kabru (21,290 and 24,015 feet respectively) but Kangchenjunga itself was hidden in clouds. I have rarely enjoyed a mountain walk so thoroughly and my heart was uplifted by the excellence of our prospects.

It sang within me. I was already at fourteen or fifteen thousand feet, less than a fortnight from our base, in perfect physical condition, not an ounce of my reserve of strength yet called upon; a perfectly clear course to the peak in front of me, the mountain scarcely five miles away, the weather looking better all the time, and none of the extremes of temperature which had been so frightful on Chogo Ri. No sign that wind was likely to give any trouble. In short, not one dark spot upon the horizon.

Camp 2, though no place for a golf course, as the game is at present played, possesses the great advantage of being a perfect Pisgah. The summit of Kangchenjunga is only two miles away and I am able to see almost the whole of the debatable ground which my reconnaissance from above Darjeeling had denied me. I climbed to a short distance above the camp: the last doubt disappeared. The level glacier stretched less than a mile away. Thence rose a ridge covered by steep glacier except at its eastern edge, where there was a patch of bare rock with scarcely any interruption from ice. This rock was cut away on its right by a terrific precipice, sheer to the lower glacier, but there was no reason why anyone should fall off. The rocks were of the character—easy slabs—of those of the Eiger above the little Scheideck, the precipice being on the right hand instead of on the left. The slabs ended in a level space of snow jutting beyond the glacier above, and therefore safe from any possible avalanche. The place would make an admirable camp.

Thence, one could work a way to the west; and, avoiding a patch of séracs, ascend steep slopes of ice (covered at present by snow) which led directly to the great snow basin which lies, as one may say, in the embrace of Kangchenjunga. These slopes were the critical point of the passage. I intended to fix a long knotted rope at the top, if necessary, to serve as handhold for the coolies, it being now certain that we could establish our main camp at the foot of Jacob's Rake. Certain, that is, bar the interference of absolute perversity.

The following day showed me that such perversity was only too likely to put a spoke in the wheel. The arrangement was that I was to find my way to Camp 3, which I had already been able to choose through my glasses. I left Tartarin and Reymond in charge of the bulk of the coolies, having pointed out to them the best way across the glacier. It was more or less intricate going compared with Piccadilly, but it was certainly less trouble than an average march on the Baltoro. My object in going ahead was merely to make sure that Camp 3 was as favorable as it looked from a distance. It was. There was a broad level plateau of loose stones marked by a big boulder, which I called Pioneer Boulder, for a variety of reasons, all referring ironically to "Pioneer Peak." This plateau was perhaps seven hundred to a thousand feet above the glacier ...

I settled down quite comfortably at Camp 3 and sent a man down to find the main body and tell them it was all right, and they were to come up. Most unfortunately, it was misty. I could not see what had happened. And if I had been able to, I might almost have doubted my eyes. The coolies were coming—Oh ho! oh ho!—in a long circular route round the head of the glacier, for no reason at all. The weather cleared toward evening and there they were, within shouting distance, within three quarters of an hour's easy going for the slowest men, up excellent slopes on firm rocky ground.

To my amazement, I saw the doctor preparing to pitch camp. It was inexplicable imbecility. Shouts produced no effect and there was nothing for it but for me to go down. He had chosen a bivouac on bare ice, where there was hardly sufficient level ground to pitch the tents, but it was too late to pack up again, so I had to make the best of it. I asked him the reason for his extraordinary conduct. He replied that there was a rumor that I had broken my leg on a moraine. This was as antecedently unlikely as anything could possibly be; and anyhow he could see perfectly well with his own eyes that I had done nothing of the sort; and thirdly, if I had done it, all the more reason for coming to my assistance. I began to think there was something seriously wrong with the man.

On the top of this, there was bad news from the rearguard. Righi sent up bitterly quarrelsome messages. His antics had made all sorts of trouble with the coolies, who were at one time in open revolt. Pache managed to get them into good humor again. He was a gentleman; he understood the oriental mind instinctively. He was, in fact, making extremely good. As soon as he saw that Righi was half insane with the fear that comes to people of his class in the absence of a chattering herd of his fellows, and in the presence of the grandeur of nature, he assumed moral charge of him. The difficulties with the rearguard disappeared immediately. Unfortunately, I did not understand at the time what was happening, or I should have gone down and sent Righi back to his kitchen. Pache himself did not realize his own importance and took it upon himself to come up. The moment his back was turned, Righi became insane.

Everyone had passed a most uncomfortable night at the absurd bivouac. I decided to go no further than Camp 3 the next day. Tartarin was absolutely astonished that the men with whom he had been having such trouble behaved quite simply and naturally as soon as I was on the spot. He claimed that they had positively refused to go further, but they picked up their loads and strolled cheerfully up the slopes without so much as a word of admonition.

Not understanding the secret of my power, though he had seen it exercised so often by Eckenstein and myself, he imagined that I must be terrorizing the men by threats and beatings. In point of fact, I never struck a man during the entire expedition, save on one occasion to be described presently.

Camp 3 was extremely pleasant. It afforded magnificent views in every direction and one had one's choice of sun or shade. I spent the day in taking advantage of the amenities of the situation. I took pains to fix up an excellent shelter for the men by means of large tarpaulins, and saw to their comfort in every way. We had even the advantage of song, for the camp was a haunt of small birds. Its height cannot have been far short of eighteen thousand feet.

It was urgent that the march to Camp 4 should be started at the earliest glimmer of light, for though the route lay almost entirely over rock, there were a few short snow passages which would become dangerous after sunrise, and the hanging glacier on our left might conceivably discharge some of its superfluous snow across one or two points of the route. I explained these points carefully to the men, who were for the most part quite intelligent enough to understand. Moreover, they were already aware of the general principles, a number of them having already traveled, if not on glaciers, at least on winter snow. They were eager to start, but Tartarin deliberately hindered them. I had awakened at three o'clock and got them off by six. It had not been a cold night—none of the men showed any signs of suffering or made any complaint—but the doctor said that they ought to be allowed to warm themselves thoroughly in the sun before starting. He suggested that the march should begin at about eleven o'clock. These were words of sheer insanity. Even on Chogo Ri, where the nights were really cold, no such nonsense had ever been suggested.

I led at once on to the glacier. There was no difficulty of any sort; the snow being in excellent condition, it merely required a little scraping and stamping. But at the point where it becomes necessary to take the rocks on the right so as not to be under a small patch of séracs, the slope is in the direction of the tremendous precipice previously described. It was there that I gave an exhibition of glissading. I do not think the men would have been afraid at all if the excited shouts and gesticulations of Reymond and the doctor had not demoralized them. These celebrated climbers were themselves actually afraid for their own skins. And this, if you please, on a slope down which I could glissade head first! Having got the men across, we proceeded up the rocky slopes. I must confess that here I had misjudged the difficulty.

I had expected to find quite easy walking, but there were a few passages where it amounted to scrambling from the point of view of a loaded man. I decided to arrange for a fixed rope as a measure of safety, it being my plan to send the picked coolies up and down regularly to bring up supplies as they were needed. In the meantime, the men behaved magnificently, laughing and joking and giving each other a helping hand whenever required. I posted the Kashmiris and the other personal servants at the *mauvais pas*, but there was no hint of any real danger.

Camp 4 is at the top of this rocky slope on a level ridge, level enough, but not as broad as I could have wished. There was, however, a certain amount of natural shelter afforded by rocks and I was able to construct a fairly comfortable place for the night. There was a better camp three hours higher; but the weather, after a fine morning, had begun to look bad and the snow was in bad condition. The men, too, though perfectly happy, were most of them very tired, and some of them knocked over by what they supposed to be mountain sickness—symptoms of exhaustion, headache, pains in the abdomen, dizziness, and so forth. I knew what the trouble was and went round to the sufferers and dropped a little atropine into their eyes. Half an hour later they were all perfectly restored. The alarming symptoms were all due to the glare.

I sent down to Pache to come up to Camp 3 as better in every way than Camp 2. I asked Tartarin and Reymond if they had any messages to send. They were too exhausted to reply to their names. I was utterly bewildered. The previous day had been a bare hour, and the march to Camp 4 perfectly easy and by no means long or trying for men without loads. I myself, though I had borne the burden and heat of the day more than anyone, was as fresh as paint and as fit as a fiddle. I had never felt better in my life. I was in perfect condition in every respect. I spent the afternoon nursing the invalids.

Tartarin recovered by the next morning sufficiently to curse. I could not imagine what his grievance was and cannot imagine it now. The most charitable explanation of his conduct that I can give is that he was mentally upset, partly no doubt due to psychical distress, and to some form of heat stroke. I have always been satanically happy in the hottest sunshine, but the slopes of Kangchenjunga on a fine day at noon were near my limit. Both the doctor and Reymond were unquestionably very ill. It was impossible to think of going on to the next camp that day. We rested accordingly. Late in the day, to my surprise, Pache arrived with a number of coolies—I had asked him to send up the sirdar and one other man. I wanted to give Naga personal instructions about the management of his men. It had been no part of my plan for any of the others to come beyond Camp 3. I wanted to make Camp 3 the base until we found a good place on the snow basin above. The arrival of Pache and his men overcrowded Camp 4.

The root of the trouble, apart from any ill-feeling, was that none of my companions (except Pache) understood that I expected them to keep their word. I had arranged a plan, taking into consideration all sorts of circumstances, the importance of which they did not understand and other of which they did not even know, and they did not realize that to deviate from my instructions in any way might be disastrous. Their disobedience having resulted in things going wrong, they proceeded to blame me. Righi had refused point blank to send Naga on my express command; he had failed to send up any supplies, so that we were absolutely out of petroleum and short of food, both for ourselves and for our men.

Pache reported that some of the men had deserted. It was never cleared up why they should have done so. But one of them, in disobedience to orders, had gone off by himself—I never discovered exactly where—and had fallen and been killed. This man, it was said, was carrying Pache's sleeping valise. This at least was certain, that the valise was missing.

An accident being alleged, I sent down the doctor on the following morning to make an inquiry into the matter, and also to send up supplies of food and fuel which we needed urgently. Pache told me that Righi was deliberately withholding food from us. His conduct was murderously criminal, if only because we might have been prevented by bad weather from descending in the last resort.

That afternoon Reymond and I made a little excursion up the slopes. We found that the snow was not as bad as might have been expected, and the gradients were so easy and the glacier so free from icefall that there would be no danger for a prudently conducted party, even when the snow was soft.

On this slope of Kangchenjunga one occasionally meets a condition of snow which I have never seen elsewhere. Rain or sleet blows against the face of the mountain and is frozen as it touches. The result is to produce a kind of network of ice; a frozen drop serves as a nucleus from which radiate fine filaments of ice in every direction. It is like a spider's web in three dimensions. A cubic foot of network would thus be almost entirely composed of air; the ice in it, if compact, would hardly be bigger than a tennis ball, perhaps much less. With the advance of the evening, the rain turns to snow; and in the morning it may be that the network is covered to a depth of several inches. The temperature possibly rises a few degrees and the surface becomes wet. It then freezes again and forms a hard crust. Approaching a slope of this kind, it seems perfectly good névé. One strikes it with one's ax and the entire structure disintegrates. In front of one is a hole as big as a cottage and as the solid slope disappears, one hears the tinkle of falling ice. It is a most astonishing and disconcerting phenomenon.

During the whole time that I was on the mountain, I experienced no high wind and no unpleasant cold. But the heat of the day was certainly very severe. My skin had gradually become inured to the sun. I had not been burnt painfully in ten years. I simply browned quietly and pleasantly. But on Kangchenjunga it got me—not badly enough to cause sores, but enough to make the skin somewhat painful and brittle. Here was another reason for starting early in the day and reaching camp, if possible, by noon at the latest.

On the nineteenth, having dispatched Tartarin to the rear, Reymond, Pache, and myself went on with our small party. The doctor was, of course, to make sure of sending up supplies and Pache's valise. We reached Camp 5 in about three hours. It was situated on a little snowy hump below a small peak on the ridge. We intended to make our way to the path between this peak and the main spur. The slopes were rather steep in one or two places, but quite without danger, as they eased off a short distance below (about two hundred fifty feet) to a practically level part of the glacier. I should, in fact, have preferred to go straight up them instead of making the detour by the rocks on the edge of the big precipice, had it not been that a small patch of sérac overhung them.

No valise arrived for Pache that night, and no petrol or rations. We were accordingly obliged to rest the next day. I had given Pache my eiderdown sleeping bag and one of my blankets. He was thus quite comfortable physically; but he was, of course, anxious about his effects. All his spare boots, clothes, etcetera, were in the missing bag, and all his private papers.

During the day a few provisions arrived, but no rations for the men, and no petrol. I sent back one of the men with urgent orders and several others to assist in carrying the supplies. (Also because we could not feed them where we were.) I wrote a second letter to Tartarin the same day; a man arrived at last with the petrol. In this letter which was signed by Pache as well as myself, the blame for the failure of the bandobast was given entirely to Righi.

> It seems to me and to Pache also that the shortage of food is the fault of M. Righi who refused to send Naga when Pache told him to do so. This disobedience, which has come so near to involving us in disaster, must not be repeated. All the loads should be sent to Camp 3 except those which are under shelter. Righi must be responsible for carrying this out. For yourself, you should join us as soon as you can with at least ten loads of sattu and Naga to help us. The next three days will be the crisis of the expedition.
>
> With cordial friendship, yours.

There was no difficulty whatever in carrying out these perfectly simple, normal instructions.

Camp 5 is at the height of twenty to twenty-one thousand feet and certainly not more than two to three thousand feet above Camp 3. We had taken the first ascent very easily, it having been transformed into a regular snow track with immense steps made solid by repeated regelation. It might be called two hours' easy going. The doctor had recovered his health and his good humor, and we had none of us a moment's doubt that he would put the fear of God into Righi and carry out the above instructions promptly and efficiently.

On Thursday, August 31, I started up the slopes with six men and a perfectly light heart. The problem was, of course, how to get the coolies up with the minimum of trouble. I sent Salama ahead with an ax and shovels on a rope. Their job was to clear away all loose snow and to enlarge the steps made by Salama so that the way up the mountain should be literally a staircase of the easiest kind. Their leader was a man named Gali. I remained close to him throughout so that if by any chance he fell I could catch him.

I would not rope myself, so as to be able to go to the rescue instantly in case Salama got tired or came to a passage too difficult for him. We advanced very rapidly. We were certainly over twenty-one thousand and possibly over twenty-two thousand feet. There were no symptoms of the slightest deficiency of physical energy on the part of anyone. I have never seen a man ply an ice ax faster than Salama did that day. I was, of course, very carefully on the lookout for the slightest tendency on the part of the snow to slip.

We had reached a shallow couloir. Reymond and Salama had got some distance ahead of the coolies. Some of the chips of ice dislodged by their step-cutting were sliding down in our direction and they began to carry some of the surface with them. I was warned by the gentle purring hiss, rather like a tea kettle beginning to sing, which tells one that loose snow is beginning to move. Gali saw the little avalanche coming toward him, was frightened, and fell out of his steps. I caught him, put him back, and hastily anchored the rope to a wedged ax. But the man had completely lost his nerve and, by the operation of that instinct which makes a drowning man throw up his hands, began to do the one thing that could possibly have brought him to harm—to untie himself from the rope. I ordered him to desist, but he was quite hysterical, uttered senseless cries, and took no notice. There was only one thing to do to save him from the consequences of his suicidal actions, and that was to make him more afraid of me than he was of the mountain; so I reached out and caught him a whack with my ax. It pulled him together immediately and prevented his panic from communicating itself to the other men. Things then went on all right.

Some of the slopes were really very bad—deep soft snow on ice. One short patch was at an angle of fifty degrees. It was a question of fixing a rope or finding a new route to the left, which I did not want to do as I was in doubt about the glacier above. There were some séracs which might or might not be stable. We went down to Camp 5 without further adventure, but the morale of the men had been shaken by the incident of the toy avalanche. Their imaginations got out of hand. They began to talk nonsense about the demons of Kangchenjunga and magnified the toy avalanche and Gali's slip and wallop to the wildest fantasies. During the night some of them slipped away and went down to Camp 3.

On September 1 we renewed the assault. Reymond, Pache, and Salama went up the sloes on the rope and got over the bad patch. They were so much encouraged by their success that they went out of sight and hearing, contrary to my instructions. I needed them to help the three coolies with loads over the bad part. They preferred to leave the whole responsibility to me, but I could not bring three heavily loaded men up such slopes without assistance, and there was nothing to do but await their return. In the meantime, I saw to my surprise that a large party had arrived at Camp 5. When I got down I found that Tartarin's hysteria and Righi's malignant stupidity had created yet another muddle.

They had arrived at the camp, bringing with them some seventeen or twenty coolies, and they had not brought any of the things of which we stood in such need. Their behavior was utterly unintelligible. The doctor did not seem to know what he was saying; his remarks were merely confusedly irritated. He did not seem to be able to answer any of my questions or give any explanation of what had happened in the past. His one idea was to hold a durbar and have himself elected leader in my place. There was no provision in our agreement for any such folly. He pointed out that it was merely a scrap of paper. When the others arrived, an excited argument began. There was no suggestion that I had acted improperly in any way. From first to last it was merely the feeling of foreigners against being bossed by an Englishman. The same thing had happened with Pfannl on Chogo Ri.

On the present occasion, however, the Englishman was in a minority of one. Fortunately I had never heard that a fact of that sort makes any difference to an Englishman. I did my best to reason with them and quiet them, like the naughty children they were. Reymond had nothing to complain of and was actively friendly.

Indeed, I had much more to worry me than the nonsense of Tartarin and Righi. They had brought up all these men without any provisions for food or shelter and it was now late in the day. The snow was in an absolutely unsafe condition and though I had chosen the route so as to minimize the danger, it was absolutely criminal to send men down. But the mutineers were utterly insensible to the voice of reason. I told the coolies that since they could not stay at Camp 5, the best thing they could do was to shelter under the rocks at Camp 4, and they went off and did so. I warned the mutineers that they would certainly be killed if they tried to go down that night; it was perhaps more or less right for coolies, but for *them*—I knew only too well the extent of Tartarin's ingenuity in producing accidents out of the most apparently unpromising material. They stormed all the more. I ought to have broken the doctor's leg with an ax, but I was too young to take such a responsibility. It would have been hard to prove afterward that I had saved him by so doing.

To my horror, I found that Pache wanted to go down with them. The blackguards had not even had the decency to bring up his valise. I implored him to wait till the morning. I told him he could have the whole of my sleeping kit. But nothing would move him. I explained the situation, but I suppose he could not believe that I was telling the literal truth when I said that Guillarmod was at the best of times a dangerous imbecile on mountains, and that now he had developed into a dangerous maniac. I shook hands with him with a breaking heart, for I had got very fond of the man, and my last words were, "Don't go: I shall never see you again. You'll be a dead man in ten minutes." I had miscalculated once more; a quarter of an hour later he was still alive.

Less than half an hour later, Reymond and I heard frantic cries. No words could be distinguished, but the voices were those of Tartarin and Righi. Reymond proposed going to the rescue at once, but it was now nearly dark and there was nobody to send, owing to Righi's having stripped us of men. There was, furthermore, no indication as to why they were yelling. They had been yelling all day. Reymond had not yet taken his boots off. He said he would go and see if he could see what was the matter and call me if my assistance were required. He went off and did not return or call. So I went to sleep and rose the next morning at earliest dawn and went to investigate.

The task was easy. About fifteen minutes below Camp 5 the track had been carried away over a width of twenty feet (seven short paces). The angle of the slope was roughly twenty degrees (limits of error twenty-five degrees and twelve degrees). The avalanche had stopped two hundred fifty feet below, and at this point it was from forty to sixty feet in width; that is to say, it was an absolutely trivial avalanche. A single man could have ridden it headfirst without the slightest risk of hurting himself. The width of the avalanche (and other signs) showed that six men on a 120-foot rope had been walking on each other's heels, the rope being festooned so as to be worse than useless. A man struggling in a loose-snow avalanche has a fair chance of getting to the top, but if every time he does so he is jerked away by the rope, it will be the greatest piece of luck if he is not killed. Tartarin, who should have been the last man on a descent in order to watch the others, to see that the rope was kept stretched, and to check any slip at the outset, was leading.

Here is Righi's account of the accident.

> Suddenly the four men above us began to slide; we hoped they would be able to stop themselves, but the slope was too steep. They swept past us like lightning. The doctor and I did the best we could to stop them, but in vain; for, as they rushed downward, they started an avalanche (the snow being in such a moist condition from the afternoon sun, and easily moved). I was torn away from my anchor, head downward, the doctor vainly calling to me to hang on as we might be able to stop the others. I was pulled down in what seemed a whirlwind of snow. I remember nothing during the fall. The doctor followed and fell farther down. I came to a few minutes after, hearing the doctor calling and telling me to get up. I could not do so, being pinned down on one side by the rope which was straight into the avalanche, and on the other I was keeping the doctor from falling farther down the slope. Had he been killed by the fall, I should have been helpless and most likely would have been frozen where I lay.

It is noteworthy that some seventeen coolies without ropes, axes, boots, claws, and Tartarin had crossed the fatal spot quite safely.

I found these men perfectly happy. They had taken my advice and passed the night under the rocks by Camp 4. I slowly descended, they following at a short distance. Presently I came to a place where the snow had slipped off the glacier ice for some distance. The angle was decidedly steep, and though I was able to cross it easily enough in my claws, it would not do for the coolies; so I called to them to go higher up over the glacier. But they were afraid to do this. They said they wanted to follow me, which they did, after enlarging my steps with an ax. At the time, I had no doubt that this place was the scene of the accident, if there had been one, of which I was not sure. Anyhow, I could not see how even Tartarin could have come to grief on so easy and safe a slope as the other. But on arrival at Camp 3 I was able to understand what had happened. Thanks to my habits of accuracy, I had taken careful measurements.

Pache and three of my best coolies had been killed. Tartarin was badly bruised, and thought his spine was damaged. The accident had brought him completely to his senses. He realized that I had been right all along, and was appalled by the prospects of returning to Switzerland and meeting Pache's mother.

Righi, on the other hand, showed only the more what an ill-conditioned cur he was. He had not been hurt at all badly, but his ribs were slightly bruised; he claimed that he had "rupture of the heart," and spent his time moaning and bellowing. That his sufferings were mostly pure funk was evident from the fact that he forgot all about them directly when he was engaged in conversation.

I ought to have been much angrier than I was, for the conduct of the mutineers amounted to manslaughter. By breaking their agreement, they had assumed full responsibility. It was impossible for me to continue with the expedition. My authority had been set at naught, and I would not risk any man's life.

———•———

THE SUMMIT*

Edmund Hillary

At 6:30 a.m. we crawled slowly out of the tent and stood on our little ledge. Already the upper part of the mountain was bathed in sunlight.

* Excerpted from *High Adventure: The True Story of the First Ascent of Everest* (1955).

It looked warm and inviting, but our ledge was dark and cold. We lifted our oxygen onto our backs and slowly connected up the tubes to our face masks. My thirty-pound load seemed to crush me downwards and stifled all enthusiasm, but when I turned on the oxygen and breathed in deeply, the burden seemed to lighten and the old urge to get to grips with the mountain came back. We strapped on our crampons and tied on our nylon rope, grasped our ice axes and were ready to go.

I looked at the way ahead. From our tent very steep slopes covered with deep powder snow led up to a prominent snow shoulder on the southeast ridge about a hundred feet above our heads. The slopes were in the shade and breaking trail was going to be cold work. Still a little worried about my boots, I asked Tenzing to lead off. Always willing to do his share and more than his share if necessary, Tenzing scrambled past me and tackled the slope. With powerful thrusts of his legs he forced his way up in knee-deep snow. I gathered in the rope and followed along behind him.

We were climbing out over the tremendous south face of the mountain and below us snow chutes and rock ribs plummeted thousands of feet down to the Western Cwm. Starting in the morning straight on to exposed climbing is always trying for the nerves and this was no exception. In imagination I could feel my heavy load dragging me backward down the great slopes below; I seemed clumsy and unstable and my breath was hurried and uneven. But Tenzing was pursuing an irresistible course up the slope and I didn't have time to think too much. My muscles soon warmed up to their work, my nerves relaxed, and I dropped into the old climbing rhythm and followed steadily up his tracks. As we gained a little height we moved into the rays of the sun and although we could feel no appreciable warmth, we were greatly encouraged by its presence. Taking no rests, Tenzing plowed his way up through the deep snow and led out onto the snow shoulder. We were now at a height of 28,000 feet. Towering directly above our heads was the South Summit—steep and formidable. And to the right were the enormous cornices of the summit ridge. We still had a long way to go.

Ahead of us the ridge was sharp and narrow, but rose at an easy angle. I felt warm and strong now, so took over the lead. First I investigated the ridge with my ice ax. On the sharp crest of the ridge and on the right-hand side loose powder snow was lying dangerously over hard ice. Any attempt to climb on this would only produce an unpleasant slide down toward the Kangshung Glacier. But the left-hand slope was better—it was still rather steep, but it had a firm surface of wind-blown powder snow into which our crampons would bite readily.

Taking every care, I moved along onto the left-hand side of the ridge. Everything seemed perfectly safe. With increased confidence, I took another step. Next moment I was almost thrown off balance as the wind-crust suddenly gave way and I sank through it up to my knee. It took me a little while to regain my breath. Then I gradually pulled my leg out of the hole. I was almost upright again when the wind-crust under the other foot gave way and I sank back with both legs enveloped in soft, loose snow to the knees. It was the mountaineer's curse—breakable crust. I forced my way along. Sometimes for a few careful steps I was on the surface, but usually the crust would break at the critical moment and I'd be up to my knees again. Though it was tiring and exasperating work, I felt I had plenty of strength in reserve. For half an hour I continued on in this uncomfortable fashion, with the violent balancing movements I was having to make completely destroying rhythm and breath. It was a great relief when the snow conditions improved and I was able to stay on the surface. I still kept down on the steep slopes on the left of the ridge, but plunged ahead and climbed steadily upward. I came over a small crest and saw in front of me a tiny hollow on the ridge. And in this hollow lay two oxygen bottles almost completely covered with snow. It was Evans's and Bourdillon's dump.

I rushed forward into the hollow and knelt beside them. Wrenching one of the bottles out of its frozen bed I wiped the snow off its dial—it showed a thousand-pounds pressure—it was nearly a third full of oxygen. I checked the others—it was the same. This was great news. It meant that the oxygen we were carrying on our backs only had to get us back to these bottles instead of right down to the South Col. It gave us more than another hour of endurance. I explained this to Tenzing through my oxygen mask. I don't think he understood, but he realized I was pleased about something and nodded enthusiastically.

I led off again. I knew there was plenty of hard work ahead and Tenzing could save his energies for that. The ridge climbed on upward rather more steeply now and then broadened out and shot up at a sharp angle to the foot of the enormous slope running up to the South Summit. I crossed over on to the right-hand side of the ridge and found the snow was firm there. I started chipping a long line of steps up to the foot of the great slope. Here we stamped out a platform for ourselves and I checked our oxygen. Everything seemed to be going well. I had a little more oxygen left than Tenzing, which meant I was obtaining a slightly lower flow rate from my set, but it wasn't enough to matter and there was nothing I could do about it anyway.

Ahead of us was a really formidable problem and I stood in my steps and looked at it. Rising from our feet was an enormous slope slanting steeply down onto the precipitous east face of Everest and climbing up with appalling steepness to the South Summit of the mountain 400 feet above us. The left-hand side of the slope was a most unsavory mixture of steep loose rock and snow, which my New Zealand training immediately regarded with grave suspicion, but which in actual fact the rock-climbing Britons, Evans and Bourdillon, had ascended in much trepidation when on the first assault. The only other route was up the snow itself and still faintly discernible here and there were traces of the track made by the first assault party, who had come down it in preference to their line of ascent up the rocks. The snow route it was for us! There looked to be some tough work ahead and as Tenzing had been taking it easy for a while I hard-heartedly waved him through. With his first six steps I realized that the work was going to be much harder than I had thought. His first two steps were on top of the snow, the third was up to his ankles, and by the sixth he was up to his hips. But almost lying against the steep slope, he drove himself onward, plowing a track directly upwards. Even following in his steps was hard work, for the loose snow refused to pack into safe steps. After a long and valiant spell he was plainly in need of a rest, so I took over.

Immediately I realized that we were on dangerous ground. On this very steep slope the snow was soft and deep with little coherence. My ice ax shaft sank into it without any support and we had no sort of a belay. The only factor that made it at all possible to progress was a thin crust of frozen snow which tied the whole slope together. But this crust was a poor support. I was forcing my way upward, plunging deep steps through it, when suddenly with a dull breaking noise an area of crust all around me about six feet in diameter broke off into large sections and slid with me back through three or four steps. And then I stopped; but the crust, gathering speed, slithered on out of sight. It was a nasty shock. My whole training told me that the slope was exceedingly dangerous, but at the same time I was saying to myself: "Ed, my boy, this is Everest—you've got to push it a bit harder!" My solar plexus was tight with fear as I plowed on. Halfway up I stopped, exhausted. I could look down 10,000 feet between my legs and I have never felt more insecure. Anxiously I waved Tenzing up to me.

"What do you think of it, Tenzing?" And the immediate response, "Very bad, very dangerous!" "Do you think we should go on?" and there came the familiar reply that never helped you much but never let you down: "Just as you wish!" I waved him on to take a turn at leading. Changing the lead much more frequently now, we made our unhappy way upward, sometimes sliding back and wiping out half a dozen steps and never feeling confident that at any moment the whole slope might not avalanche. In the hope of some sort of a belay we traversed a little toward the rocks, but found no help in their smooth, holdless surfaces. We plunged on upward. And then I noticed that, a little above us, the left-hand rock ridge turned into snow and the snow looked firm and safe. Laboriously and carefully we climbed across some steep rock and I sank my ice-ax shaft into the snow of the ridge. It went in firm and hard. The pleasure of this safe belay after all the uncertainty below was like a reprieve to a condemned man. Strength flowed into my limbs and I could feel my tense nerves and muscles relaxing. I swung my ice ax at the slope and started chipping a line of steps upward—it was very steep, but seemed so gloriously safe. Tenzing, an inexpert but enthusiastic step-cutter, took a turn and chopped a haphazard line of steps up another pitch. We were making fast time now and the slope was starting to ease off. Tenzing gallantly waved me through and with a growing feeling of excitement I cramponed up some firm slopes to the rounded top of the South Summit. It was only 9:00 a.m.

With intense interest I looked at the vital ridge leading to the summit—the ridge about which Evans and Bourdillon had made such gloomy forecasts. At first glance it was an exceedingly impressive and indeed a frightening sight. In the narrow crest of this ridge, the basic rock of the mountain had a thin capping of snow and ice—ice that reached out over the east face in enormous cornices, overhanging and treacherous and only waiting for the careless foot of the mountaineer to break off and crash 10,000 feet to the Kangshung Glacier. And from the cornices the snow dropped steeply to the left to merge with the enormous rock bluffs which towered 8,000 feet above the Western Cwm. It was impressive all right! But as I looked my fears started to lift a little. Surely I could see a route there? For this snow slope on the left, although very steep and exposed, was practically continuous for the first half of the ridge, although in places the great cornices reached hungrily across. If we could make a route along that snow slope, we could go quite a distance at least.

With a feeling almost of relief, I set to work with my ice ax and cut a platform for myself just down off the top of the South Summit. Tenzing did the same and then we removed our oxygen sets and sat down. The day was still remarkably fine and we felt no discomfort through our thick layers of clothing from either wind or cold. We had a drink out of Tenzing's water bottle and then I checked our oxygen supplies. Tenzing's bottle was practically exhausted, but mine still had a little in it. As well as this, we each had a full bottle. I decided that the difficulties ahead would demand as light a weight on our backs as possible so determined to use only the full bottles. I removed Tenzing's empty bottle and my nearly empty one and laid them in the snow. With particular care I connected up our last bottles and tested to see that they were working efficiently. The needles on the dials were steady on 3,300 pounds per square inch pressure—they were very full bottles holding just over 800 liters of oxygen each. At three liters a minute we consumed 180 liters an hour and this meant a total endurance of nearly four and a half hours. This didn't seem much for the problems ahead, but I was determined if necessary to cut down to two liters a minute for the homeward trip.

I was greatly encouraged to find how, even at 28,700 feet and with no oxygen, I could work out slowly but clearly the problems of mental arithmetic that the oxygen supply demanded. A correct answer was imperative—any mistake could well mean a trip with no return. But we had no time to waste. I stood up and took a series of photographs in every direction, then thrust my camera back to its warm home inside my clothing. I heaved my now pleasantly light oxygen load onto my back and connected up my tubes. I did the same for Tenzing and we were ready to go. I asked Tenzing to belay me and then, with a growing air of excitement, I cut a broad and safe line of steps down to the snow saddle below the South Summit. I wanted an easy route when we came back up here weak and tired. Tenzing came down the steps and joined me and then belayed once again.

I moved along onto the steep snow slope on the left side of the ridge. With the first blow of my ice ax my excitement increased. The snow—to my astonishment—was crystalline and hard. A couple of rhythmical blows of the ice ax produced a step that was big enough even for our oversize high-altitude boots. But best of all the steps were strong and safe. A little conscious of the great drops beneath me, I chipped a line of steps for the full length of the rope—forty feet—and then forced the shaft of my ice ax firmly into the snow. It made a fine belay and I looped the rope around it. I waved to Tenzing to join me and as he moved slowly and carefully along the steps I took in the rope. When he reached me, he thrust his ice ax into the snow and protected me with a good tight rope as I went on cutting steps. It was exhilarating work—the summit ridge of Everest, the crisp snow and the smooth easy blows of the ice ax all combined to make me feel a greater sense of power than I had ever felt at great altitudes before. I went on cutting for rope length after rope length.

We were now approaching a point where one of the great cornices was encroaching onto our slope. We'd have to go down to the rocks to avoid it. I cut a line of steps steeply down the slope to a small ledge on top of the rocks. There wasn't much room, but it made a reasonably safe stance. I waved to Tenzing to join me. As he came down to me I realized there was something wrong with him. I had been so absorbed in the technical problems of the ridge that I hadn't thought much about Tenzing, except for a vague feeling that he seemed to move along the steps with unnecessary slowness. But now it was quite obvious that he was not only moving extremely slowly, but he was breathing quickly and with difficulty and was in considerable distress. I immediately suspected his oxygen set and helped him down onto the ledge so that I could examine it. The first thing I noticed was that from the outlet of his face mask there were hanging some long icicles. I looked at it more closely and found that the outlet tube—about two inches in diameter—was almost completely blocked up with ice. This was preventing Tenzing from exhaling freely and must have made it extremely unpleasant for him. Fortunately the outlet tube was made of rubber and by manipulating this with my hand I was able to release all the ice and let it fall out. The valves started operating and Tenzing was given immediate relief. Just as a check I examined my own set and found that it, too, had partly frozen up in the outlet tube, but not sufficiently to have affected me a great deal. I removed the ice out of it without a great deal of trouble. Automatically I looked at our pressure gauges—just over 2,900 pounds (2,900 pounds was just over 700 liters; 180 into 700 was about 4)—we had nearly four hours' endurance left. That meant we weren't going badly.

I looked at the route ahead. This next piece wasn't going to be easy. Our rock ledge was perched right on top of the enormous bluff running down into the Western Cwm. In fact, almost under my feet, I could see the dirty patch on the floor of the Cwm which I knew was Camp 4. In a sudden urge to escape our isolation I waved and shouted and then as suddenly stopped as I realized my foolishness. Against the vast expanse of Everest, 8,000 feet above them, we'd be quite invisible to the best binoculars. I turned back to the problem ahead. The rock was far too steep to attempt to drop down and go around this pitch. The only thing to do was to try to shuffle along the ledge and cut handholds in the bulging ice that was trying to push me off it. Held on a tight rope by Tenzing, I cut a few handholds and then thrust my ice ax as hard as I could into the solid snow and ice. Using this to take my weight, I moved quickly along the ledge. It proved easier than I had anticipated. A few more handholds, another quick swing across them, and I was able to cut a line of steps up onto a safe slope and chop out a roomy terrace from which to belay Tenzing as he climbed up to me.

We were now fast approaching the most formidable obstacle on the ridge—a great rock step. This step had always been visible in aerial photographs and in 1951 on the Everest Reconnaissance we had seen it quite clearly with glasses from Thyangboche. We had always thought of it as the obstacle on the ridge which could well spell defeat. I cut a line of steps across the last snow slope and then commenced traversing over a steep rock slab that led to the foot of the great step. The holds were small and hard to see and I brushed my snow glasses away from my eyes. Immediately I was blinded by a bitter wind sweeping across the ridge and laden with particles of ice. I hastily replaced my glasses and blinked away the ice and tears until I could see again. But it made me realize how efficient was our clothing in protecting us from the rigors of even a fine day at 29,000 feet. Still half blinded, I climbed across the slab and then dropped down into a tiny snow hollow at the foot of the step. And here Tenzing joined me.

I looked anxiously up at the rocks. Planted squarely across the ridge in a vertical bluff, they looked extremely difficult and I knew that our strength and ability to climb steep rock at this altitude would be severely limited. I examined the route out to the left. By dropping fifty or a hundred feet over steep slabs, we might be able to get around the bottom of the bluff, but there was no indication that we'd be able to climb back on to the ridge again. And to lose any height now might be fatal. Search as I could, I was unable to see an easy route up to the step or, in fact, any route at all. Finally, in desperation I examined the right-hand end of the bluff. Attached to this and overhanging the precipitous east face was a large cornice. This cornice, in preparation for its inevitable crash down the mountainside, had started to lose its grip on the rock and a long narrow vertical crack had been formed between the rock and the ice. The crack was large enough to take the human frame and though it offered little security, it was at least a route. I quickly made up my mind—Tenzing had an excellent belay and we must be near the top—it was worth a try.

Before attempting the pitch, I produced my camera once again. I had no confidence that I would be able to climb this crack and with a surge of competitive pride which unfortunately afflicts even mountaineers, I determined to have proof that at least we had reached a good deal higher than the South Summit. I took a few photographs and then made another rapid check of the oxygen—2,550-pound pressure. (2,550 from 3,300 leaves 750. 750 over 3,300 is about two-ninths. Two-ninths off 800 liters leaves about 600 liters. 600 divided by 180 is nearly 3½.) Three and a half hours to go. I examined Tenzing's belay to make sure it was a good one and then slowly crawled inside the crack.

In front of me was the rock wall, vertical but with a few promising holds. Behind me was the ice wall of the cornice, glittering and hard but cracked here and there. I took a hold on the rock in front and then jammed one of my crampons hard into the ice behind. Leaning back with my oxygen set on the ice, I slowly levered myself upward. Searching feverishly with my spare boot, I found a tiny ledge on the rock and took some of the weight off my other leg. Leaning back on the cornice, I fought to regain my breath. Constantly at the back of my mind was the fear that the cornice might break off and my nerves were taut with suspense. But slowly I forced my way up—wriggling and jambing and using every little hold. In one place I managed to force my ice ax into a crack in the ice and this gave me the necessary purchase to get over a holdless stretch. And then I found a solid foothold in a hollow in the ice and next moment I was reaching over the top of the rock and pulling myself to safety. The rope came tight—its forty feet had been barely enough.

I lay on the little rock ledge panting furiously. Gradually it dawned on me that I was up the step and I felt a glow of pride and determination that completely subdued my temporary feelings of weakness. For the first time on the whole expedition I really knew I was going to get to the top. "It will have to be pretty tough to stop us now" was my thought. But I couldn't entirely ignore the feeling of astonishment and wonder that I'd been able to get up with such difficulty at 29,000 feet even with oxygen.

When I was breathing more evenly I stood up and, leaning over the edge, waved to Tenzing to come up. He moved into the crack and I gathered in the rope and took some of his weight. Then he, in turn, commenced to struggle and jam and force his way up until I was able to pull him to safety—gasping for breath. We rested for a moment. Above us the ridge continued on as before—enormous overhanging cornices on the right and steep snow slopes on the left running down to the rock bluffs. But the angle of the snow slopes was easing off. I went on chipping a line of steps, but thought it safe enough for us to move together in order to save time. The ridge rose up in a great series of snakelike undulations which bore away to the right, each one concealing the next. I had no idea where the top was. I'd cut a line of steps around the side of one undulation and another would come into view. We were getting desperately tired now and Tenzing was going very slowly. I'd been cutting steps for almost two hours and my back and arms were starting to tire. I tried cramponing along the slope without cutting steps, but my feet slipped uncomfortably down the slope. I went on cutting. We seemed to have been going for a very long time and my confidence was fast evaporating. Bump followed bump with maddening regularity. A patch of shingle barred our way and I climbed dully up it and started cutting steps around another bump. And then I realized that this was the last bump, for ahead of me the ridge dropped steeply away in a great corniced curve and out in the distance I could see the pastel shades and fleecy clouds of the highlands of Tibet.

To my right a slender snow ridge climbed up to a snowy dome about forty feet above our heads. But all the way along the ridge the thought had haunted me that the summit might be the crest of a cornice. It was too late to take risks now. I asked Tenzing to belay me strongly and I started cutting a cautious line of steps up the ridge. Peering from side to side and thrusting with my ice ax, I tried to discover a possible cornice, but everything seemed solid and firm. I waved Tenzing up to me. A few more whacks of the ice ax, a few very weary steps and we were on the summit of Everest.

⟜

It was 11:30 a.m. My first sensation was one of relief—relief that the long grind was over; that the summit had been reached before our oxygen supplies had dropped to a critical level; and relief that in the end the mountain had been kind to us in having a pleasantly rounded cone for its summit instead of a fearsome and unapproachable cornice. But mixed with the relief was a vague sense of astonishment that I should have been the lucky one to attain the ambition of so many brave and determined climbers. It seemed difficult at first to grasp that we'd got there. I was too tired and too conscious of the long way down to safety really to feel any great elation. But as the fact of our success thrust itself more clearly into my mind, I felt a quiet glow of satisfaction spread through my body—a satisfaction less vociferous but more powerful than I had ever felt on a mountaintop before. I turned and looked at Tenzing. Even beneath his oxygen mask and the icicles hanging from his hair, I could see his infectious grin of sheer delight. I held out my hand and in silence we shook in good Anglo-Saxon fashion. But this was not enough for Tenzing and impulsively he threw his arm around my shoulders and we thumped each other on the back in mutual congratulations.

But we had no time to waste! First I must take some photographs and then we'd hurry down. I turned off my oxygen and took the set off my back. I remembered all the warnings I'd had of the possible fatal consequences of this, but for some reason felt quite confident that nothing serious would result. I took my camera out of the pocket of my windproof and clumsily opened it with my thickly gloved hands. I clipped on the lens hood and ultraviolet filter and then shuffled down the ridge a little so that I could get the summit into my viewfinder. Tenzing had been waiting patiently, but now, at my request, he unfurled the flags wrapped around his ice ax and standing on the summit held them above his head. Clad in all his bulky equipment and with the flags flapping furiously in the wind, he made a dramatic picture and the thought drifted through my mind that this photograph should be a good one if it came out at all. I didn't worry about getting Tenzing to take a photograph of me—as far as I knew, he had never taken a photograph before and the summit of Everest was hardly the place to show him how.

I climbed up to the top again and started taking a photographic record in every direction. The weather was still extraordinarily fine. High above us were long streaks of cirrus wind cloud and down below fluffy cumulus hid the valley floors from view. But wherever we looked, icy peaks and somber gorges lay beneath us like a relief map. Perhaps the view was most spectacular to the east, for here the giants Makalu and Kanchenjunga dominated the horizon and gave some idea of the vast scale of the Himalayas. Makalu in particular, with its soaring rock ridges, was a remarkable sight; it was only a few miles away from us. From our exalted viewpoint I could see all the northern slopes of the mountain and was immediately struck by the possibility of a feasible route to its summit. With a growing feeling of excitement, I took another photograph to study at leisure on returning to civilization. The view to the north was a complete contrast—hundreds of miles of the arid high Tibetan plateau, softened now by a veil of fleecy clouds into a scene of delicate beauty. To the west the Himalayas stretched hundreds of miles in a tangled mass of peaks, glaciers, and valleys.

But one scene was of particular interest. Almost under our feet, it seemed, was the famous North Col and the East Rongbuk Glacier, where so many epic feats of courage and endurance were performed by the earlier British Everest Expeditions. Part of the ridge up which they had established their high camps was visible, but the last thousand feet, which had proved such a formidable barrier, was concealed from our view as its rock slopes dropped away with frightening abruptness from the summit snow pyramid. It was a sobering thought to remember how often these men had reached 28,000 feet without the benefits of our modern equipment and reasonably efficient oxygen sets. Inevitably my thoughts turned to Mallory and Irvine, who had lost their Jives on the mountain thirty years before. With little hope I looked around for some sign that they had reached the summit, but could see nothing.

Meanwhile Tenzing had also been busy. On the summit he'd

scratched out a little hole in the snow and in this he placed some small offerings of food—some biscuits, a piece of chocolate, and a few sweets—a small gift to the gods of Chomolungma which all devout Buddhists (as Tenzing is) believe to inhabit the summit of this mountain. Besides the food, I placed the little cross that John Hunt had given me on the South Col. Strange companions, no doubt, but symbolical at least of the spiritual strength and peace that all peoples have gained from the mountains. We made seats for ourselves in the snow and sitting there in reasonable comfort we ate with relish a bar of mint cake. My camera was still hanging open on my chest so I decided to put it safely away. But my fingers seemed to have grown doubly clumsy. With slow and fumbling movements, I closed the camera and did up the leather case. I suddenly realized that I was being affected by the lack of oxygen—it was nearly ten minutes now since I'd taken my set off. I quickly checked the gauges on our bottles—1,450-pound pressure; roughly 350 liters of oxygen; nearly two hours' endurance at three liters a minute. It wasn't much, but it would have to do. I hastily put my set on and turned on the oxygen. I felt better immediately. Tenzing had removed the flags from his ice ax and, as there was nothing to tie them to, he thrust them down into the snow. They obviously wouldn't stay there for long. We slowly got to our feet again. We were tired all right and all my tension and worry about reaching the summit had gone, leaving a slight feeling of anticlimax. But the smallness of our supply of oxygen filled me with a sense of urgency. We must get back to the South Summit as quickly as possible.

I took up my ice ax, glanced at Tenzing to see if he was ready, and then looked at my watch—it was 11:45 and we'd only been on top fifteen minutes. I had one job left to do. Walking easily down the steps I'd made in the ridge I descended forty feet from the summit to the first visible rocks, and taking a handful of small stones, thrust them into my pocket—it seemed a bit silly at the time, but I knew they'd be rather nice to have when we got down. Then, wasting no time, I set off along the ridge. Fortunately my steps were all intact and we cramponed along them quickly and safely. We knew we had to hurry and, tired as we were, we drove ourselves hard. In what seemed an astonishingly short time, we were climbing down toward the top of the difficult rock step. I could see from here the frail fashion in which the cornice was attached to the rocks, but with the confidence of familiarity I plunged down into the chimney and wriggled my way between the rock and the ice to the bottom. Tenzing quickly followed and we climbed on again. The ridge was now much steeper and more exposed, so we moved one at a time, each man belaying the other as he moved. We were going very quickly indeed, but at the same time taking every care. We cautiously shuffled our way across the rock ledge and then moved on to the steps crossing the last steep slopes. Once again I could see far below us in the Western Cwm the dirty smudge of Camp 4 and I thought how pleased they'd all be at our news. With a feeling of relief I cramponed on to the little saddle at the foot of the South Summit and then slowly climbed up the generous stairway I'd whacked out in its icy side nearly four hours before. I sat down beside our discarded oxygen bottles and Tenzing joined me there. It had only taken us one hour from the top.

Once again I checked our oxygen bottles—there was only about an hour's endurance left, but this should get us down to our reserve supply on the ridge. Tenzing offered me his water bottle and I had a long swig out of it. It was a delicious brew of water, sugar, lemon crystals, and raspberry jam. I looked back up the ridge and saw that our steps were clearly outlined in the snow, so I got out my camera once again and photographed them. Despite the cold conditions, my camera seemed to be working very well, which was most encouraging, as I realized how important these summit photographs were. Our rest was very short— only a few minutes—and then we were on our feet again and starting down.

The thought of this descent had never been far from my mind throughout the day and I viewed it with fearful anticipation. It had seemed so difficult and dangerous on the ascent that I was very much afraid that when we came down it tired and much less alert, one of us might slip and precipitate a disastrous avalanche. I was determined to pack the treacherous snow into safe and stable steps as if our lives depended, as they probably did, on not one of them breaking. Tenzing looked as strong and staunch as ever and I felt I could confidently rely on him as a stout anchor. I started cramponing carefully down the first steep slopes of frozen snow. The wind was now a good deal stronger and occasional strong gusts made us feel uncomfortably off balance. I soon reached the first line of steps down the steep ridge at the top of the great slope. Steadying myself against the slope with my ice ax, I climbed carefully down from step to step. And then I muttered a hearty curse! I'd come to the steps Tenzing had cut on the way up and which had been all right on the ascent but were too widely spaced for a safe or comfortable trip down. Rather reluctantly I decided to take care and set to work to re-cut them again. Cutting steps down a steep slope when you are laden with cumbersome gear is always a tedious business, especially in a gusty wind, and I wasn't sorry to move back onto my own steps again and drop rapidly down to where the ridge petered out in the great slope.

Now the unpleasant moment had arrived and we had 300 feet of steep and dangerous snow to deal with. First of all, we had to get onto the slope and this entailed a traverse over some steep rocks. Tenzing belayed me carefully and I started across them. Using every meager handhold I could find I inched my way along, very conscious of the tremendous drops beneath and realizing for the first time just how tired I was. To reach the snow slope from the rocks was a tricky move, but with a long step I lowered myself reluctantly into its snowy grip. As I stood there looking downward, all my earlier fears returned. The slope dropped away with startling abruptness and our deep upward tracks looked hazardous in the extreme. Ten thousand feet below us was the avalanche-strewn Kangshung Glacier, coldly and impersonally waiting to receive a toppling cornice or a careless climber. I hastily shrugged these morbid thoughts out of my mind and started packing the loose snow into a little ledge so that I could safely belay Tenzing across the rock pitch. My stance was far from perfect, but I put the rope over my shoulders and waved to Tenzing to cross. He moved slowly onto the traverse and laboriously began to work his way over. With a sudden shock I realized how tired he was—how tired we both were! It seemed a long time before he stepped across to join me.

With a tense feeling in the pit of my stomach I started down the slope, packing the loose snow with my boot into a step that would take my weight. Each time I changed my weight into a new step, I had a moment of fear to see if it would hold. We were going very slowly, but we couldn't afford to hurry. I glanced behind. Grimly silent, Tenzing was climbing down the steps with great care. He was obviously tired, but was still strong and safe. I went on packing steps and lowering my-self into them. Time lost its meaning and the great slope turned into an eternal and endless nightmare. It was with an astonished feeling of relief that I suddenly realized we were nearly at the bottom. I started traversing carefully over to the right, plunging now with renewed vigor through the deep snow and then, with an enormous feeling of thankfulness, I stepped onto the ridge again and sank the shaft of my ice ax deeply into the firm snow. I took in the rope as Tenzing moved up beside me. We looked at each other and we didn't need to speak—our faces clearly showed our unrestrained relief.

Almost casually I started down the ridge—it seemed so easy now after what we'd just come down—but a sudden fierce gust of wind brought me sharply to my senses and I started concentrating again. I knew our oxygen must be nearly exhausted and that we had to reach the dump left by Evans and Bourdillon before it ran out. I pushed on as hard as I could. The wind had wiped out a lot of our tracks in the snow, but it didn't take long to remake them. And then we reached the oxygen dump and another nagging worry lifted from my mind. I checked the sets on our backs. We still had a few liters of oxygen left and couldn't afford to waste it. We continued on down carrying the life-saving reserve bottles in our hands. The ridge broadened and I realized we'd reached the snow shoulder above Camp 9. I plunged down the steep slope off the ridge, sidled around a rock bluff, and then saw our tent only a hundred feet away. I moved eagerly toward it, but suddenly felt very tired and weak. My load felt like a ton and my boots were as heavy as lead. I realized that my oxygen bottle had run out. I climbed slowly on to our tent platform, took off my oxygen set, and slumped down in the snow. Tenzing wearily sat down beside me. It was good to be back.

Our tent was flapping furiously in the wind and already many of the guy lines had come undone. Tenzing crawled inside it and started getting the cooker going for a hot drink. I removed the empty bottles from our oxygen sets and connected up our last meager reserves. I reduced the rate of flow to two liters a minute and tested both the sets out. Frequent gusts of wind were whipping across the ridge, pelting me with stinging particles of snow, but I was too tired to worry very much. Far below on the South Col I could see the tents flapping and thought I saw some figures moving. It was nice to know there was someone there to help us, but it looked a long way down. Tenzing handed out a large mug of warm, sweet lemon-flavored water and I drank it with relish. We rolled up our sleeping bags, our air mattresses, and our personal gear and tied them onto our oxygen sets. We needed them for sleeping in the lower camps. We heaved our loads onto our backs and turned on our oxygen and then, with no feelings of regret, I took one last glance at our forlorn little camp that had served us so well and started off down again.

There were no tracks visible on the slopes below us, but I knew that once we had worked across onto the ridge we could stick to it until we reached the remains of the highest Swiss camp. I forced a deep trail across the slope, very conscious of the weakness in my limbs and the extra weight on my back. The ridge itself dropped away in an unhealthy-looking sweep of snow-covered rocks. I knew Evans and Bourdillon had had some unpleasant slips on this part of the ridge and I was determined that we shouldn't do the same—we mightn't be so lucky! We made our way slowly down, moving very carefully but steadily. It wasn't particularly difficult, just rather unpleasant, and we knew we couldn't afford to slip. Our first objective was the remnant of the Swiss tent about 700 or 800 feet below us. For a long time it never seemed to get any closer, but all of a sudden it grew much larger and there we were, right beside it.

Now we had to branch off to the right to the head of the great snow couloir leading down to the South Col. We crossed slowly over easy snow and rock slopes to the little rock ledge which gave access to the couloir and then we looked down our last problem—the long steep slopes beneath us. With a sudden start I realized there wasn't a step showing—for some reason I had expected George Lowe's steps still to be intact. My heart sank! I was deadly tired and had no desire for another bout of step-cutting. I tried the snow with the hope that it would be soft enough to kick steps down it, but it was as hard as a board. It was far too steep to attempt to crampon it in our weak condition. I had no alternative but to start cutting again. I had only chipped down about ten feet into the couloir when I heard a high-pitched roar from the bluffs above us and next moment I was hit by a terrific gust of wind and almost torn from my steps. As I braced myself against the slope with the pick of my ice ax dug into the hard snow as a belay, I was peppered with a barrage of small ice particles dislodged from the battlements above. After a few moments the wind disappeared as quickly as it had come.

I went on cutting step after step and Tenzing moved into the couloir behind me. A few moments later we were once again clinging to the slope, being buffeted unmercifully by a powerful gust. It seemed as though the couloir was acting as a wind tunnel and intensifying the wind to dangerous proportions. I continued hacking a path downward, but when I'd done over 200 feet I'd just about had enough. Tenzing—tired though he was—offered to take a turn and cut down for nearly another hundred feet. Then he moved ten feet out to the right and started kicking steps down a softer layer of snow. Thankfully I moved down behind him and we lost height quickly. I noticed that a small figure had appeared on the icy slopes above the South Col and somehow I knew it was George Lowe. We stopped and had a rest at the crevasse at the foot of the couloir and then moved on again. We knew we were safe now and with the disappearance of our tension the last of our energy went too. But, stiff-legged and weary, we thumped on down automatically.

George's tall, strong figure was now much closer and the thought struck me that there wasn't anyone I'd rather tell the news to first. George and I had been through a lot together in the mountains. We'd had a lot of success together and we'd had our tough moments; no one had done more than George to make this final success possible. Already I could see his cheerful grin and next moment his strong vigorous voice was shouting out a greeting. To my tired mind he looked an absolute tower of strength. In rough New Zealand slang I shouted out the good news and next moment we were all talking at once and slapping each other on the back. I could feel a warm glow of contentment creeping over me and for the moment at least quite forgot that I was at 26,000 feet with a fifty-mile-an-hour wind whistling around my ears.

TO NAMDAPHA AND TAWANG*

Anil Yadav

My newfound brother Rupah-da turned me over to Nature's Beckon in front of the Tinsukhia Railway Station. When the Tata 407 minibus finally left—after having waited interminably for flustered passengers

* A journey in the Eastern Himalaya, part of a larger account of travels in northeast India, excerpted and translated from *Woh Bhi Koi Des Hai Maharaj!* (2012).

arriving from god knows where—fowl stuffed into a wicker basket underneath a seat cackled. There was a sack of potatoes with a hole in it; some popped out and rolled about on the floor. We were eighteen passengers in all, including a ten-year-old, traveling with a group of experts who worked for Nature's Beckon, an NGO working to build environmental awareness. Our destination: the jungles of Namdapha on the Changlang plateau in Arunachal Pradesh—Namdapha is the highest peak in the region. These jungles, abutting Burma, rise up from swampy wetlands in the plains to snow-covered mountains and span 2,000 square kilometers. There is such geographic diversity that multiple seasons co-exist over contiguous territory. From the jhapi hats, binoculars, packets of crisps, and the keen desire to hear the opinions of strangers on the varieties of forests found in different geographical regions of the world, it was clear everyone had done their homework well.

The young director of Nature's Beckon, Soumyadeep, tried to lighten the atmosphere with well-timed jokes and tales of travels in the wild but his narration was stolid, and his manner that of a tour guide in a hurry. No tales were told him in reply. A freshly minted young journalist, Pem Thi Gohain, launched an interrogation: What was my salary break-up at the paper I worked for; and who was the editor brilliant enough to send me on this assignment? I distanced myself from him by speaking in English and by shrinking into myself and looking out the window, pretending to be absorbed in the landscape. It was impossible to tell any more lies.

A tire punctured in Digboi. The diver propped the vehicle on a makeshift jack built out of a pile of bricks and stood on the side of the road, thumbing down trucks to borrow a tire iron from. This was going to take a while so I left for a brief walkabout.

Digboi is full of oil wells; its neighborhoods are named after the bends in the roads next to which they stand. Small hills are dotted with bungalows from the British era. Each bungalow once occupied by a single British family is now shared by many households. Digboi is a sleepy town, one where from the looks of things a heavy breakfast is all that is needed to send one back to bed.

We left and soon after the driver stopped in Margherita. While the rest of us ate, he went off to have the puncture repaired. Santwana Bharali, aka Poppy, was our tour coordinator. She had an MSc in botany; her cheeks dimpled prettily when she smiled. One of our co-passengers was a psychology nut. According to him, Poppy had followed the driver to the puncture-repair shop only because she wanted to see the tire tube fill up with air and become tumescent. I concurred. But when she opened her purse and paid the mechanic, I silently chided the influence of Freud on the manner in which I had agreed with his assessment of Poppy. Archana Niyog, another co-passenger, was what you might call a homely girl; she was serving food to her fellow passengers, urging each to eat some more.

The large yellow signboard which marks the beginning of the Stilwell Road flashed past us near the railway crossing in Lido. The road, built during the Second World War at enormous cost in terms of the lives of soldiers and laborers, begins in Jairampur in Arunachal Pradesh, enters Burma, spans Kachin territory, and terminates in the Kunming province of China. One of the longstanding demands in the region is the reopening of the road so that trade may flourish, but our relations with China remain rocky.

Lido is a vast colliery. Coal dust rained upon me from impossibly tall heaps in a black billowing mist. The practice of open-cast mining gives this town a mysterious, suspicious air.

The olive-green of battle fatigues became increasingly more concentrated once we entered Arunachal Pradesh. A state of high alertness has become the norm here after 1962 when China defeated India in war. We were stopped at every checkpoint to be interrogated and for our permits to be examined; it was night by the time we were done. When twilight fell everyone looked up at the sky in complete silence. Perhaps its color reflected our most inward moods. Afterward, everyone dozed.

Red points of light flickered deep within the forests. To avoid the telltale thwack-thwack of ax on tree trunk, a small hole is drilled and a fire set within. The embers smolder for many days before the tree finally comes crashing down. In many places forests were being burned down to make way for jhum cultivation. Those fires were much more widespread and malignant. Only 2 percent of land in the state is under permanent cultivation, either as small terraced fields or as bigger plots in the lowlands.

The bus entered one of the gates to Namdapha. A shaggy animal bolted across the front of the truck and was spotlit by its headlamps. Eyes opened wide, shoulder joined shoulder in anticipation, and heads came together as everyone peered out the windows. Poppy quacked in a sleep-laden voice: "Porcupine! Porcupine! I know very well that was a porcupine."

The hedgehog vanished under the bushes on the side of the road. The ten-year-old found his long-awaited opportunity to lay hands upon his father's binoculars—so what if it was dark? The minibus halted near a waterfall. The air was rank with the odor of swamp deer, of which there must have been a herd nearby. Jain-ul-Abedeen, aka Benu Daku, is an experienced hunter who quit his hereditary profession to become an environmentalist. He said, snorting, "They are foolish animals. Once spooked by torches, they can't run. Hunters get them easy."

It was a four-kilometer hike from the waterfall to the rest house. Bags on backs, we trooped into the darkness in single file, our path lighted by torches. The drone of crickets vibrated through the forest. On our left was a deep gorge at the bottom of which rushed the Dihang River. The pauses in between the crump-crump of footsteps were deafening in their silence. In those moments it was easy to imagine the act of measuring time as a joke which man plays to keep himself deluded. Elephant dung, a deer's hoofprints, and tire marks became mysteries to be deciphered at leisure. Benu shone his light into the gorge, looking for something. He stopped, then said sotto voce, "There might be a tigress nearby."

A commotion followed; it crumpled up our single file and brought us into a huddle. The effect of torchlight on tigers was discussed in whispers, with books being quoted and their publishers and prices mentioned. This was a serious moment but something seemed out of joint. I don't know why a thought occurred to me: "This is a new profession for Benu. He and Soumyadeep are injecting a dose of excitement into these middle-class nature-lovers so their trip becomes memorable."

As soon as we reached the rest house, the sweat-soaked trekkers called out to their gods and collapsed, using their backpacks as cushions upon which to stretch their strained backs. Bricks were collected, makeshift stoves hurriedly set up, and rice put on to boil. A safe corner for the women to sleep in was scouted. A whistle went off shrilly and at length; everyone gathered round and the experts answered questions on Namdapha in the dim light of a kerosene lantern.

The tiger and three species of leopard inhabit Namdapha: the common leopard, the clouded leopard, and the rare snow leopard. The red panda is also to be found here.

The Namdapha Tiger Reserve was set up because this area is the perfect habitat for felines: it has flowing water, shade, and abundant prey. These make up the ideal environmental cycle.

Some creatures such as the flying squirrel, the white hornbill, and the howler monkey make the reserve their home because of geographical features which are unique to the area.

Chakma refugees from Bangladesh have been rehabilitated in the Gandhi Gram village located inside the forest. They hunt and eat elephants. Hunting has put the elephant population under stress.

Lisu refugees from Burma live in the jungle, too. They are skilled at hunting tigers.

Tiger-bone liquor is much in demand in China. Tiger whiskers are used to manufacture sex toys.

The wide expanse of the jungle is manned by just thirteen employees who can't even manage to shut all the gates of the reserve. There is no electricity and all the drinking water must be brought from the Noa-Dihing River . . .

After these stark truths were underlined in many different ways, the dancing flames reflected on the walls took on a new meaning. The deep silence of the forest invaded our tired minds. The whistle went off again, shrill and long; rice and flat-bean curry was served. Later, everyone pitched in to wash the dishes in candlelight. Soon I could hear snores.

It was raining in the morning. Binoculars and cameras jumped out of their carrying cases and kept waiting for a long time. Later, we were ferried across the Noa-Dihing in two batches under a steady drizzle. Bimal Gogoi and Mridul Phukan identified birds and animals from their calls. The deep silence of the forest made itself felt once more. In a crowd, we lose the ability to feel because all of us are trying frantically to communicate something or the other and this takes up all our attention. Yet, walking underneath the dripping forest canopy on the thick carpet of fallen leaves and sodden mulch, I felt regret: this place had everything, but that which I find in a tree standing alone on the side of a road, it couldn't give me.

Poppy showed us a twig on which grew a layer of what looked like white mold. She said, "Look, there is no pollution here. This lichen is proof." She picked up a berry from the ground and said in chaste

Assamese, "The pahu eats the flesh of this fruit and the porcupine its pit. In this manner they help propagate these seeds all over the forest."

"This pahu, is it a bird?" She laughed. I understood I had made yet another mistake in wringing meaning from the Assamese language.

"Pahu is not a bird. *Pahu* is Assamese for 'deer,'" Archana corrected me.

We had climbed from a height of forty meters to two hundred fifty meters over rocky, uneven terrain. Thin red leeches swarmed up our shoes. They soon crawled into our socks and everyone looked around for salt—the best antidote for leeches—which we had all forgotten to bring. Tikendrajit, from Barpeta, had long been scratching his head. A leech had fastened itself to his scalp and was turgid with blood. I pulled it off.

A tribal, Lat Gam Singpho, was accompanying our party as guide. Using his dao he cut green cane into strips and fashioned himself a hat. When everyone crowded around demanding a hat, he made one for each. A lengthy photo session ensued. The hats which adorned the people's heads deranged the balance of chemicals within their brains. They capered about spouting gibberish: "He hai hua, chi chai chung!" In those green-cane hats they had found an excuse to express their truest, their innermost reactions to the Singpho's illiteracy and backwardness. Later, all the men took turns to wield the keen Singpho dao on the surrounding trees.

The sun came out in the afternoon and the forest took on new colors. We heard the cracking of bamboo. A small herd of elephants was crashing through, though we saw them only in our imaginations. A sudden shower drenched us in the evening and we didn't need the services of a boat to cross the Noa-Dihing on our way back. Many other environmentalists came to us at night and—eating chicken curry and rice—gave us much useful information on crocodiles, hornbills, and elephants. In one later session, people narrated their experiences of the jungle. Some-one was terrified by the sight of an elephant brought up close by his binoculars, another slyly transformed anecdote into personal experience. Archana told us the heartrending story of the death of a calving cow and her attachment to the orphaned calf. Soumyadeep often dreamt of wild elephants surrounding him and of a forest goddess who would come to his rescue. Lat Gam Singpho, who now lived in the forest, had once been ward boy in a hospital. He had a remarkable story.

"I can face down a tiger with a dao in hand but ghosts scare me to death. There were some doctors in the hospital who conspired so I would lose my job. They put a new shirt on a corpse and propped it against the wall. A burning cigarette was wedged between its fingers, some loose change was put in its pocket, and a dao slung from a belt at its waist. The corpse was pointed out to me from afar and I was sent to summon it. When he didn't hear my calls I put a hand on his shoulder and then took off running. That day, for the first time in my life, I drank a boiling cup of tea in one breath."

This was the first true story I had heard of a tribal wandering about in a jungle of dead souls.

Amid a marathon of snores, the ten-year-old snuggled up to me and demanded a story. He seemed unhappy and was unable to sleep. I scoured the corners of my memory but found no tale suitable for a young child—all my stories were rated "A." I first felt a surge of self-pity, then came a glimmer of self-realization: As a child, I would doubt every story I heard. And because I kept neglecting them, kept hating them, they had evaporated. The child said to me, "Let's go for a stroll outside. Maybe you will remember one."

Outside the resthouse, a furry creature floated across the milky-white beam cast by the flashlight, followed by another—a pair of flying squirrels were playing catch. An entire team of experts tramping about all day hadn't been able to spot even one. A thin membrane connects the fore- and hind legs of the rodent on both sides. Using tree branches as a runway, it gathers speed and launches itself. The membrane fills up with air and the squirrel glides from tree to tree.

My work had been made easy. I adorned the boy's shoulder with the cloak of a forest god, slung a Singpho dao around his waist, and put him on the back of a flying squirrel. Now he could himself describe the mysteries of the jungles to me.

⌒

The first batch of one thousand plastic replicas of hornbill beaks which had arrived from Delhi had been distributed in the Nyishi villages around Namdapha. And Lat Gam Singpho had a question for Bharat Sundaram, project officer with the Asian Elephant Research and Conservation Center, Bangalore: "Will elephants made out of plastic be distributed among the Chakma refugees who live in the west of

Namdapha?" The Chakmas hunt elephants with poisoned arrows. It takes them half an hour to bring down an animal but preparation for the hunt lasts many days.

Young Bharat Sundaram was then on a trek in the Northeast, accompanied by porters laden with provisions and tents. He was tracking footprints and sampling elephant dung to determine their numbers. A nationwide elephant census was underway. The Northeast is a special zone where the very existence of elephants is under threat in many areas; many of their old stomping grounds and corridors of passage have been wiped out. However, it was the hornbill that Bharat was most interested in because of those traits in the bird which are expected only of humans. Bharat had photographed a rufous-headed Hornbill in Namdapha. This species of hornbill had never been spotted in India and the event was being treated as a new find.

The hornbill is a colorful, beautiful bird with an extraordinarily large beak. When the female lays eggs, she goes on a four-month-long maternity leave. The young emerge from the nest only once they have fully fledged. During this time the male guards the nest. He brings food for his wife and children. Some species of hornbill form cooperative societies. Many pairs get together to hatch eggs and to look after the brooding mothers. Pairs mate for life, and remain faithful to each other.

The beauty of the hornbill is also its curse. Nagas use their feathers to adorn their headdresses. Many tribes of Arunachal Pradesh, including the Nyishi, use hornbill beaks as ornaments on their crowns. They lie and wait for the male; when it returns to the nest with food for its brooding mate, they kill it. The flesh of the hornbill and oil extracted from its fat are considered an aphrodisiac. Unani hakims, wandering ayurvedic vaids who examine people on roadsides in full view of curious gawkers, and quacks of all varieties possess hornbill beaks with which they lure the loveless and the superstitious. This bird is rapidly dwindling in numbers; it is a rare sight even in dense forests.

Forest officers and the World Wildlife Trust of India jointly came up with the idea of replicas after a great deal of thought. The beaks distributed in the Nyishi villages had been manufactured in Delhi on order. Each had cost fifteen rupees to make. Since one can't make money off hornbills, they were being distributed gratis. The officers and the NGOs were certain that the tribals would reconcile these plastic toys with their religious beliefs and stop hunting the bird. There were some organizations, too, which held that plastic is harmful to the environment and the tribals should be given wooden beaks. Even better, they should be trained to carve beaks so that they could find employment.

Some people in the villages had accepted the plastic beaks, but the ones with the original article made fun of them. Now the danger was that the remaining hornbills in the forest would also be wiped out due to this conflict between the villagers. This was why Lat Gam Singpho wanted to pose his question to Bharat Sundaram.

Bharat had also visited Gandhi Gram, the furthest village on India's frontier, in the far south of Namdapha. Lisu refugees from Burma have been settled there. Anyone who visits carrying kerosene and sugar is welcomed in the village as an honored guest. The nearest weekly market is a three-day walk each way. They barter goods with local fish which they hunt with an anesthetic. The Lisu examine the moss which grows on the rocks standing mid-river. From the marks made on the moss by the fishes' mouths as they graze upon them, they gauge the size of the fish. They then take the leaves of a particular tree which has narcotic properties, grind them up, and stir the paste into the water. The drugged fish belly-up on the surface. The fish are not for sale but, yes, they can be bartered for kerosene.

∽

The Apatani tribe was yet to come across that important invention known as the wheel in the year Kuru Hasang was born in the Ziro valley. Still, the Apatani are considered the most modern among the tribes of Arunachal for having innovated the concepts of fixed—non-jhum—cultivation and irrigation. When Hasang was admitted to the Army School, Bhubaneshwar, in 1963, his father ritually sacrificed an egg on the village border before letting him go out into the limitless, unknown world. Within five years of leaving his village, Hasang was commissioned into the Air Force, became a fighter pilot, and flew MIGs. He came back to his village in Arunachal in 1978—once the state was formally formed—having retired as flight lieutenant, to try his hand at politics. When I was traveling in the area, the middle-aged Kuru Hasang, after having lost multiple elections, was the chief secretary of the Arunachal Pradesh Congress Committee. His wife ran a medical store in the Hapoli neighborhood of Ziro.

Many tribes of Arunachal Pradesh, including the Nocte, the

Khampti, the Nyishi, and the Tagin, have their own fading heroes who, because of coincidences, have managed to cram many lives into one. They have vaulted distances which takes the rest of humanity many thousands of years to trudge over. More than sixty tribes live in Arunachal and the state has more than fifty known languages. Yet the written history of the area is merely three hundred years old. Every old officer who has served in the area has a story which begins: "When we first came here, accustomed as we were to the sensations which nudity arouses, we wouldn't even look at the tribals. And, when we began to look at them, what happened was . . ."

The state of Arunachal has itself similarly launched headlong into democracy. Before independence, the region was officially known as a "Tribal Area." A few British surveyors would travel in the area accompanied by armed battalions, scouting for opportunities to build roads and lay down railway lines. They wanted to extend trade possibilities for the East India Company further into countries in the east. In 1954 the Kameng, Siang, Subansiri, Lohit, Tirap, and Tuensang divisions were combined into the North East Frontier Agency (NEFA) which was administered by the Foreign Ministry for a long time. After 1972 Tuensang went to Nagaland and the rest of the divisions coalesced into Arunachal Pradesh. Post-1962, after the debacle with China, the central government invested blindly in roads and communication networks, and the investment shows. A population of merely nine lakh lives in an area of 78,000 square kilometers but telephone poles stand tall in every jungle. The army regularly flies sorties from bases in Siliguri and Dibrugarh, ferrying rations, political leaders, officers, and soldiers—an exercise that costs an average of four crore rupees per day. There are close to one hundred helipads in the state. In all of India, the maximum number of mishaps—mainly due to helicopters losing their way in fog and crashing—in which ministers, chief ministers, and pilots have lost their lives have occurred in Arunachal.

I wanted to visit Hapoli and meet Kuru Hasang and his wife. The idea was to conduct a long interview on his memories of the time when he came back to Ziro on his first furlough from the Air Force. But I got distracted and reached Tawang instead.

It happened in this manner. One day in Bhalukpong, the remains of a poet interred within the soul of a Buddhist monk of the Mahayana order decided to draw breath. And all he said was "Tawang will have played for two hours in the light of the new sun by the time dawn breaks over the rest of the world." More prosaically, friends in Benares had given me the names of lamas who had gone to Sarnath to study theology and who now lived in monasteries in Arunachal. So, naturally, I set out on a very long, serpentine road shrouded in fog which threaded through a desert of snow and ice. I have never seen more shades of blue in the sky since.

Before I reached Bomdila, I could never have imagined that a Tata Sumo, grinding along in the first and second gears, is like a faithful horse which responds to its rider's most urgent wishes, his most fleeting whims. It takes a special set of ears to drive on these remote mountains—ears which can discern the whispers, wails, and sobs of an engine underneath its overpowering roar. And it takes a special kind of sensitivity which detaches the accelerator and the brake from the vehicle, makes them part of the driver's being, and instantaneously transmutes the smallest tremor, the least vibration, into crystal-clear thought. It is not without reason that in the couplets and verses inscribed on windscreens and bumpers— usually dismissed as slight and even cheap—the vehicle is often cast in the role of lover or mistress. At their base is the living, breathing relationship between man and machine, and their pact to live and die as one.

Descending from the 6,000-foot-high Nechi Phu pass, I would occasionally visualize the Tata Sumo drifting down the gorge like an unmoored kite and children standing at the bottom of the valley, waving, imagining it to be a helicopter. At each instance I would stare hard at the driver and think: Was I projecting my innermost fear and influencing him in any way? But he was in a deep trance. He was lost in a time and space where his passengers had no existence any longer.

From Bomdila (8,500 feet) an infinite variety of clouds billow and play. Fog descends without warning and obscures the world; when it parts the dazzling Himalaya stands tall and close. Bomdila is the district headquarters of the West Kameng district, home to the Monpa, Sherdukpen, Aka, Mijia, and Bugun tribes. The dogs of Bomdila are infamous—they prowl the streets on sub-zero nights and can easily take down a man and feed on his flesh. There is an abundance of flora. Some quite lucrative. A truckload of *Taxus baccata*—from which the anti-cancer chemical Taxol is extracted and exported to Europe— delivered to Guwahati can fetch enough money to buy a brand-new truck chassis.

There was an old man in Bomdila market who said to me in the manner of one demonstrating an invisible monument, "The Chinese had marched down to here during the war."

I found a place to bed down in a slate-roofed dhaba in the Dirang valley. A wild wind sprang up and whistled as night descended; the temperature dropped sharply and it was difficult to keep one's feet in that gale outside. I piled two quilts over my sleeping bag but the cold bore into my bones. The mistress of the dhaba allowed me to move my sleeping bag close to the fireplace but before going to bed issued strict instructions to her terrifying mastiff: "Keep sharp; no one should go outside!" I'd make a move to walk out, driven by the desire to view the silvery Himalaya in moonlight, but the dog would bristle, bare its teeth, and growl imperiously: "A fleeting glimpse, cooling balm to the eyes, or your life. Make up your mind about what you want." I'd resign myself and come back to my sleeping bag.

In the morning I made my way to a gompa—established by the Buddhist guru Padmasambhava in the eighth century inside the Dirang dzong, an ancient fort—to look for Lama Nawang Lamsang. In this area, which seems more Tibet than India, Padmasambhava is known as Lopon Rinpoche. Young novice monks were seated in the sanctum sanctorum of that small gompa, reading from ancient scriptures. An elderly monk informed me that monk Lamsang was traveling outside the Dirang valley. After a moment's thought he opened a battered tin box, took out a very old piece of stone, and, placing it on my palm, said, "This is the heart of a demon which was killed here. After it was killed, the Mon people converted to Buddhism."

"How did its heart turn to stone?"

"What then, if not a stone . . . it was a demon!"

With that piece of irrefutable logic, he left no reason for me to doubt that symbol of the victory of Buddhism.

As one climbs up the Dirang valley toward the Sela Pass, the vegetation thins out, disappears, and is replaced by snow-topped granite mountains and, in a very few places, by densely growing grass which appear as soft as mattresses. Hidden by dense fog, army trucks scream and wail their way up in an ant-crawl; grazing yaks occasionally heave into view; the thin oxygen makes breathing difficult. The Sela (14,000 feet) is the second-highest motorable pass in the world. These winding high roads, made possible by the prowess of the Border Roads Organization, resemble tangled kite cord wound around one's fingers and then carelessly tossed aside. To the left, immediately after the Sela gate, was a lake which had frozen inward from its shores. In the middle was clear blue water which seemed to reflect the universe itself. Some new army recruits were playing with snowballs and taking pictures. From the window of a small tea shop in a stone hut near the gate I could see valleys shimmering through gaps in the layers of cloud which covered them. The tea shop was run by a family which made a living selling tea to tourists and soldiers. Looking out at the soldiers, the tea maker said sagely even as vapor billowed from his mouth, "The more difficult a place is to reach, the more its beauty is enhanced . . . But for how long?"

The most reassuring sight in this bleak mountain desert were the white flags which flapped restlessly in the icy wind. This is a custom in these parts: whenever one asks for something from the gods he erects a white flag. Perhaps he lives with the conviction that his prayer will someday ride the winds to its intended address.

The driver slipped into a trance once more as the descent commenced. It had rained recently. The water dripping off the rocks and boulders on the sides of the road had pooled in the middle and frozen over, creating strange shapes—mostly in the shape of daggers. Greenery made an appearance after Jaswantgarh. In Jang we stopped in an old Monpa house where a bottle of rum stood next to a kettle of water bubbling on a wood fire. A cat was perched on a stool next to the stove to keep count of the pegs consumed. The valleys spread out around us sighed and moaned as they endured the relentless assaults of the wind. The owner of the establishment sat outside; she was convinced that life-threatening cold is enough to ensure honesty.

We caught occasional glimpses of the golden roofs of the Tawang Monastery—one of the most important and famous centers of Mahayana Buddhism—in the falling twilight as our vehicle rounded corners; the collector had already been contacted and a grand suite booked in the Circuit House.

↬

Gulping down pure mountain air in the pauses afforded to me by my lungs which struggled in the thin air, I reached the monastery in the afternoon, looking for a Sarnath-returned lama. The prayer wheel mounted on the front gate was freezing. Teenage monks were sitting in the lawn in front of the prayer hall, eating porridge. The prayer flag towering above them was straining in the wind, blowing with sufficient force to sway the sixty-foot pole to which the flag was attached. Behind them was the Tawang Monastery museum. Among the exhibits were an enormous elephant tusk, ancient musical instruments, monks' belongings, and human skulls covered over with gold and silver leaf and exquisitely carved. There was also a library which included silk-wrapped religious manuscripts seven centuries old. The prayer hall was awash in the glow of a statue of Buddha that had been brought from Tibet three hundred years earlier. On the walls were murals depicting tantric scenes.

There used to be many legends about how such a massive statue reached Tawang. About half a century earlier, when a strong earthquake jolted the region, the statue split and even more stories were added to the legends and fed them. In 1997, His Holiness the Dalai Lama visited Tawang Monastery; under his orders, skilled sculptors were invited from Nepal to restore the Buddha statue. During the restoration, certain documents were recovered from the belly of the statue; from them it was learnt that different parts of Buddha's body were interred separately in southern Tibet by followers of the Gelugpa sect, which had been brought there on horseback.

I asked the lama in charge of the museum why so many skulls were displayed. He pointed out Panden Lhamo, the guardian deity and protectress of Tibet, in a mural and said, "Earlier, lamas used them to offer liquor to the deities during tantric worship; but Pepsi or Coke is offered nowadays."

"Where do you get that from?"

"From the general store in the bazaar, of course!" the lama said, staring at me in astonishment.

After the Potala Palace in Lhasa, Tawang is the oldest monastery in the Mahayana tradition. It was established in the seventeenth century by Merag Lama Lodre Gyatso. He is said to have been inspired and guided by his horse to do so. In the Tibetan language, *Tawang* means "chosen by a horse." Tawang is famous all over the world as a center of tantric worship; seventeen monasteries fall under its direct administration. Until not very long ago, collectors from Tibet would come to villages in Tawang to collect land tax. As far as China is concerned, Tawang is northern Tibet. Based on this claim, when Arunachal Pradesh became a state in the Indian union, China registered an official protest about India's claim on certain parts of the area.

That evening in the bazaar I met a red-robed monk astride a motorcycle. He told me that Jaspinder Narula, a Bollywood playback singer of Punjabi origin, would be performing at the Buddha Purnima festival. Udit Narayan—another Bollywood playback singer—had already performed once. He also told me that the actors Shahrukh Khan and Madhuri Dixit had shot scenes for the movie *Koyla* here.

I asked the monk, "Why is multinational Pepsi offered to the gods instead of homebrew?"

He winked and, with the look of a man enjoying himself, replied, "Buddhism is also a multinational religion, where's the problem!"

MEDITATIONS

When the sight-obscuring veil
Thinned
All at once the wordless nothingness
Turned loquacious.
The soughing pines sent heady scented wind-messages
—though unseen.
Birds huddled in the shrubbery
Called out to me in God's own tongue.

In the distance, a Pahadi song.

—Dharamvir Bharati

FRAGMENT FROM THE ADI PURANA
Jinasena

The Himvaan range stands tall indeed and radiantly united. It is king among mountains, as if it has modeled itself upon you (you who are a king among kings).

Its peaks are golden, jewel-studded, and extend upward to a height of one hundred yojanas. It is as if a (skilled sculptor) has chiseled it into being.

Standing with its eastern and western extremities bathed in the water of briny seas, so magnificent is the range, it is as if it was created to measure the span of earth itself.

Siddhas, scholars, and naag live upon it forever; such are the jewels which adorn the forests upon its slopes.

Precious stones glow upon its slopes in magnificence, as if they have been crafted from the reflections of the very damsels of heaven.

The forests spread around it smile among the blooms and, with their radiance, seem to mock Nandan Van itself, the Forest of Immortals.

At its brow is the Padmasarovar, a lake of many excellent qualities and bearing the purest of waters upon which float radiant golden lotuses.

This mountain bears upon itself the Great River Ganga, which flows from the eastern end of the Padmasarovar, and the Great River Sindhu, which flows from the western end of the Padmasarovar.

The river Rohitasya, which emanates from the northern end of the Padma Lake, is also borne by this mountain.

By adorning itself with these three insurmountable Great Rivers, it is as if this mountain wishes to demonstrate (through mantra, vitality, and sheer dominance) its ability to bear the weight of the earth upon itself.

JUST A STRAND IN SHIVA'S HAIR
FACE-TO-FACE WITH THE AXIS OF THE WORLD

Arundhathi Subramaniam

AUGUST 18, 2011

A mountain is a mountain. Or so I've always believed. Despite all that Sadhguru says about scaffolds and knowledge repositories, a mountain is still a mountain, as far as I can see.

It is true, some are endowed with more height, more girth, more grandeur. But in this pageant spread out before us, Kailash isn't short on competition.

But there is the obvious difference. Even with the sinister blanket of cloud that hangs heavily across our landscape this morning, it is evident that this mountain allows itself some distinction. Amid these mountains of snow-lathered green and garnet, this is the only granite mountain we can see. Dark, crenellated, forbidding, cloud-smothered, it stands implacably, a postcard pinned to our grimy window, a reminder of why we are here.

Meru, Shambhala, sky pillar, Shiva linga—I don't know about any of that, but the view at my window is proof that Kailash exists. Or perhaps it is just that we have entered the postcard ourselves. That seems equally possible. Breathing this rarefied air, it is possible we have stumbled into a subtler dimension and are now postcard pilgrims about to participate in a collective optical illusion, about to discover that the divide between fact and fiction has always been obscure, cloudy, snow-congealed.

The Tibetans believe, in fact, that this still point in a turning world is actually a visitor, an alien—a flying mountain that had to be tethered to the earth by the gods and finally secured by the Buddha's four decisive footprints. It is a reluctant visitor, too. In Kaliyuga, the age of degeneration, it yearns to be elsewhere and is likely to take wing at any time. For all its solidity, that is also easy to believe. One day, the denizens of this hotel could well wake up to find their windows have turned into empty slates, wiped clean of eons of visual habit.

And it is for this that we made this trip, I reflect as I stand at our first-floor landing before breakfast. It is for this black convulsion of earth with its endless train of legend, its reputation stretching across millennia, way back into ancestral memory.

Is it worth the journey?

I decide to suspend judgment. I might not be able to take the burden of anticlimax right now. I don't have the breath for it. All I know over breakfast is this: I am colder than I have ever been. Manasarovar is a tropical paradise in comparison. I yearn nostalgically for my tent and its sleeping blanket. I cannot eat a bite. I am down to tea and periodic infusions of hot water and honey. The slightest exertion makes me aware of my lungs like never before. The bathrooms are unspeakable. The yard in front of the hotel is a picturesque riot of human and yak shit. The rain is incessant. Everyone around me looks the way I feel—bewildered, battered, in varying states of medical disrepair. Two of our group have been on oxygen all night. Conversation is sporadic. The Sound of Isha music team is rehearsing, trying feebly, if valiantly, to infuse some nirguna bhakti into the dining room (the one which doubles up as a dormitory and pantry and smells like it, I think uncharitably). It's difficult to ignore the wheezing breaths and occasional nosebleeds amid the strains of Kumar Gandharva's bhajans.

And yet, oddly enough, we are whole. Smiles are wan but they haven't disappeared yet. If I could sit motionless through the day, nursing a mug of tea, I tell myself, it's possible that I'll survive. My breath is reasonably even when I sit still. The cold could be manageable if I don't leave this space. (There are advantages of having a versatile single room; never unused, it carries the residual warmth of continued human habitation.)

It is at 1:00 p.m. that we get the news. Sadhguru has announced that he is making a one-kilometer trek uphill toward Kailash. Those of us who are inclined can join him. The clouds have cleared. The sun—Aparna pops her head in to announce with admirable cheeriness—is out. Kailash is visible. Come on!

An uphill trek when climbing to my first-floor room feels like an expedition to the stars.

I remember Sadhguru's words the evening before. "Don't force yourself. I want to take everyone back alive. Right now we're probably at

16,300 feet. When we climb to the highest point, we're going to touch around 17,600 feet. After this point, every fifty feet will make a big difference in terms of how your body behaves with the change in oxygen levels. So those of you that have taken ponies or yaks to get here, don't push yourselves any further."

I stare at my shoelaces and slowly shake my head. Each time it feels like the demands can't get more preposterous, they do.

And so, of course, I spend the next hour following Sadhguru up the mountain.

◦

It is at this point that I probably should abandon understatement. It is time to let go of the last vestige of self-respect. To claim to be witness-archivist any more would be a sham.

I may have started out on this trip as a seeker-observer. A sympathetic one, it is true. Committed to my guru, it is true. But still, if I were honest, I have been oscillating for the large part of this week between respectful observer and cautious participant.

At some point yesterday, however, I realized the extent to which the journey had diminished me. I had been pared down to a pilgrim. Nothing more and nothing less. Footsore, travel-weary, breath-rationed, bewildered, like everyone else around me. Helpless, ineffectual, leaning on wooden staffs and sturdy Sherpas, the stoic strength of yaks, and the goodwill of fellow travelers for support.

But at this point, I have been whittled down even further. There isn't much of a choice about it either. If I were to look at the path winding endlessly before me, it wouldn't take much time before I sink down and accept defeat.

The only strategy, I discover, is one step at a time. And one breath— one shuddering breath—at a time.

But of course, the mind that is wily enough to think up strategies is also wily enough to see through them. And so it is a matter of minutes before I give in to the inevitability of failure and beat a retreat.

The fact is I don't.

I admit that this has nothing to do with tenacity or courage. After the Manasarovar dip, I carried a soupçon of pride, perhaps not entirely unpardonable. Pride at my capacity for endurance, for being game enough to brave the elements, for midlife recklessness. But at this point, I know that not a single step I take has anything to do with me.

Which brings me to my confession: I am now, quite simply, whether I like it or not, a devotee. The only way I make this ascent—past a twisting, winding panorama of stream and crag, glade and rock—is by pinning my gaze on the guru. It is the sight of his form ahead of me, sure of foot, long of stride, nimbly negotiating the path ahead, that keeps me going. Each time it feels like agony to put the next foot forward, each time it feels like my lungs are going to burst, I focus on him. In savage terror, in desperate trust. If he is my guru, he has to ensure I make it. I don't have much mind left now, or much body, or very much breath. If he is my guru, he has to carry me along.

And I find that although the prospect of a trek is still hair-raising, I am able somehow to take the next step. The next breath. And then the next.

Periodically, he turns. His gaze sweeps over us all, alert, calm, dispassionate. On a couple of occasions it rests on me. I realize then that he knows the truth as well as I do—the fact that I am, in fact, subsisting on his presence. Perhaps others are too.

It feels like an era before we halt. In actuality, it has taken us just a little over an hour. Sadhguru decides that we should stop by a waterfall. As I take my last few steps, faltering and stumbling, he looks down at me, his gaze not unkind.

"You're doing well," he says quietly.

It takes me time to reply. "Because of you," I say inarticulately, short on breath.

His eyes glimmer with amusement. He is not unaccustomed to my longstanding distaste for overstatement. This clearly doesn't sound like me. It is now, however, a fact, a bald statement of truth.

I manage to add, "And my back. The pain. It's gone."

"So miracles do happen," he says lightly. He has turned away before I can respond.

I subside on a rock. We are now at the highest point of our journey—over 17,500 feet. When I look down, I marvel at how far we have climbed. The hotel now seems like a distant speck below us. Looking at the path we have taken uphill, it feels we have traveled more than a kilometer. But it is not the hotel or the path behind us that commands our attention after a moment. It is what lies before us: this towering presence, striated by snow, swathed in endless diaphanous tissues of mist. Black, enormous, emphatically present.

If the invariable human problem with the sacred is its intangibility, its elusiveness, here all complaints are surely laid to rest. For here is reality in capital letters. Here is mountain—solid, physical, eminently tactile. And here is metaphor—richly veined, textured, inflected by eons of spiritual folklore. The result of this conjunction between the physical and the metaphysical, between the literal and the emblematic, is Shiva frozen eternally in form. Or to put it another way, here is simply the staggering sight of centuries of abstraction—of incredible mythological and mystical sophistication—embodied in unequivocal stone. Here is idea made image. The conceptual made concrete. Thought turned thingy. Miracle as mountain.

No pilgrim, no aesthete—no one, I decide—could ask for more.

For the next hour, twenty of us sit meditating on the mountain. The chant of "Tryambakaya Mahadevaya" accompanies us.

Later, I ask others in the group what this experience meant to them. "Magic," says S. "The deepest meditation I've ever had," says A. "Time stood still," says T. "It was my seventh time," says M, "and it still took my breath away." "Bliss," says N. Swami. Nirvichara merely smiles. Our young "non-meditator" photographer from Delhi grins. "I was busy shooting Sadhguru and all of you in your meditative trances and explosive states," he says mischievously. "But then I started shooting Kailash. And the closer I went to the mountain, something began to happen . . ." He pauses. "Man, that mountain's alive."

In my case, I'm not sure what exactly that hour meant. But with Sadhguru seated a few feet behind and the mountain in front, I do remember being aware that this was the defining moment of my journey, the point of my pilgrimage—a pilgrimage that began much earlier than ten days ago. This is the hour I will look back on, I told myself, the hour I will remember, the hour that I will wonder at for the rest of my life. This is the stuff of personal myth, the point at which a bunch of seemingly random human histories—mine and the rest of the group's—intersects with the beyond without any of us ever being any wiser of what that intersection really means.

The mountain begins to pulsate. Perhaps it is the effect of moving cloud and shifting light. The effect of being in a place that swims between fact and symbol. Or perhaps it's just the altitude and Diamox. Or perhaps it's the two accomplices at work yet again: the master and his "50 percent partner," Shiva. I wonder if they even know, as partners in crime, where one's sphere of influence ends and the other's begins.

Then the tears start. And great wracking sobs. And so prose ends and another language takes over.

—◈—

HIMALAYA ON A PUSHCART*

Dharamvir Bharati

"Himalaya on a Pushcart"—a most interesting title, isn't it? And believe me, I did not have to seek it at all. It arrived fully formed.

It was only yesterday. I was standing at a paan shop with a senior novelist—a friend too—when an ice seller came along, pushing a cart laden with blocks of ice—gleaming, freezing, billowing clouds of vapor. Almora being my friend's birthplace, he gazed at the ice for a moment, lost among the vapors, and said absently, "It is ice that is the jewel of the Himalaya." The title leapt up at me: "Himalaya on a Pushcart." Why am I telling you all this? If you are an amateur poet, just starting out, bhai, take this title and pen down some lines—one hundred, two hundred even—lines unrefined, meaningless. This title is for you. And if a brand-new poem is an overly vexatious enterprise, there is an opportunity for competent songwriters, too. Let's address these blocks of ice. Come down, come down here. Why are you perched up there like the monkeys which make the high peaks their home? O poets new, climb onto the pushcart, let your creations find buyers at paan shops.

All of this occurred to me, and I immediately told my senior friend everything. Outwardly he laughed, but I felt that the ice had scored his heart. In all honesty, anyone who has seen the cloud-wreathed peaks of the Himalaya conversing with the moon and the stars—even from fifty

* Written in praise of the Himalayan snows, this essay has been excerpted and translated from *Thele Par Himalaya* (1968).

miles away—has witnessed pristine white snow shimmer and sparkle like an ocean of milk under the glow of a new moon; the snows of the Himalaya will score his heart, too, and at every remembrance of it, a sharp ache will rise. I know, for I too have witnessed those snows.

～

The truth is that we had traveled to Kausani only to gaze upon snow and ice from up close. From Nainital we went to Kosi village, having negotiated the terrifying twists and turns on the road from Nainital to Ranikhet and from Ranikhet to Majhkhali. The road forks at Kosi; one goes to Almora and the other to Kausani. A more back-breaking, ugly, and drought-stricken route would be difficult to imagine. Not a drop of water or a speck of greenery, and hemmed in all around by dust-brown mountains. The reckless novice bus driver from Almora hurtled us at such speed along the twisty road cut into the mountainside that all of us had a yellow tinge to our faces when we reached Kosi. We were the only two travelers for Kausani, so we disembarked. The bus sped along to Almora. We ducked under a tin-roofed shed and, parking ourselves on a wooden bench, whiled away our time. We were tired and the weather was humid. A lorry arrived after two hours and when we saw Shukla-ji climb down from it, we heaved sighs of relief. A traveling companion such as Shukla-ji is can only be found if good karma has accrued over many past lives. It was he who had enthused us to visit Kausani; tired-ness never found expression on his face nor did laziness—one look at him would drive all our fatigue away.

But who was this with Shukla-ji? Tall, thin; a slim face adorned with an Emile Zolaesque beard; in loose trousers, a woolen jerkin flung over his shoulder; and slung by his side—was it a thermos, a camera, or binoculars? The gentleman had an insouciant air about him. The man, his slim-trim frame—much like mine—and his casual swagger! Gaug-ing the ever-increasing curiosity on my face, Shukla-ji said, "Sen is one of the most famous painters of our city. He has been awarded by the Academy for his work. He is using that money to travel." Sen quickly became one of us—what a clear-hearted man he was! And we were soon to witness his antics.

The view transformed as soon as we left Kosi—the river gurgling between rocks rounded smooth by friction, small villages flourishing on its banks, and fields like crumpled green muslin. What a beauty Someshwar Valley is! Green and lush. We passed one bus station after the next, small hill post offices, and tea shops, and occasionally drove over bridges spanning either the Kosi or one of its tributaries. The road sometimes pierced desolate pine forests. The bus groaned over the road that twisted and turned like it was traversing the pitted, scaly back of an ancient dragon. Yet it was pleasant and, after the fatigue of our earlier journey, the bus ride induced a stuporous lassitude. But at the same time an anxiety gripped our hearts. We were nearing Kausani, having left Kosi eighteen miles behind. Wasn't Kausani only six miles away? The magical beauty of the place that we had heard so much about . . . where was it? Before we left, a colleague had told me that Kausani had entranced him more than Kashmir had; Gandhi-ji wrote his treatise on Anasakti Yoga here and declared that to live in Kausani was to feel like one was living in Switzerland. These rivers, valleys, fields and villages were beautiful but hardly deserving of such high praise. We expressed our anxiety to Shukla-ji off and on and, as Kausani approached ever nearer, our anxiety transformed into impatience, then dissatisfaction, and soon, our faces began to reflect distress. We couldn't be certain of Shukla-ji's reaction because he remained silent.

All at once the bus rounded a large bend and began climbing steadily.

Kausani is situated at the very top of the high mountain ranges to the north of the Someshwar Valley. Beyond Kausani, the terrain falls away steeply. The bus stopped at its station. It was a small, quite decrepit village and there was no sign of snow anywhere. We had been thoroughly cheated. How disappointed I was! I clambered down from the bus, fuming, and stood transfixed, a statue engraved in stone. The valley spread out before me was of incomparable splendor. This was the gloriously colorful Katyur valley which the Kausani range had shielded from our view; surely only demigods and the glorious Kinner people of legend made their home here. The valley was tens of kilometers wide and spread over with fields like green muslin carpets; it was crisscrossed with ocher pathways lined with white stones and by rivers which were like vines that grow and double back upon themselves until they are inextricably intertwined. A quick thought came to me: I should pick these vines up and wind them around my wrist, hold them to my eyes.

We had been transported to a new world altogether. So ethereal, so beautiful, so exquisitely adorned and blemishless ... I felt I must take my shoes off and wipe my feet before even setting a single step upon that earth. My eyes scanned the valley inch by inch and crossed it; and where the verdant fields, the rivers, and the woods dissolved in the haze and the indigo mist of the horizon, I could make out the dim outlines of some small hills; beyond the hills were clouds and beyond the clouds, nothing. My eyes restlessly scanned the billows until, all at once, my heart felt a small jolt. What is it that stands firm and unmoving among the shifting clouds, itself a fragment of cloud? And what amazing color it has: neither white, nor silver, not even light blue, yet all three at once. What *is* it? Can't be snow. Yes sir! What is it if not snow? A thought struck like a bolt of lightning: Beyond this valley stands the Himalaya—King, Emperor, among mountains. These clouds hide it but it is there, in front of us, and one of its smaller peaks peeks childlike from a cloud-window. I shouted in excitement, "Snow! Look!" Shukla-ji, Sen, and everyone else looked but by then the snow had been hidden from sight. Almost as if someone had pulled the small peak inside, thinking it to be a mere child which might tumble out the window in its excitement.

What roaring life that one audience with the Himalaya filled us with. The disappointment, the discouragement, fatigue—everything vanished in a flash, as if by magic. We were all eager and excited. Now the clouds would part and the Himalaya would stand before us, uncovered . . . a boundless beauty would unveil herself, inch by inch, and . . . then? And then? My heart galloped.

Shukla-ji was calm; he would only glance at me and smile, as if to say, "Such impatience, such restlessness. . . You hadn't even reached Kausani that your face fell. Now do you understand? The magic of this place?" The khansama at the dak bungalow said to us, "You are fortunate indeed, sahib. Fourteen tourists arrived and stayed for weeks; not one glimpse of the snows. You've arrived only today and it looks like the weather will clear and the clouds part."

We put away our luggage. But all of us sat in the verandah up front, without even a cup of tea at hand, and kept staring at the shrouded mountains. The clouds slid down and, one by one, one new peak after the other showed its outline. Then all stood revealed—a sensational, mysterious, jagged row which began on our left, sped to our right, and disappeared into the depthless nothingness. If I could express the emotions that were bubbling up within us at that time, I wouldn't be feeling these scars on my heart, I wouldn't be feeling this heartache. The only certain, though faint, realization was that just as standing before a block of ice bathes one's face in cooling vapors, the breeze blowing in from the Himalaya was touching my forehead and evaporating all my struggles and my inner turmoil, all the "taap"—the restless heat within. I understood for the first time why seekers of yore thought of bodily, spiritual, and material turmoil as taap and why they found their way to the Himalaya to quench those restless fires. Yet another truth rose, a new sun on my mind-horizon. How ancient are these snow masses! Who can plumb the depths of that primeval time from which these ageless indestructible snows have gathered on these massifs? It is because of this that some foreigners have given the snows on the Himalaya a special name; they call it the Eternal Snows. The sun was on its way down and momentarily lighted up the crevasses, the glaciers, the sheer cliffs, and the gorges on the distant peaks. I thought with a slightly panicked heart: Has a human ever set foot upon these peaks or is it only snow which blizzards upon them, howling and moaning?

The sun set out on its downward path and, gradually, liquid saffron flowed in the glaciers. The snows turned red, the color of lotus blossoms, the valleys and gorges deep yellow. As night descended we rose, washed up, and took tea. But everyone was quiet, inward, as if each had lost something of his; or, rather, each had found something, such a thing that he was immersed in his soul, and was busy securing it within his heart.

The moon rose and we stepped out again . . . everything was peaceful now. It was as if the snows were asleep. I pulled an armchair a little to the side and sat upon it. Why has my mind become so bereft of imagination? It is in sight of these mountains that so many have written so much and here I am: a poem a far cry; not a verse, not even a word wells up within. But this is of no consequence—nothing is of consequence before the Emperor of Snows. The clouds shrouding my inner being are slowly parting. Something rises within, something akin to these peaks, and tries to soar ever upward so it can match their loftiness. I felt: Himalaya is an elder brother and has progressed upward, much above me, and seeing me—the younger brother—at a level lower than him, frustrated and abashed, is inspiring me and throwing me an affectionate challenge: "Do you want to soar? Do you have the courage for it?"

All at once Sen sang a few verses of Rabindrasangeet and a spell broke. We became charged with energy, all of us, and brimmed over with irrepressible power, euphoria, and joy. Sen was happiest—restless as a child, like a small bird. He chirped: "Sirs, I am wonderstruck! What miracles of God in the Himalaya." Our laughter hadn't died down when he stood upon his head in the shirshasan pose. On being asked why, he replied, "I want to see the Himalaya in a new perspective." We later came to know that he was vexed with the ultra-modernist style of painting in Bombay. "All them genius people view the world standing on their heads. So I also look at the Himalaya like that."

The following day we climbed down the valley and walked twelve miles to Baijnath where the Gomti flows. The image of the Himalaya floated upon the sparkling waters of the river. There was no telling when—if—I would reach the white peaks and so I gazed upon the reflection of the mountains shimmering on the surface and remained immersed within it.

∽

Even today I remember and an ache rises in my heart. My friend the novelist saw the ice on the pushcart the other day and slipped into a sea of memories. I understand his pain. When I speak of the Himalaya on a pushcart and laugh it is simply a ruse to forget my heartache. The snow peaks call out to me. And I? I stand at a crossroads, gaze upon a few blocks of ice on a pushcart, and tell my heart it must be content. It was at such a moment, surrounded by such Himalayas laden on pushcarts, that the saint Tulsi said: "Will I ever dwell thus? Upon the lofty heights of the snow peaks?" The thought steals into my heart that I should send the Himalaya a missive: "No, friend . . . I will return. I will return again . . . and again. Your heights are my home, where my heart finds peace . . . I am helpless in this, and there is nothing I can do."

TRAVELS IN INDIA AS AN UNKNOWN SANNYASIN*

Swami Vivekananda

I was once traveling in the Himalayas, and the long road stretched before us. We poor monks cannot get anyone to carry us, so we had to make all the way on foot. There was an old man with us. The way goes up and down for hundreds of miles, and when that old monk saw what was before him, he said, "Oh sir, how to cross it; I cannot walk any more; my chest will break." I said to him, "Look down at your feet." He did so, and I said, "The road that is under your feet is the same road that you have passed over and is the same road that you see before you; it will soon be under your feet. The highest things are under your feet, because you are Divine Stars; all these things are under your feet. You can swallow the stars by the handful if you want; such is your real nature. Be strong, get beyond all superstitions, and be free."

Many times I have been in the jaws of death, starving, footsore, and weary; for days and days I had no food, and often could walk no further; I would sink down under a tree, and life would seem [to be] ebbing away. I could not speak, I could scarcely think, but at last the mind reverted to the idea: "I have no fear nor death; I never hunger nor thirst. I am It! I am It! The whole of nature cannot crush me; it is my servant. Assert thy strength, thou Lord of lords and God of gods! Regain thy lost empire! Arise and walk and stop not!" and I would rise up, reinvigorated, and here am I, living, today. Thus, whenever darkness comes, assert the reality, and everything adverse must vanish.

Once when I was in Varanasi, I was passing through a place where there was a large tank of water on one side and a high wall on the other. It was in the grounds where there were many monkeys. The monkeys of

* Excerpted from *Swami Vivekananda on Himself* (1963).

Varanasi are huge brutes and are sometimes surly. They now took it into their heads not to allow me to pass through their street, so they howled and shrieked and clutched at my feet as I passed. As they pressed closer, I began to run, but the faster I ran, the faster came the monkeys, and they began to bite at me. It seemed impossible to escape, but just then I met a stranger who called out to me, "Face the brutes!" I turned and faced the monkeys, and they fell back and finally fled. That is a lesson for all life—face the terrible, face it boldly. Like the monkeys, the hardships of life fall back when we cease to flee before them.

Once in western India I was traveling in the desert country on the coast of the Indian Ocean. For days and days I used to travel on foot through the desert, but it was to my surprise that I saw every day beautiful lakes, with trees all around them, and the shadows of the trees upside down and vibrating there. "How wonderful it looks and they call this a desert country!" I said to myself. Nearly a month I traveled, seeing these wonderful lakes and trees and plains. One day I was very thirsty and wanted to have a drink of water, so I started to go to one of these clear, beautiful lakes, and as I approached, it vanished. And with a flash it came to my brain, "This is the mirage about which I have read all my life," and with that came also the idea that throughout the whole of this month, every day, I had been seeing the mirage and did not know it. The next morning I began my march. There was again the lake, but with it came also the idea that it was the mirage and not a true lake.

So it is with this universe. We are all traveling in this mirage of the world day after day, month after month, year after year, not knowing that it is a mirage. One day it will break up, but it will come back again; the body has to remain under the power of past karma, and so the mirage will come back. This world will come back upon us so long as we are bound by karma: men, women, animals, plants, our attachments and duties, all will come back to us, but not with the same power. Under the influence of the new knowledge the strength of karma will be broken, its poison will be lost. It becomes transformed, for along with it there comes the idea that we know it now, that the sharp distinction between the reality and the mirage has been known.

Real monasticism is not easy to attain. There is no order of life so rigorous as this. If you stumble ever so little, you are hurled down a precipice—and are smashed to pieces. One day I was traveling on foot from Agra to Vrindavan. There was not a farthing with me. I was about a couple of miles from Vrindavan when I found a man smoking on the roadside, and I was seized with a desire to smoke. I said to the man, "Hallo, will you let me have a puff at your chillum?" He seemed to be hesitating greatly and said, "Sire, I am a sweeper." Well, there was the influence of old Samskaras, and I immediately stepped back and resumed my journey without smoking. I had gone a short distance when the thought occurred to me that I was a sannyasin who had renounced caste, family, prestige, and everything—and still I drew back as soon as the man gave himself out as a sweeper, and could not smoke at the chillum touched by him! The thought made me restless at heart; then I retraced my steps and came to the sweeper whom I found still sitting there. I hastened to tell him, "Do prepare a chillum of tobacco for me, my dear friend." I paid no heed to his objections and insisted on having it. So the man was compelled to prepare a chillum for me. Then I gladly had a puff at it and proceeded to Vrindavan. When one has embraced the monastic life, one has to test whether one has gone beyond the prestige of caste and birth, etcetera. It is so difficult to observe the monastic vow in right earnest! There must not be the slightest divergence between one's words and actions.

You find that in every religion mortifications and asceticisms have been practiced. In these religious conceptions the Hindus always go to the extremes. You will find men with their hands up all their lives, until their hands wither and die... I once saw a man who had kept his hands raised in this way, and I asked him how it felt when he did it first. He said it was awful torture. It was such torture that he had to go to a river and put himself in water, and that allayed the pain for a little while. After a month he did not suffer much. Through such practices powers can be attained ...

Once when traveling in the Himalayas I had to take up my abode for a night in a village of the hill people. Hearing the beating of drums in the village some time after nightfall, I came to know upon inquiring of my host that one of the villagers had been possessed by a devata or god spirit. To meet his importunate wishes and to satisfy my own curiosity, I went out to see what the matter really was. Reaching the spot, I found a great concourse of people. A tall man with long, bushy hair was pointed out to me, and I was told that person had got the devata on him. I noticed an ax being heated in fire close by the man; and after a while, I found the red-hot thing being seized and applied to parts of his body and also to his hair! But wonder of wonders, no part of his body or hair thus branded with the red-hot ax was found to be burnt, and there was no expression of any pain in his face. I stood mute with surprise. The headman of the village, meanwhile, came up to me and said, "Maharaj, please exorcise this man out of your mercy." I felt myself in a nice fix; but moved to do something, I had to go near the possessed man. Once there, I felt a strong impulse to examine the ax rather closely, but the instant I touched it, I burnt my fingers, although the thing had been cooled down to blackness. The smarting made me restless and all my theories about the ax phenomenon were spirited away from my mind! However, smarting with the burn, I placed my hand on the head of the man and repeated [Japa] for a short while . . . It was a matter of surprise to find that the man came round in ten or twelve minutes. Then oh, the gushing reverence the villagers showed to me! I was taken to be some wonderful man! But, all the same, I couldn't make any head or tail of the whole business. So without a word one way or the other, I returned with my host to his hut. It was about midnight, and I went to bed. But what with the smarting burn in the hand and the impenetrable puzzle of the whole affair, I couldn't have any sleep that night. Thinking of the burning ax failing to harm living human flesh, it occurred again and again to my mind, "There are more things in heaven and earth, Horatio, than are dreamt of in your philosophy."

But Sri Ramakrishna used to disparage these supernatural powers; his teaching was that one cannot attain the supreme truth if the mind is diverted to the manifestation of these powers. The human mind, however, is so weak that, not to speak of householders, even 90 percent of the sadhus happen to be votaries of these powers. In the West, men are lost in wonderment if they come across such miracles. It is only because Sri Ramakrishna has mercifully made us understand the evil of these powers as being hindrances to real spirituality that we are able to take them at their proper value.

Once when I was putting up at Manmatha Babu's place, I dreamt one night that my mother had died. My mind became much distracted. Not to speak of corresponding with anybody at home, I used to send no letters in those days even to our Math. The dream being disclosed to Manmatha, he sent a wire to Calcutta to ascertain facts about the matter. For the dream had made my mind uneasy on the one hand, and on the other, our Madras friends, with all arrangements ready, were insisting on my departing for America immediately, and I felt rather unwilling to leave before getting any news of my mother. So Manmatha, who discerned this state of my mind, suggested our repairing to a man living some way off from town who, having acquired mystic powers over spirits, could tell fortunes and read the past and the future of a man's life. So at Manmatha's request and to get rid of my mental suspense, I agreed to go to this man. Covering the distance partly by railway and partly on foot, we four of us—Manmatha, Alasinga, myself, and another—managed to reach the place, and what met our eyes was a man with a ghoulish, haggard, soot-black appearance, sitting close to a cremation ground. His attendants used some jargon of south Indian dialect to explain to us that this was the man with perfect power over the ghosts. At first the man took absolutely no notice of us; and then, when we were about to retire from the place, he made a request for us to wait.

Our Alasinga was acting as the interpreter, and he explained the requests to us. Next, the man commenced drawing some figures with a pencil, and presently I found him getting perfectly still in mental concentration. Then he began to give out my name, my genealogy, the history of my long line of forefathers, and said that Sri Ramakrishna was keeping close to me all through my wanderings, intimating also to me good news about my mother. He also foretold that I would have to go very soon to far-off lands for preaching religion. Getting good news thus about my mother, we all traveled back to town, and after arrival received by wire from Calcutta the assurance of my mother's doing well . . . Everything that the man had foretold came to be fulfilled to the letter, call it some fortuitous concurrence or anything you will . . .

Well, I am not a fool to believe anything and everything without direct proof. And coming into this realm of Mahamaya, oh, the many magic mysteries I have come across alongside this bigger magic conjuration of a universe! Maya, it is all Maya! . . .

I used to beg my food from door to door in the Himalayas. Most of the time I spent in spiritual practices which were rigorous; and the food that was available was very coarse, and often that too was insufficient to appease the hunger. One day I thought that my life was useless. These hill people are very poor themselves. They cannot feed their own children and family properly. Yet they try to save a little for me. Then what is the use of such a life? I stopped going out for food. Two days thus passed without any food. Whenever I was thirsty I drank the water of the streams using my palms as a cup. Then I entered a deep jungle. There I meditated sitting on a piece of stone. My eyes were open, and suddenly I was aware of the presence of a striped tiger of a large size. It looked at me with its shining eyes. I thought, "At long last I shall find peace and this animal its food. It is enough that this body will be of some service to this creature." I shut eyes and waited for it, but a few seconds passed and I was not attacked. So, I opened my eyes and saw it receding into the forest. I was sorry for it and then smiled, for I knew it was the Master who was saving me till his work be done.

—◦◦◦—

THE TRAVELS OF SWAMI HARIDAS *
Rahul Sankrityayan

SEEKING YOGIS FROM RISHIKESH TO GANGOTRI

Haridas accompanied Vaishnavdas to Rishikesh. At that time, Rishikesh was not a city; nor could it be called a town or even a large village. All it had were a dozen shops, small and big. Baba Kali Kamliwale had a presence in the area but that, too, was limited. The Punjab-Sindh Kshetra had just been initiated. There was plenty of unclaimed forest and fallow land—mark out a boundary and that land was yours. This is why half the land in Rishikesh now belongs to either the followers of the Baba Kali Kamliwale sect or to the Punjab-Sindh Kshetra. How could Haridas, or this writer who visited that area three years later, have imagined that buildings would stand where once only a couple of thatched roofs marked civilization? Or that Rishikesh would become the town of sadhus, lit up by electric lamps at night, with markets that

---

* Fragments from the life and quest of Swami Haridas, a sadhu wandering in the western Himalaya, as recorded by Rahul Sankrityayan; excerpted and translated from *Ghumakkad Swami* (1958).

would shame even those of Haridwar. If these two institutions own half the land and the shops in Rishikesh today, it has not been an unfair deal for society at large because these organizations do not work for personal gain but for the betterment of society. They are of much help to travelers to Rishikesh and other parts of Uttarakhand. The ones proficient in Sanskrit like to call it Hrishikesh—Hrishikesh being the name of Krishna—but this does not give us any insight into the history of the place. Idols from the Gupta period have also been discovered in Hrishikesh. The time to which we refer did not recognize this name; then it was only Ayodhya which was the town of sadhus. Now Rishikesh is home to thousands of sadhus. The two friends went to Bharatji's temple and stayed there. There were not many sadhus around so it was not difficult to locate the yogis whom they were seeking. The writer of these lines was almost influenced by yoga and siddhi at that stage of his life. Then, it was wanderlust accompanied by the desire to learn Sanskrit which brought him to the banks of Ganga at Haridwar from its banks at Kashi. This move was compelled by the fact that people at home would have obstructed the course of his study in many ways. In the same way as this writer had decided to travel through Uttarakhand, disappointed with his learning at Rishikesh and Haridwar, Haridas consulted Vaishnavdas and decided to travel up to Jamunotri, Gangotri, and Kedarnath and Badrinath. Vaishnavdas had been to these places before, but thinking of "more fruit with more labor," he agreed to accompany Haridas.

‍ഽ

Another motivating factor in this decision was Haridas's hope that he could meet yogis deep in the forests of the Himalaya. They traveled from Rishikesh to Laxmanjhula and stayed there for a week. They visited many sadhus living in Tapovan and Kajlivan but could not find anyone practicing yoga. The four feet traveled onward. This was Haridas's first actual travel in the mountains; first, because the Chitrakoot hills he had been on earlier couldn't be called mountains. He had heard of bears and other dangerous residents of the dense and unknown forests and his heart wasn't free of fear. In the tourist season one could expect to meet fellow travelers on the roads to the four pilgrimages, but now was not the time for pilgrims, nor were there any local or organized places of rest. This is the reason he had requested Vaishnavdas to accompany him. There were dharmshalas and sadaarwat—charities which served travelers on an ongoing basis—spread across the routes. These services provided by the Kali Kamli sect could be found every ten to fifteen miles. One could rest there and receive pulses, flour, rice, salt, oil, and wood fuel for free. The two travel mates could not avail of these facilities because they would have had to return to Rishikesh to obtain a letter for these services. This was done to ensure that the same person would not avail of the supplies again and again. Therefore, after one ration one would be given a letter that would certify him for the next and so on. Who would have bothered walking thirty miles down mountain and up mountain for this? They also did not bother because Vaishnavdas was in a mind to travel through the villages and not over main roads. This showed how strong his wanderlust was. He took Haridas along the narrow paths through the villages. Those were not the days when grains were scarce, nor were goods expensive. Therefore visiting eight or ten houses would get them enough to eat. They reached Devaprayag. From here emerged two paths; one went up the left bank of the Alaknanada to bifurcate into two paths—one leading to Kedarnath, the other to Badrinath. The other went up the left bank of the Bhagirathi to split further into two paths—one leading to Gangotri, the other to Jamunotri. They decided: now that they had set forth, they would visit all the four holy places of pilgrimage. They walked toward Tehri and found steep inclines on this route. They were not adept at climbing in the mountains and found it difficult going. Even one familiar with the mountains takes time to ease himself into the terrain. After one ascent came a descent. That was followed by other ascents which were not as difficult. They reached Tehri on the fourth day.

Perhaps no one had informed them about the popular belief that one's pilgrimage is not complete until one has paid one's respects to the king of those lands. The lands on which the four holy pilgrimages were situated belonged to the descendants of the king of Tehri. Srinagar used to be the capital then. The Gorkhas had defeated the king and taken over his lands. The king of Garhwal helped the British defeat the Gorkhas. After this, the British merged the well-populated lands (including Srinagar) into their domain and left the highlands and jungles to the descendants of the Kumaon dynasty. The king chose Tehri for his capital. Even after his defeat, the lands were believed to belong to the

Tehri dynasty. In Tehri, there was a sadaarwat which supplied them with flour, pulses, jaggery, salt, turmeric, and chillies. Because of the expertise of Vaishnavdas, they had no need to take alms from there. They rested along the banks of Bhagirathi for a couple of days and set out upward from its right bank. In two or three days, they reached Dharasu.

By now, Haridas was adept at walking in the mountains. Every now and then, some incline would test them, but he wouldn't be out of breath, nor would his feet resist. If they had wanted, they could have walked all day with a little rest in the afternoon and would have reached Dharasu the same evening. But they were in no hurry. They walked and paused as they pleased. In the villages, they would get milk in addition to pulses and flour. Grain was much easier to access fifty years ago than it is now when things have become more expensive. But wanderlust is not captive to time and place; it finds its own ways for itself.

At Dharasu, the ways parted for Gangotri and Jamunotri. They had heard much about the difficult terrain of Jamunotri. Today, one can drive up to Dharasu from Rishikesh over a proper road. Perhaps by the time this book comes off the press, cars will travel right up to Uttarkashi, too; even today, jeeps make their way there with ease. It is difficult to tell by when vehicles can travel on the road up to Jamunotri. Many people choose Gangotri over Jamunotri because of the latter's difficult terrain. Haridas and Vaishnavdas were not among them.

At Dharasu, they met a group of sadhus on their way to Jamunotri whose spirits, too, were not to be dampened by the terrain. They were now going to leave the Ganga river system behind and proceed toward that of the Jamuna. The point of separation of the two river systems lies high on a mountaintop which requires much effort to reach. They moved on. At night, they took shelter in a nearby village. The seven sadhus woke early and began their expedition. The climb began after half a mile. It was too early for the new rays of the rising sun to reflect off the sky-kissing snow peaks but the woods flanking the path were visible. The footpath climbed upward alongside a rivulet about eight feet wide. The rivulet did not carry much water but it sped down with such force, no one dared cross it. The sadhus rested their alms bowls and climbing poles on the bank of the rivulet and built a fire to light their chillums. They smoked their tobacco and dispersed for their ablutions. One of the sadhus walked a little distance, rounded a bend, and squatted to ease himself. He cast an eye at the jungle across the rivulet and saw a bear digging for roots. The sadhu thought, "It's close, but across the water; what harm can it do me?" If he had come away quietly nothing would have come of the encounter, but the sadhu tossed a stone at the bear. It saw him. The bear quit its scrabbling and leapt toward the sadhu. The sadhu tossed one more stone at the animal. By then, the bear had reached the edge of the rivulet and started to lower itself into the water. The sadhu panicked and, shouting "Bear attack! Bear attack!" scampered down to the other sadhus and fled uphill, carrying his alms bowl and climbing pole. Haridas and the rest of the sadhus also saw that the bear was trying to swim across. Now, they weren't mountain folk that they would know what to expect of wild animals. They too were all fear-struck and, carrying their respective alms bowls and climbing poles, fled uphill. The bear did not swim across but regained the bank and began tracking them. On uphill climbs one's breath becomes labored every four steps and the heart seems to leap into the throat, and at that moment all the sadhus felt themselves to be still as statues. Yamaraj was coming at them, his arms outstretched. All of them soon gained the strength of elephants. Panting and out of breath, they kept running uphill. They were drenched in sweat but unwilling to give even the tiniest quarter to their legs which were begging for mercy. Fortunately, a little ahead, the rivulet described a large curve and the path diverged from it. In this way both the rivulet and the bear passed out of their line of sight. They kept running for a while, looking back fearfully. But now they were reasonably assured that the bear wouldn't follow them. The sun was up and they could see for miles around. Yet they couldn't feel completely at ease until they met a few villagers. Almost everyone had the *Hanuman Chalisa* by heart: all believed that "ghosts and demons come not near, when the name of Mahavir is on one's lips." But, at that time, no one remembered the *Hanuman Chalisa* or the name of Mahavirji. They could depend only on their legs.

They soon reached the shores of the Jamuna via the villages of Dadal and Gangani. They had witnessed the Ganga as a foamy white river even in Dharasu and low-lying Rishikesh and Haridwar. But the Jamuna, even at this height, was a deep blue. Gazing at the river with its Krishna-like hue, its waters the color of the dark god's skin, they thought, "Is it because of Him that the river gains this color?" It was an arresting sight. She picked her way along the level but boulder-strewn valley, hemmed in on two sides by towering mountains covered over with trees and greenery among which birds flitted, chittering raucously.

They traversed the left bank of the Jamuna—which stopped, pooled, and flowed again—stopping to gaze at and refresh themselves in numerous small rivulets and falls joining the river until they reached the village of priests, Kharsali. Had they been walking in the plains, they would have come across any number of mendicants or mutths; there would be no need to seek the charity of the sadaarwat. But even without sadaarwat, the sadhus managed to find food readily. They had come far into the Himalaya but Haridas did not come across a single yogi even in these deserted climes. But he wasn't disheartened. He was beginning to enjoy the journey.

He had met the priests of Badrinath in Devaprayag. He had seen that they were extremely well versed in Sanskrit. Haridas believed all the priests of Uttarakhand to be the same. But the priests of Yamunotri, living in Kharsali, were different. They had no education worth the name; their outfits, made out of woolen blankets, were exceedingly filthy. The young men and women were all fair and good-looking, but were covered with filth and grime from head to toe. It was perfectly justified, for Haridas as well as for other travelers, to wonder why everyone was so dirty. They might have thought that it was in the nature of these people to remain filthy because of the cold climate. How could he know that with education and money, one can maintain cleanliness in the coldest wilderness; and of the sort one will not find among even the most elite men and women in the largest of Indian cities? Haridas was also astonished that come evening, these high priests, elite Brahmins all, would bring out their dhols and beat out rhythms on them. What's more, their women would join in freely. Many people find it difficult to believe that three thousand years earlier, when our Vedic ancestors made their home in the Saptsindhu (Punjab) region, their society was as free as that of the priests of Kharsali. They would organize similar gatherings, play instruments, and the Aryan men and women would dance to their hearts' content.

Yamunotri is merely four miles from Kharsali but is at such height that it receives a great deal of snowfall and is exceedingly cold. The residents of Kharsali built houses there to live all year round, anticipating the place to be less cold than Yamunotri.

Our travelers went some distance and had to ford the Yamuna. They then took a path upward from the right bank of the river. It was a steep climb but by now they were well practiced. Their climb ended at an immensely tall rock face down which the Yamuna plunged in multiple streams, as if dropping down from the sky itself. This wondrous avatar of the Yamuna did not attract Haridas as much as the hot spring close by did, into which he intended to dip a measure of rice wrapped in muslin. The water was so hot, it could cook not only rice but also potatoes; actually, anything which could be wrapped in muslin and dipped. He believed this to be one of the miracles wrought by Mother Yamuna. How could Haridas know that a sulfurous fire burns underground, heats groundwater, and sends it bubbling up to the surface? Such hot springs are to be found not only here, or at Manikaran in Kullus but in other parts of the world, too. People even take baths in springs where the heat can be easily borne. Haridas and his friends took a dip in a pool where scalding water from the hot spring had been mixed with cold river water and made bearable.

In Yamunotri, Haridas felt as if he was experiencing the piercing cold of the Magh-Paush months when, in the plains, the summer skies were raining fire. He didn't have much bedding with him, having deemed them excess load. Sadhus usually own a shawl in which they place a few essentials, a blanket, and tie up into a bundle. This bundle they sling over one shoulder. In the other they carry a sling-bag. They are used to traveling thus laden, an alms bowl in one hand and a pair of tongs in the other. An especially devout sadhu might put a statue of Thakurji in another bag and sling it around his neck. A marginally literate sadhu might also carry a copy of Tulsidas's *Ramayan* along. Sadhus have been described as laden jackfruit trees. It is the stuff they carry slung from their shoulders, necks, and arms which makes them seem so. But Haridas and his friends favored carrying as little as possible. And now they cursed their shortsightedness. Had they not found an abundance of dry firewood, the nights would have been difficult to endure. They reached Yamunotri before afternoon. The sky was calm, and the noontime cold wasn't excessive but was increasing in intensity as the sun slid down to the western horizon. They couldn't be sure about the conditions at night, or they would have immediately set out for Kharsali again. But the Vedic sages have declared: "Fire cures snow." Fire really did prove the ideal antidote to cold for the party. Having built a roaring fire of massive logs, they spent the night basking in its warmth.

During a brief stay in Uttarkashi, they were assured that yogis and mahatmas were to found in good numbers ahead. They set out eagerly. At their first halt they were told that a mahatma lived in a village close by, near a freshwater spring. The village fell three miles off their route. Haridas was extremely pleased. Vaishnavdas, too, did not want to disappoint his young traveling companion. They reached the village. The mahatma turned out to be a hermit. They stayed with him for three days. The mahatma's learning was limited to Tulsidas's *Ramayan*. But it was difficult to say if he completely understood the *Ramayan*. Yes, he was a practitioner of the yogic practice of pranayam and also had a smattering of Rajyoga. Haridas had already gained—under the tutelage of Baba Gopaldas—as much knowledge as the mahatma. They learned that the mahatma had lived there for a decade. And that he had traveled extensively. The man was of no use to Haridas, and he couldn't direct Haridas to an accomplished yogi either.

They enjoyed a dip in the hot springs of Gangnani and pressed on. The climb up Sukhi Chatti didn't seem excessive to them, even though it was much more difficult than the Devaprayag incline. They reached Harsil, which is also called Hariprayag by the priests who live there. Soon after, they reached the rope bridge spanning the Bhairav Valley, having crossed the Ganga in two places. The one to cross this bridge, suspended from rocky mountains which seem to touch the sky itself, used to be considered a man intrepid and great. There is no sign of the bridge now. People cross the valley over an iron bridge constructed at a lower height. That unfortunate soul who desired to stand in the middle of the structure and gaze down upon the Bhot Ganga—a silver wire meandering below him—would find his very life-force sucked out. The journey of six miles after the bridge, over paths shaded by deodar trees, was pleasurable. They reached Gangotri (height: 10,300 feet). The appeal of Gangotri had not yet reached its present proportions and, other than the temple built in honor of Mother Ganga, only a few wooden huts could be seen. Vaishnavdas and some other sadhus insisted that they should press on to Gaumukh. Gaumukh is the place where the Ganga issues forth from a huge hunk of ice. A distance of perhaps sixteen or eighteen miles. And no roads. They had to pick their way among boulders. In some places, patches of unmelted snow still remained. They had their audience with Mother Ganga. It wasn't possible to walk back the same day so they had to spend the night where there was neither a village nor shelter. They spent the night in a hollow, shivering from the cold.

At that time there were no sadhus of the Digamber sect in Gangotri. How would they dare to live there, being forbidden by their faith to wear clothes? Even the thickest of blankets and quilts could offer no protection from the cold there. But, with practice, one can endure cold to a large extent. This is evidenced by the fact that, now, more than half a dozen Digambers live in Gangotri. About twenty or twenty-five years earlier, it was Swami Krishnashram alone who demonstrated such courage. But even he would climb down to Harsil or one of the other villages in winter. Which is where he now stays the year round with his woman disciple, submerged in an uninterruptible trance.

MEDITATING IN DEVAPRAYAG

Haridas—Baba—did not want to move on from the forests of Kunao at all. It was an ideal spot to conduct meditative exercises. He spent a week there, subsisting on leaves and herbs. But hunger began to affect his meditative exercises. It was the Kartik month of 1977. And so Baba departed Kunao, casting longing eyes at his little meditation hut. It wasn't suitable for him to continue living in Lakshmanjhula. He climbed uphill and reached Devaprayag on the third day. Some sadhus told him that half a mile from Devaprayag—across the Ganga—was a cave in which a sadhu once meditated. Haridas Baba had come to Devaprayag for him. About a quarter mile from Devaprayag, right on the bank of the Ganga, was a hollow which could be made habitable. There was no other cave for at least two miles around that spot. He couldn't arrange for meals there either. But he would surely find alms in Devaprayag. If he reached the priests' houses at either 10:00 or 11:00 a.m., they would give him a roti without too much fuss. His spot, on the shore of the Ganga, wasn't perfect but since he couldn't find another he decided to winter there. With a little labor, it wasn't difficult for him to make his cave habitable. A man from the village nearby pitched in too, and soon his cave was windproof and insulated. Baba possessed two blankets and an alfee, a garment made out of blankets, which he could use against the cold. Other than these he had two shoulder cloths, two loincloths, and a kamandal. He would go seeking alms two or three days, and receive roti or rice from about four households with ease. This food was enough for twenty-four hours. A footpath near the cave led up to the village but no one seemed to use it.

The priests had come to know that a baba had taken up residence on the riverbank but no one visited him all winter. Baba lived there for a little more than six months. He enjoyed his meditation practice and made significant progress as well. Yet he wasn't entirely satisfied. Thoughts of mealtimes would keep distracting him. The facilities of the forests of Kunao didn't exist on the riverbank. Summer arrived. The doors of Badrinath opened for darshan. Pilgrims began to make their way from and to the plains. These pilgrims were the people off whom the priests of Devaprayag would make their money. A pilgrim on his way up might ask: "Are meditators, saints, or yogis to be found in caves around here?" The priests would take their clients to the Pretshila (Spirit Rock) and other places of pilgrimage in and around the area. They began to include Hari-baba's site of meditation on their itinerary. Seeking darshan with hands folded in veneration, some would offer a few rupees before going on their way. The priests' sons or others from the village would come back and take the money away. Baba had nothing to do with money. Things might have been bearable had they been limited to occasional audiences but there were some pilgrims who would refuse to budge until they had heard a few sage words from Baba. This soon began to irk him. He undertook a vow of silence and even had this information written out on a board. But there were some imbecilic pilgrims who would say, "It's all right if you can't speak. Write out a few words of wisdom; that will serve our purpose." One pilgrim pursued him for three days and left only after Baba scribbled a few words.

Baba now had no choice but to leave his spot. Pretshila is about two miles from Devaprayag on a bank of the Alaknanda river. There was a small unoccupied hut with a temple nearby. Baba arrived in the month of Saavan and took up residence. He began to be known as "Mauni Baba" on account of his vow of silence. There was a village nearby which included a few priestly households—alms wouldn't be a problem. The priests would bring travelers to the Pretshila in the daytime. While Gaya is the "official" site from where the spirits of the dead find deliverance, not every Hindu priest recognizes and upholds this monopoly. So they have established "shila"—consecrated stones dedicated to the worship of spirits—in various places. Badrinath, too, has Pretshilas and the priests of Badrinath live in Devaprayag. Naturally, they had established a Pretshila in Devaprayag, too. The hill inhabitants may be backward in many areas of life but their priests are very advanced in establishing dubious centers of pilgrimage. It is because of this that there is a rash of Kashis and Prayags in the region. The offering of rice and pulses is specific to Jagannathji but these offerings can be monetized and are now hugely popular in Badrinath, too. The Pretshila terrified people. After all, it was the spot where spirits from all directions—east-west, north-south—would be brought and set free. They would hardly let go of their ancient habits. They could catch hold of anyone at all, and thus no one would dare come to the Pretshila in the evening. There was an uproar among the villagers: they said spirits gather at the Pretshila for a nightly conference. Any unfortunate who might stumble upon the conference wouldn't return with his life intact. But Mauni Baba lived there. He was indeed a master, which was why the ghosts and spirits could do him no harm. And because of this, people began to revere Mauni Baba more and more. It was also widely held that the area was infested with scorpions, so poisonous that a sting to a man's vital parts could even kill him. There were many in the hut Baba occupied. He lived there for two months and the scorpions were kind to him, just as the ghosts and spirits were. Baba would sleep through the day and carry out his meditative exercises through the night. At times he would lie down at noon—after lunch—through to evening, meditating. This was the time when the pilgrims would visit. Thinking that Baba was asleep, they would leave him be.

The practice of the focusing of the senses is such that it can be accomplished sitting or lying down. But it's true that, performed lying down, sleep is a tremendous impediment to meditation. Therefore, of the five base conditions which impede meditation, sleep is considered the topmost. But in reality, sleep is itself a meditative state reached once the trammels of illusion and the claims of the world have fallen away. When a man is in deep sleep, all his mental processes are at a near cease. That state we seek by stilling the mind, sleep brings to us daily, unfailingly, as a way to calm the body and give it rest. However, when meditating, the attempt is to bring about that state even as the mind and the body remain conscious and aware. When one meditates, continually negotiating the push and pull of sleep and wakefulness, and seeks to unite the mind and its distractions in one seamless whole, sleep casts its shadow upon the mind, banishes it from existence, and reveals itself. The opportunity which nature has granted us, to give all the organs of our body rest and rejuvenation through sleep, is itself a barrier to meditation. On lying down, the entire body becomes motionless and one is sleepier then than when one is sitting and the mind, instead of centering, becomes enwrapped in slumber. Once fatigue falls away, sleep no longer affects the mind. Hari-baba would frequently fall asleep while meditating. But how long could sleep keep him in its clutches? As soon as it would leave him, he would make all efforts to center his mind once more. Haridas somehow stretched his time in Devaprayag for two more months, dealing with constant interruptions to his practice of meditation. Thus, when winter set in, he returned to Rishikesh, and his little meditation hut in Koyalghati.

——≡◦≡——

IN SEARCH OF THE SNOW LEOPARD*
Peter Matthiessen

OCTOBER 21

We leave Rohagaon as the first light tints the snow peaks to the south.

Outside the village, two little girls in wool boots and bead necklaces, carrying water, tarry on a corner of the trail to watch us go; minutes later, I look back, and they still stand there, little ragged stumps on the daybreak sky.

All around, the sun fires the summits, yet these steep valleys are so shut away from light that on this trail above the Suli Gad we walk for two hours in dim daybreak shadow. Here and there wild roses gather in clear pale-yellow bloom, and a flight of snow pigeons wheels up and down over the canyon far below; we look in vain for tahr or other

* The account of a 1973 expedition to the Crystal Mountain, Mount Kailash, to study wildlife, and as much a spiritual journey as a field trip, *The Snow Leopard* (1978) is a classic of Himalayan writing.

creatures on the slopes across the valley. Wildlife has been scarce all along the way, with no sign at all of exotic animals such as the moon bear and red panda.

The trail meets the Suli Gad high up the valley, in grottoes of bronze-lichened boulders and a shady riverside of pine and walnut and warm banks of fern. Where morning sun lights the red leaves and dark still conifers, the river sparkles in the forest shadow; turquoise and white, it thunders past spray-shined boulders, foaming pools, in a long rocky chute of broken rapids. In the cold breath of the torrent, the dry air is softened by mist; under last night's stars this water trickled through the snows. At the head of the waterfall, downstream, its sparkle leaps into the air, leaps at the sun, and sun rays are tumbled in the waves that dance against the snows of distant mountains.

Upstream, in the inner canyon, dark silences are deepened by the roar of stones. Something is listening, and I listen too: Who is it that intrudes here? Who is breathing? I pick a fern to see its spores, cast it away, and am filled in that instant with misgiving: the great sins, so the Sherpas say, are to pick wildflowers and to threaten children. My voice murmurs its regret, a strange sound that deepens the intrusion. I look about me—who is it that spoke? And who is listening? Who is this everpresent "I" that is not me?

The voice of a solitary bird asks the same question.

Here in the secrets of the mountains, in the river roar, I touch my skin to see if I am real; I say my name aloud and do not answer.

By a dark wall of rock, over a rivulet, a black-and-gold dragonfly zips and glistens; a walnut falls on a mat of yellow leaves. I wonder if anywhere on earth there is a river more beautiful than the upper Suli Gad in early autumn. Seen through the mist, a water spirit in monumental pale gray stone is molded smooth by its mantle of white water, and higher, a ribbon waterfall, descending a cliff face from the east, strikes the wind sweeping upriver and turns to mist before striking the earth; the mist drifts upward to the rim, forming a halo in the guarding pines.

Leaving the stream, the trail climbs steeply through the trees, then down again under the rock of a dripping grotto, a huge cave of winds. Beyond rises a grassy hill set about with red cotoneaster berries and the yellows, blues, and whites of alpine flowers, and above the hill, like an ice castle set atop a nearer peak, soars Kanjiroba. In twilight, the path descends again to the upper Suli, where camp is made beside the roaring water. We shout to one another and cannot be heard; we move about like shades in the dark canyon.

OCTOBER 22

At dawn on this east side of the canyon, the ground is frozen, making a ringing sound under the stave, and ice slivers glimmer in the brooks that flow into the torrent. Moving upriver in near darkness, we find a bear's nest in a hackberry—our first sign of the Asiatic black bear, called the "moon bear." The bear sits in the branches and bends them toward him as he feeds on the cherry-like fruits; the broken branches make a platform which the bear may then use as a bed. In a corner of this nest, a blue rock dove—the wild ancestor of the street pigeon—has late-October young, as yet unfledged. We make a bear's breakfast of wild berries touched by frost.

A forest of dead pines, dank river caves, and hearths of travelers; two caves are fitted with wood shelves, as if these places had been hermit habitations. The shelves are marked with the swastika, that archaic symbol of creation that occurs everywhere around the world except south of the Sahara and in Australia. It was taken to North America by the ancestors of the American aborigines; in the Teutonic cultures, it was the emblem of Thor; it appeared at Troy and in ancient India, where it was adopted by Hindus, then Buddhists. The reversed swastika is also here, in sign of the B'on religion, still prevalent in old corners of these mountains; since it reverses time, it is thought to be destructive to the universe, and is often associated with black magic.

Faint musical cries ring through the trees above the water noise. In the dim light, I cannot find the caller, and walk on. He calls again, and now I see him, in a small woodland grove across the river; he is a settler, cutting the wild grass for winter hay. I am glad to see him, yet sad that he is here; even this wild region of the Suli Gad will disappear. Because we cannot speak over the river, we merely smile, and he puts his sickle down and lifts his hands, placing his palms together in simple greeting. I do the same; we bow, and turn away.

Near a fork where a tributary stream flows down from the B'on village at Pung-mo, the deep forest across the torrent has been parted by avalanche, and on this brushy slope, a dark shape jumps behind a boulder. The slope is in bright morning sun, but I glimpse the creature only for an instant. It is much too big for a red panda, too covert for a musk deer, too dark for wolf or leopard, and much quicker than a bear. With binoculars, I stare for a long time at the mute boulder, feeling the presence of the unknown life behind it, but all is still, and there is only the sun and morning mountainside, the pouring water.

All day I wonder about that quick dark shape that hid behind the rock, so wary of a slight movement on the far side of a rushing torrent; for I was alone, and could not have been heard, and was all but invisible in the forest shades. In the list of Himalayan mammals, black bear and leopard seem the best choices, but no bear that I ever saw moved like this animal, and no leopard is a uniform dark red or brown. Could it have been a melanistic leopard—a "black panther"? But I have seen leopards many times in Africa, where the species is the same; in rough terrain of bush and boulders, the leopard is much less apt to spring for cover than to crouch, flatten, and withdraw.

And so—though I shall assume it was a musk deer—it is hard to put away the thought of yeti. This forested ravine of the upper Suli Gad is comparable in altitude to the cloud forests of eastern Nepal that are thought to shelter "the man-thing of the snows"; so far as I know, no yeti have been reported from west of the Kali Gandaki, but in reference to a creature as rare and wary as the yeti is presumed to be, this may only mean that these northwestern mountains are far less populous, far less explored.

At 10,800 feet, the canyon opens out into high valleys. A herd of the black shaggy oxen known as yaks are moving down across a hillside of cut barley, preceded by a cold thin tinkle of bells; in these mountains, a faint bell is often a first sign of human presence. The lead animals, carrying packs, are decked out in red collars and bright tassels, and soon a man and wife come down the path in full Tibetan dress, the man in blanket, belted cloak, and baggy pants tucked into red wool boots tied around the calf, the woman in striped apron and black cloths.

On a long slope, in buckwheat fields, is the settlement called Murwa, which takes its name from a kind of mountain millet. The Murwa folk are very clean by comparison to the people of Rohagaon, and their stone houses, yards, and fields are well ordered and well kept; they have red dogs and well-fed stock, and sell a few eggs and potatoes to Phu-Tsering. The sunny hillside is protected all around by snow peaks, and down the high wall to the west roars the great waterfall from Phoksumdo Lake, joining the Murwa stream to form the Suli. I am sorry we must march straight up through this restful place in order to reach Phoksumdo Lake before the evening.

In a cold wind at the Murwa stream, we take off boots and pants and wade the current, which is strong and swift, over slick rocks. I hurry in the icy water, for my numb feet find no footing; suddenly I am plunging like a horse, on the brink of a frigid bath, or worse. Moving diagonally upstream, I make it safely after some bad moments and dry myself on a sunny rock, out of the wind.

From Murwa there is a steep climb through scrub juniper and deodar cedar to a ridge at 12,500 feet—the natural dam that holds Phoksumdo Lake among the snow peaks. I am some distance ahead of GS when a man on horseback, crossing the ridge, demands to know my destination. "Shey Gompa," I declare—the Crystal Monastery. "Shey!" he repeats doubtfully, looking behind him at the peaks to the northwest. He points toward the south and then at me. "Tarakot," I say, "Dhorpatan." Nodding, he repeats, "Dhorpatan." Probably he is going there, and is glad to learn that we have got across Jang La; I neglect to warn him that his pony will not make it.

A boy and girl appear among the cedars. In her basket is a cask of goat cheese, and cheese wrapped in birch bark; she presents me with a bit, and I buy more, and out of the wind, on warm needles in the shelter of evergreens, I eat it up, with half of a big raw radish from Rohagaon.

From the forest comes the sound of bells, and horse hooves dancing on the granite: a man in a clean cloak and new wool boots canters up on a pony with silver trappings. This horseman, too, demands to know my destination, and he, too, frowns to learn that it is Shey. With a slashing movement of his hand across his throat, he indicates the depth of snow, then rides off in a jangle of bright bells.

Clouds loom on the mountains to the south; the cold wind nags me. Soon GS comes, having had the same report: he fears we may have trouble getting in. I nod, though what concerns me more is getting out. The snow already fallen at Kang La will not melt this late in the year; it can only deepen. To be trapped by blizzard on the far side of the Kang would be quite serious, since the food that remains cannot last more than two months.

Northward, the ridge opens out in a pine pasture at 12,000 feet where a herd of yaks, like so many black rocks, lies grouped in the cold sun. The yak has been domesticated from wild herds that still occur in remote parts of Tibet. The female yak is called the bri, and her bushy-tailed, short-faced calf looks like a huge toy. Among these yaks are some yak-cattle hybrids, known as *dzo*. On the shaggy coats, the long hairs shine, stirred by the wind; one chews slow cud. Manure smell and finch twitterings, blue sky and snow: facing the cold wind from the south, the great animals gaze down across the cliff to where the Bauli Gad, descending from Phoksumdo, explodes from its narrow chute into two, then three broad waterfalls that gather again at the Murwa stream below.

In the granite and evergreen beyond the yaks, a lake of turquoise glitters beneath the snow peaks of the Kanjirobas. I walk down slowly through the silent pines.

A geologist would say that Phoksumdo Tal, three miles long, a half-mile wide, and reputed to be near a half-mile in depth, was formed when an earthquake collapsed the mountain on this side of the high valley, blocking the river that comes down from the Kanjirobas at what is now the north end of the lake. But local tradition has a different explanation:

> When B'on was the great religion of the Land of B'od, of which this region was once part, there was a village where this lake now lies. In the eighth century, the great Buddhist saint Padmasambhava, the "Lotus-Born," came to Phoksumdo with the intent of vanquishing the mountain demons. To this end, he persecuted a B'on demoness who, fleeing his wrath, gave these villagers a priceless turquoise, making them promise not to reveal that she had passed this way. But Padmasambhava caused the turquoise to be turned to dung, upon which the villagers, concluding that the demoness had tricked them, betrayed her whereabouts. In revenge, she wreaked upon them a disastrous flood that drowned the village beneath turquoise waters.[*]

Be that as it may, B'on has persisted in this region, and there is a B'on monastery near Ring-mo, a village at the eastern end of the lake that cannot differ much from the eighth-century village that vanished in the deluge. From a distance, Ring-mo looks like a fortress in a tale, for the walls are built up like battlements by winter brushwood stacked on the flat roofs. Sky-blue and cloud-white prayer flags fly like banners in the windy light, and a falling sun, pierced by the peaks, casts heraldic rays.

From the pine forest comes a woodcutter in boots and homespun, uttering barbaric cries that go unanswered in the autumn air. I follow

---

[*] See David Snellgrove, *Himalayan Pilgrimage* (Oxford: Cassirer, 1961).

this moonstruck figure down the path toward two white entrance stupas. The stupas, ringed and decorated in warm red, are fat and lopsided, like immense gingerbread houses, and it seems fitting that, nearby, a cave beneath a giant boulder is walled up with stones in which a small crooked wooden door has been inset. All about are red-gold shrubs— barberry, gooseberry, and rose—and a glistening of the last silver wisps of summer's caper blossoms. Beyond the stupas, protecting the walled town like a moat, is the Bauli torrent that falls down from Phoksumdo. A bridge with flags crosses the torrent where it narrows to enter its mile-long chute down around the west end of the ridge to the great falls, and just above this bridge, in the roaring waters, is a boulder that was somehow reached by a believer, and OM MANI PADME HUM has been carved there in mid-torrent, as if to hurl this mantra down out of the Himalaya to the benighted millions on the Ganges Plain.

Across the bridge, a third entrance stupa is built in an arch over the path up to the town. There are snowdrifts under the north walls, and three immense black yaks stand there immobile. Beyond are small patches of barley and buckwheat, and potato, which came to these mountains in the nineteenth century. A boy leads a team of *dzo* through the potatoes, hauling a crude harrow with wood blade; other children ride the harrow handles to keep the blade sunk in the flinty soil. In their wake, an old man, kneeling, scavenges stray potatoes with a hand hoe, though barely fit to manage his own body. Seeing a stranger, he offers a broken yellow smile by way of apology for his old age.

On the village street stands a tall figure in a red cloak flung over a sheepskin vest that is black with grime; a lavender turban with tassles and once-colorful wool boots deck the extremities of this bandit, who hails me in a wolfish, leering way. Now pretty children run out, smiling, and a silent mastiff runs out, too, only to suffer a rude yank from its chain; its lean jowls curl in a canine smile of pain. Everyone in Ring-mo smiles, and keeping a sharp eye out, I smile, too.

The rough brown buildings have wood doors and arches, and filthy Mongol faces, snot-nosed, wild, laugh at the strangers from the crooked windows. Strange, heavy thumpings come from an immense stone mortar: two girls strike the grain in turn with wood pestles four feet long, keeping time with rhythmic soft sweet grunts, and two carpenters hew rude pine planks with crude adzes. Among the raffish folk of Ring-mo, dirt is worn like skin, and the children's faces are round crusts of sores and grime. Both sexes braid their long hair into pigtails and wear necklaces of beads and dark bits of turquoise, silver, and bone, as well as small amulet packets of old string around their necks. The dress here is essentially Tibetan—cloaks, apron belts, and red-striped woolen boots with yak-twine soles.

Through Jangbu, we question everyone about Kang La and Shey Gompa, as the crowd gives off that heartening smell of uncultivated peoples the world over, an earthy but not sour smell of sweat and fire smoke and the oil of human leather. Goats, a few sheep, come and go. Both men and women roll sheep wool on hand spindles, saying that blizzards have closed Kang La for the winter. On the roofs, culled buckwheat stacked for winter fodder has a bronze shine in the dying sun, and against a sunset wall, out of the wind, an old woman with clean hair turns her old prayer wheel, humming, humming.

October 23

The Tamangs will turn back at Ring-mo, for they are not equipped for the Kang Pass. A goat has been found, and some wood flagons of *chang*, to celebrate our weeks together, and they butcher this billy goat with glee. The Sherpas don't participate in the taking of its life, but they will be happy to help eat it.

In early afternoon, bearing away the goat's head and forequarters and five bellyfuls of *chang*, Pirim and his companions cross the torrent and go chattering uphill, past the cake-colored stupas, to vanish among the sunny pines; freed of their loads, they fairly dance. And though I smile to see the way they go, I feel a sinking of the spirit.

Tukten is our sole remaining porter, and he will be paid henceforth as a Sherpa, as he is much too valuable to lose. The decision to keep Tukten on was mine, as despite his ambiguous reputation I find him the most intelligent and helpful of our men; also, I feel that in some way he brings me luck. He will go with me in case I depart from Shey before GS, for Dawa and Gyaltsen speak no English whatsoever, and GS will need both Jang-bu and Phu-Tsering.

A wind out of the north is cold, but behind the high stone walls of the stock compound where the tents are pitched, the sun is warm. Despite all the reports of heavy snow, we have decided against using yaks, which can plow through new snow up to their bellies but are soon immobilized by ice and crusts. And so Jang-bu is organizing a new lot of porters, who are demanding twenty-five rupees a day. Already these noisy fellows lay the groundwork for malingering at the Kang Pass— "What will you pay us if we must turn back?" They say two days are needed to prepare food and patch their clothes, and one man has been all day in our compound, sewing hard gray wool from a spindle whorl (much like that used by the Hopi) into his calf-high woolen boots, and meditating on our gear the while.

All but the porters have lost interest in us quickly, now that it's clear just how and where the money will be made. In costumes, attitudes, and degree of filth, these Ring-mos cannot have changed much from the eighth-century inhabitants who betrayed the demoness when her turquoise turned to dung. At this season, they live mostly on potatoes, ignoring the autumn bounty of wild fruit that is everywhere around the village. Down by the stream, I persuade two girls to try the gooseberries that grow there. The children are suspicious, tantalized, astonished; in their delight, they stare at each other, then begin to laugh.

While GS climbs the mountainside in search of bharal, I explore the stupas and the town. Even to my untutored eye, the ancient frescoes on the stupa walls, and the ceiling mandalas especially, seem intricate and well designed, for the culture of this region was formerly more vital than it is today. The dominant colors are red ochers, blues, and whites, but yellow and green are also used for certain Buddha aspects and manifestations. The confusion of Buddha figures is compounded here because B'on still prevails, despite the eighth-century inundation of the B'on villagers beneath Phoksumdo. At Ring-mo, Sakyamuni is called Shen-rap, and the faithful swing their prayer wheels left about and circumambulate prayer walls and stupas with left shoulder to the monument instead of right. The swastikas here in the main stupa are reversed, and the prayer stones bear such B'on inscriptions as OM MATRI MUYE SA LE DU ("In clarity unite"),* said to derive from the language of Sh'ang Sh'ung, the mysterious kingdom of western Tibet where, according to B'on-pos, the great B'on teachings usurped by the Buddhists first appeared.

"There is no word for Buddhism in Tibet. Tibetans are either *chos-pa* (followers of *chos*—the Dharma or Universal Law as revealed by Buddha)

* Ibid.

or *b'on-pos* (followers of B'on)."* Yet in practice, B'on has adapted itself so thoroughly to Buddhism, and vice versa, that in their superficial forms they are much the same.

At Ring-mo, OM MANI PADME HUM is carved on the river rock, and a blue Buddha manifestation on the frescoes represents the great scourge of B'on, Padmasambhava; incidental decorations inside and outside the stupas are common symbols of Tibetan Buddhism, such as the conch-shell trumpet of victory, the intertwined snakes, the four-way yin-yang, and the four- and eight-petaled lotuses. B'on has degenerated into a regressive sect of Buddhism and is so regarded, here at least, by its own practitioners. As one of the townsmen says, a little sheepishly, "I am Buddhist, but I walk around the prayer stones the wrong way."

The path to the B'on monastery crosses the torrent, traversing potato fields and pasture to the evergreen forest by Phoksumdo Lake. Ring-mo is a quarter mile or more south of the lake, yet the inhabitants use its Tibetan name, Tsho-wa, or "Lakeside"—could this have been the name of the drowned village? Except for the monastery, there is no habitation near the water, and no boat has ever sailed its surface; its translucent blue-green color must reflect a white sand on the lake floor far below. There are no aquatic animals, and even algae find no place in this brilliant water rimmed around by stone. Truly it is a lake without impurities, like the dust-free mirror of Buddhist symbolism which, "although it offers an endless procession of pictures, is uniform and colorless, unchanging, yet not apart from the pictures it reveals."

The sacred eyes on small stupas by the water's edge follow me along a path of lakeside birch. On the far side of this wood stand the monastery buildings, backed up against the cliffs of the lake's east wall. Seventeen years ago, there were two B'on lamas and twelve monks at Ring-mo, but now it is locked shut, all but abandoned. An ancient caretaker, plagued by goiter, makes wood water casks and prayer stones of poor quality; his old wife squats in a potato patch so small that she can hoe all comers of it from the center. There is a B'on lama up at Pung-mo—they point toward the western peak—but they have no idea when he will come. I go away disappointed. Two days north of Shey is the monastery of Samling, which is said to be the seat of B'on in these far mountains. But if we are to believe these people, our chance of reaching Shey is very small.

* David Snellgrove, *The Nine Ways of B'on* (London: Oxford University Press, 1967).

October 24

A cold wind out of the north. I wash my head. To reduce the drain on our food supplies, Tukten and Gyaltsen leave today for Jumla, where they will obtain rice and sugar and perhaps mail; if all goes well, they will join us at Shey about November 10.

Yesterday I wrote letters to send off with Tukten, and the writing depressed me, stirring up longings, and worries about the children, and bringing me down from the mountain high.

The effort to find ordinary words for what I have seen in this extraordinary time seems to have dissipated a kind of power, and the loss of intensity is accompanied by loss of confidence and inner balance; my legs feel stiff and heavy, and I dread the narrow ledge around the west walls of Phoksumdo that we must follow for two miles or more tomorrow. This ledge is visible from Ring-mo, and even GS was taken aback by the first sight of it. "*That's* not something you'd want to do every day," he said. I also dread the snow in the high passes that might trap us in the treeless waste beyond. These fears just worsen matters, but there's no sense pretending they are not there. It is one thing to climb remote mountains if one has done it all one's life; it is quite another to begin in middle age. Not that forty-six is too old to start, but I doubt that I shall ever welcome ice faces and narrow ledges, treacherous log bridges across torrents, the threat of wind and blizzard; in high mountains, there is small room for mistake.

Why is death so much on my mind when I do not feel I am afraid of it?—the dying, yes, especially in cold (hence the oppression brought by this north wind down off the glaciers, and by the cold choppiness on the cold lake), but not the state itself. And yet I cling—to what? What am I to make of these waves of timidity, this hope of continuity, when at other moments I feel free as the bharal on those heights, ready for wolf and snow and leopard alike? I must be careful, that is true, for I have young children with no mother, and much work to finish; but these aren't honest reasons, past a point. Between clinging and letting go, I feel a terrific struggle. This is a fine chance to let go, to "win my life by losing it," which means not recklessness but acceptance, not passivity but non-attachment.

If given the chance to turn back, I would not take it. Therefore the decision to go ahead is my own responsibility, to be accepted with a whole heart. Or so I write here, in faint hope that the words may give me courage.

I walk down around the ridge to where the torrent falls into the Suli. Beneath evergreens and silver birch, ripples flow along the pale gray rocks, and a wren and a brown dipper come and go where water is pouring into water. The dipper is kin to the North American water ouzel, and the tiny wren is the winter wren of home—the only species of that New World family that has made its way across into Eurasia.

Drowned boulders knock beneath the torrent, and a rock thuds at my back. Transfixed by the bright gaze of a lizard, I become calm. This stone on which the lizard lies was under the sea when lizards first came into being, and now the flood is wearing it away, to return it once again into the oceans.

———

SUNLIGHT ON KINCHINJUNGA*

Francis Younghusband

From Kurseong we ascend through a magnificent forest of chestnut, walnut, oaks, and laurels. [John Dalton] Hooker, when he subsequently visited the Khasia Hills in Assam, said that though the subtropical scenery on the outer Himalaya was on a much more gigantic scale, it was not comparable in beauty and luxuriance with the really tropical vegetation induced by the hot, damp, and insular climate of those perennially humid Khasia Hills. The forest of gigantic trees on the Himalaya, many of them deciduous, appear from a distance as masses of dark gray foliage, clothing mountains 10,000 feet high. Whereas in the Khasia Hills the individual trees are smaller, more varied in kind, of a brilliant green, and contrast with gray limestone and red sandstone rocks. Still, even of the forest between Kurseong and Darjeeling, Hooker says that it is difficult to conceive a grander mass of vegetation—the straight shafts of the timber trees shooting aloft,

* Selections from *The Heart of Nature, or the Quest for Natural Beauty* (1921).

some naked and clean with gray, pale, or brown bark; others literally clothed for yards with a continuous garment of epiphytes (air-plants), one mass of blossoms, especially the white orchids, coelogynes which bloom in a profuse manner, whitening their trunks like snow. More bulky trunks bear masses of interlacing climbers—vines, hydrangea, and peppers. And often the supporting tree has long ago decayed away and their climbers now enclose a hollow. Perpetual moisture nourishes this dripping forest, and pendulous mosses and lichens are met with in profusion.

For this forest life, however, we cannot at present spare the attention that is its due, for we want above all things to see the mountains on the far side of this outer ridge. Tropical forests may be seen in many other parts of the world. But only here on all the Earth can we see mountains on so magnificent a scale. So we do not pause, but cross the ridge and come to the slopes and spurs which face northward, away from the plains and toward the main range of the Himalaya.

Here is situated Darjeeling, which ought to be set apart as a sacred place of pilgrimage for all the world. Directly facing the snowy range and set in the midst of a vast forest of oaks and laurels, rhododendrons, magnolias, and camellias, the branches and trunks of which are festooned with vines and smilax and covered with ferns and orchids, and at the base of which grow violets, lobelias, and geraniums, with berberries, brambles, and hydrangeas—it is adapted as few other places are for the contemplation of Nature's Beauty in its most splendid aspects.

Its only disadvantage is that it is so continually shrouded in mist. The range on which it stands being the first range against which the moisture-laden currents from the Bay of Bengal strike, the rainfall is very heavy and amounts to 140 or 160 inches in the year. And even when rain is not actually falling there is much cloud hanging about the mountains. So the traveler cannot count upon seeing the snows. There is no certainty that as he tops the ridge or turns the corner he will see Kinchinjunga in the full blaze of its glory. He cannot be as sure of seeing it as he is of seeing a picture on entering a gallery. During the month of November alone is there a reasonable surety. All the rest of the year he must take his chance and possess his soul in patience till the mountain is graciously pleased to reveal herself.

Perhaps because of the uncertainty of seeing Kinchinjunga, the view when it is seen is all the more impressive. The traveler waits for hours and days, even for only a glimpse. One minute's sight of the mountains would satisfy him. But still the clouds eddy about in fleecy billows, wholly obscuring the mountains. Six thousand feet below may now and then be seen the silver streak of the Rangit River and forest-clad mountains beyond. Around him are dripping forests, each leaf glistening with freshest greenness, long mosses hanging from the boughs, and the most delicate ferns and noblest orchids growing on the stems and branches. All is very beautiful, but it is the mountain he wants to see; and still the cloud-waves collect and disperse, throw out tender streamers and feelers, disappear, and collect again, but always keep a veil between him and the mountain.

Then of a sudden there is a rent in the veil. Without an inkling of when it is to happen or what is to be revealed, those mists of infinite softness part asunder for a space. The traveler is told to look. He raises his eyes but sees nothing. He throws back his head to look higher. Then indeed he sees, and as he sees he gasps. For a moment the current of his being comes to a standstill. Then it rushes back in one thrill of joy. Much he will have heard about Kinchinjunga beforehand. Much he will remember of it if he has seen it before. But neither the expectation nor the memory ever comes up to the reality. From that time, henceforth and forever, his whole life is lifted to a higher plane.

Through the rent in the fleecy veil he sees clear and clean against the intense blue sky the snowy summit of Kinchinjunga, the culminating peak of lesser heights converging upward to it and all ethereal as spirit, white and pure in the sunshine, yet suffused with the delicatest hues of blue and mauve and pink. It is a vision of color and warmth and light—a heaven of beauty, love, and truth.

But what really thrills us is the thought that, incredibly high though it is, heaven is part of earth, and may conceivably be attained by man. It is nearly double the height of Mont Blanc and more than six times the height of Ben Nevis, but still it is rooted in earth and part of our own home. This is what causes the stir within us.

Hardly less striking than its height is its purity and serenity. The subtle tints of color and the brilliant sunlight dispel any coldness we might feel, while the purity is still maintained. And the serenity is accentuated by the ceaseless movements of the eddying clouds through which the vision is seen. There is about Kinchinjunga the calm and repose of stupendous upward effort successfully achieved.

A sense of solemn elevation comes upon us as we view the mountain. We are uplifted. The entire scale of being is raised. Our outlook on life seems all at once to have been heightened. And not only is there this sense of elevation: we seem purified also. Meanness, pettiness, paltriness seem to shrink away abashed at the sight of that radiant purity.

The mountain has made appeal to, and called forth from us, all that is most pure and most noble within us, and aroused our highest aspirations. Our heart, therefore, goes out lovingly to it. We long to see it again and again. We long to be always in a mood worthy of it. And we long to have that fineness of soul which would enable us to appreciate it still more fully. Glowing in the heart of the mountain is the pure flame of undaunted aspiration, and it sets something aglow in our hearts also which burns there unquenchably for the rest of our days. We see attainment of the highest in the physical domain, and it stirs us to achieve the highest in the spiritual. Between ourselves and the mountain is the kinship of common effort toward high ends. And it is because of this kinship that we are able to see such lofty Beauty in the mountain.

For only a few minutes are we granted this heavenly vision. Then the veil is drawn again. But in those few minutes we have received an impression which has gone right down into the depths of our soul and will last there for a lifetime.

⌇

It will be still night—a starlit night. The phantom snowy range and the fairy forms of the mountains will be bathed in that delicate yellow light the stars give forth. The far valley depths will be hidden in the most somber purple. Overhead the sky will be glittering with brilliant gems set in a field of limpid sapphire. The hush of night will be over all—the hush which heralds some great and splendid pageant.

Then, almost before we have realized it, the eastward-facing scarps of the highest peaks are struck with rays of mingled rose and gold, and gleam like heavenly realms set high above the still, night-enveloped world below. Farther and farther along the line, deeper and deeper down it, the flush extends. The sapphire of the sky slowly lightens in its hue. The pale yellow of the starlight becomes merged in the gold of dawn. White billowy mists of most delicate softness imperceptibly form themselves in the valley depths and float up the mountainsides.

The deep hum of insect life, the chirping of the birds, the sounds of men, begin to break the hush of night. The snows become a delicate pink, the valleys are flooded with purple light, the sky becomes intensest blue, and the sun at last itself appears above the mountains, and the ardent life of day vibrates once more.

∽

In the full glare of day the mountains are not seen at their very best. The best time of all to see them is in the evening. If we go out a little from Darjeeling into the forest to some secluded spur we can enjoy an evening of rare felicity. On the edge of the spur the forest is more open. The ground is covered with grass and flowers and plants with many-colored leaves. Rich orchids and tender ferns and pendant mosses clothe the trees. Graceful vines and creepers festoon themselves from bough to bough. The air is fragrant with the scent of flowers. Bright butterflies flutter noiselessly about. The soft purr of forest life drones around. Rays from the setting sun slant across the scene. The leaves in their freshest green and of every shade glitter like emeralds in the brilliant light.

Through the trunks of the stately trees and under their overarching boughs we look out toward the snowy mountains. We look over the brink of the spur, down into the deeps of the valleys richly filled with tropical vegetation, their eastward-facing sides now of purplest purple, their westward-facing slopes radiant in the evening sunshine, with the full richness of their foliage shown up by the dazzling light. Far below we see the silver streak of some foaming river, and then as we raise our eyes we mark ridge rising behind ridge, higher and higher and each of a deeper shade of purple than the one in front. The lower are still clothed in forest, but the green has been merged in the deep purple of the atmosphere. The higher are bare rock till the snow appears. But just across them floats a long level wisp of fleecy cloud, and apparently the limits of earth have been reached and sky has begun. We would rest content with that. But our eyes are drawn higher still. And high above the cloud, and rendered inconceivably higher by its presence, emerges the snowy summit of Kinchinjunga, serene and calm and flushed with the rose of the setting sun. As a background is a sky of the clearest, bluest blue.

These are the chief elements of the scene, but all is in process of incessant yet imperceptible change. The sunshine slowly softens, the purples deepen, the flush on the mountains reddens. The air becomes as soft as velvet. Not a leaf now stirs. A holy peace steals over the mountains and settles in the valleys. The snow mountains no longer look cold, hard, and austere. Their purity remains as true as ever. And they still possess their uplifting power. But they now speak of serenity and calm—not, indeed, of the unsatisfying ease of the slothful, but of the earned repose of high attainment. Great peace is about them—deep, strong, satisfying peace.

The sun finally sets. Night has settled in the valleys. The lights of Darjeeling sparkle in the darkness. But long afterward a glow still remains on Kinchinjunga. Lastly that also fades away.

—➤•◦⇒—

LADAKH SOJOURN*

Andrew Harvey

"Every object in the light of Ladakh seems to have something infinite behind it; every object, even the most humble, seems to abide in its real place."

Francois's words and his voice came back to me as I walked, in the early evening light, to the stupa at the edge of town and sat down in its warm shadow. A stupa is a building of plaster and brick that has four stages: a large cubic foundation, rising diminishing cubes that support a wide, empty, bun-like middle portion, which supports in its turn a long spire that comes to a point in the symbol of a crescent moon cradling a sun. It is a building in which relics are kept, the relics of saints or kings or very holy teachers, and each stage of the building symbolizes a different state of consciousness. All over Ladakh, there are stupas of every shape and size; in mountain passes, on the long slopes up to monasteries, along the banks of rivers, at the entrance to secluded villages, sometimes

* Excerpted from *A Journey in Ladakh: Encounters with Buddhism* (1983).

with small shrines attached to them, as in the stupa at the entrance to Sankar, where a few badly painted smiling Bodhisattvas raise their hands in blessing. Wherever you walk in the lower parts of this landscape, you are never far from the softly rising brick-red spire of the stupa, from the flash of its crescent moon and sun in the light, from the eye, the Bindu, at the center of that union of sun and moon, that is an ancient symbol of Universal Consciousness, of the Awareness that is Nirvana. Wherever you walk, you are reminded, in the carefully calculated shape of the stupa, of the different stages of illumination that end in the experience of liberation; each of its different parts is dedicated to a different element, a different Buddha, a different ecstasy. It is a simple building, but its shape represents a whole philosophy, *is* that philosophy in one of its purest statements, crumbling white plaster and brick, against rock and sky.

The stupa at the edge of Leh stands separately on a small raised hill. I noticed as I walked up to it, seeing it against the wide spread of the Karakorams, that its shape was a meditation on the wild forms of the mountains behind it. The stupa echoes the mountains and the mountains are stupas also. Everything in this world is linked.

∽

Everything is dark by ten. Leh is given over to the night—vast, cloudless, soaked in moonlight and starlight, the Milky Way lustrous in this high mountain air, each cluster of stars, each swirling nebula, precise and dazzling . . .

You walk into the main street and look up at the palace, that by day looks so dilapidated. At first you can hardly tell it from the rock it stands on. Then slowly its walls emerge; night gives them back some of their old grandeur. Starlight salts them brightly . . .

Hardly anyone in the street. A few Kashmiris sitting under an extinguished streetlamp talking in low voices and smoking. An old woman who passes and stares at you, her face mysterious and sibylline in that light, until she smiles. A dog you cannot see, that brushes past you suddenly and barks in fear.

There is one café that is always the last to close. It is at the beginning of the main street. At the time I go there, usually about nine, there is no one else there except the young Sikh who is sitting on a table in his dirty yellow turban, making samosas for the next day. We are friends.

He has taught me how to make samosas—how to mold the batter, how to fill them with vegetables. But I am ashamed of my slowness, my lack of expertise. He can sit and talk and laugh and his hands move instinctively, shaping, filling, conjuring samosa after samosa out of the chipped white bowls of batter and vegetable . . . I have to watch all my movements. My samosas are lumpy. He laughs at me gently.

Sometimes when I come back to Leh late I pass him sitting alone in the window of his café, making samosas by lamplight. His fine, sad face shines in the yellow light; his hands, pianist's hands, move with an almost magical delicacy and precision . . . He looks up, calls me in, and we talk. An hour or two later, I walk back to my hotel. I can never sleep at once; my mind is too full to read. I lie on the roof and look up at the night, breathing in its mist of stars.

⌒

You see and hear water everywhere in Leh. Under all talk, every silence, all slow, sensuous watching, runs the murmur and flash of water. Every street glitters with snow water, racing from the mountains into the ragged stone channels that lead it through the town into the fields below. I wake up and walk to town. The first thing I see is the morning river, leaping in the light over its smooth rocks. I walk up to Pamposh; water, noisy and brilliant, runs down the hill on both sides of the street. I sit in Pamposh and look out at the old lama passing, or the woman sitting on the corner selling cabbages, or a young Kashmiri squatting outside his shop and singing, and in everything I see there is a flash of running water. I walk in the late afternoon to the Tibetan Restaurant, just down the street from Pamposh, and wait for friends, and try to write; every time I look out of its wooden windows onto the street I see the small turbulent stream outside with a child dabbling in it, or a dog wading through it, or two old Muslims sitting by it under a tree and smoking their evening hookah. And when at night I am walking, alone or with friends, through Leh up the small streets behind and round the main street, or outside to Sankar or Changspa, the villages that are only a few hundred yards away, it is always to the noise of water, shaking in moonlight and starlight, coursing in untidy channels through darkening corn, between moon-washed poplars and willows, bringing a flickering life to paths lined by shrines and small stupas that in the moonlight seem hardly more solid than the stream that runs by them.

Surrounded by so much water, the mind becomes water, hindered by nothing, abandoned, happy.

⟡

At this time of year many Ladakhi roofs are bright with drying apricots—circles and squares and lozenges of burning orange. I keep for dark days my glimpses of them from the inside of buses, from the tops of passes, or standing on the walls of a monastery: shouts of wild color in a wilderness of ocher.

Today I found a spoon in the bazaar for an old friend in Oxford. The spoon is only a long copper handle with a roughly hammered end. All it has for decoration is a linked series of askew triangles indented, unevenly, on the handle. And yet it could be Egyptian or Mayan or Amerindian or Eskimo or the latest invention of an Italian designer; its simplicity is timeless.

I saw a silver trumpet in Spituk. It was coated in massy silver, decorated with dragons and peacocks and grotesque animals (one with the head of a lion, another with the harsh eyes and beak of a King Eagle), and worked in lapis and crystal, amethyst, turquoise, and three kinds of red coral. So much disciplined exuberance and fantasy . . . I held it up against the rock of the mountains and the light of the cloudless sky, and the tails of the lions and the wings of the silver eagles broke into flame.

On the desk as I write this, a pair of antique Ladakhi chopsticks. I bought them for the son of a friend, but when it came to it I could not part with them, and gave him an old bell instead. The chopsticks are small, made of old, scarred, yellowing, thukpa- and mok-mok-stained ivory, fitted into the back of the sheath of a silver dagger. Food and death, pleasure and wariness, happiness and a proper caution ... a happy dance of opposites and paradoxes. If they were to be used in a tantric ceremony, the most elaborate symbolism could be woven around them—the knife for cutting the strings of illusion, the chopsticks for eating the food of contemplation. Their handles are of rough silver and on each there is only one ornament—a fan-tailed, fire-breathing dragon, of such power that I expect each time I pick them up to burn my hands.

Helena, Hans, and I were talking in Pamposh and Helena said, "I have been here for three weeks and I have not seen anything ugly in Leh."

But there is ugliness in Leh. There are the two great rotting green billboards outside the post office; there are the open lavatories in the bus station and along the wall of the Muslim cemetery on the way into town; there are the holes in front of Pamposh's, filled with potato peelings, slops, and newspaper; there are the mangy flea-ridden dogs nosing for food in the gutters; there are the sheep sprawled crumpled and bloody and stinking under the bridge; there are signs of poverty too—the wall eyes, the shaking hands of half-blind, stumbling old women with spectacles stuck together with sellotape, the old men with only a few black teeth left and open ulcers on their shins.

We met again that evening in Dreamland, the one half-good restaurant in town. I told them the three anti-Kashmiri expressions I had found in De Vigne. "Many fools in a house will defile it, and many Kashmiris in a city will spoil it." "If you meet a snake do not put it to death, but do not spare a Kashmiri." "Do not admit a Kashmiri to your friendship, or you will hang a hatchet over your doorway."

Hans laughed. "Actually," he said, "they are not funny. Since 1947 Ladakh has been under the 'rule' of the Kashmiris. That is what being part of the state of Jammu and Kashmir amounts to. The Kashmiris have all the power in this country—all the administrative power. Do you know, there isn't one Ladakhi minister in the state government in Srinagar? I could tell you the most hair-raising stories about the corruption, the diversion of funds from Ladakhi enterprises. For a long time the Ladakhis were patient. Many of them believed in the assurances that India made to them of a secure future, a progressive future in the Indian Republic. But nearly all Ladakhis are now angry. Angry at the Kashmiri officials who run almost every aspect of their lives and who have no sympathy for their religion and who think their country is a barren wasteland. Angry, too, that Ladakh is progressing very slowly, that there are few of the properly financed farming and irrigation schemes that are so urgently needed, angry at the lack of modern equipment, at the lack of work, at the Kashmiris who have the money to rent the shops up here for the summer season and fleece the tourists. There have been riots on and off for years, bad riots this year in January, and again in June, and there is a Protest Day scheduled later next month which could well turn violent. Many Ladakhis are secretly and illegally armed. Everyone knows that. Everyone knows too that the Ladakhi Scouts, who are here as part of the Indian Border Force, would not allow their people to be shot at by the army, and would fight if the Army were called in."

"The Ladakhis seem so friendly . . . do you really think they would fight?"

"Of course," Hans said. "How much passivity can they stand?"

"And could they win?"

"I doubt it. Their only hope is that the central government will do something about the Kashmiris. And it just might. This is a very sensitive border area, after all. But it is also true that India wants to keep Kashmir sweet, and so might turn a blind eye to what is being done here. No one can know what will happen."

There had been a power cut. The incessant noise of the powerhouse had suddenly subsided, and the restaurant was being lit with candles by the small Tibetan girl who ran it.

"The Kashmiris have almost totally pushed out Ladakhi as a language in schools," Hans said. "They only allow it to be taught up to fifth grade. And very little funds have been directed into keeping up the monasteries, or helping out the Buddhist philosophy school. The Ladakhis have already lost so much . . ."

We walked out of the restaurant and stood in the starlight. "I hope this people will preserve its identity," Hans said, "but it is a utopian hope. Besides, it is a hope I can afford; I will not have to pay for it."

The Tibetans are everywhere in Leh. They come up for the brief summer tourist season, from June to September, from places as far away as Darjeeling or Mysore. They pay exorbitant rents for rooms with one bare light bulb and a poster of Bruce Lee, or sleep in their own tattered tents in fields or by their open-air stalls. A thin Tibetan girl in faded French jeans runs Dreamland, working sixteen hours a day with her even younger brother, who at fourteen or fifteen already has the starved blank look of an opium addict; a chubby Tibetan woman of about forty, whom everyone calls "Mama," runs "The Restaurant," a wooden shack in the center of town where I eat every day. The market, the long straggling open-air market, is almost entirely run by Tibetans, of every kind and age—fat old men and thin young girls learning nervously to smoke, young Casanovas with Brylcreemed hair, American T-shirts ("I LOVE SNOOPY," "PRINCETON UNIVERSITY," "MAKE ME HAPPY"), sneakers, fat Japanese wristwatches and cassettes forever blaring out "Saturday Night Fever" or the Stones, middle-aged women selling their beads and haggling in high voices at the same time. And they sit all day with their tough, tanned faces behind heaps of silver bells and scrolls, small ivory scent boxes, waving paper flags of Amitabha or Avalokiteshvara, Buddhas of endless light and compassion, blue and green and red jade necklaces, little piles of square and oblong and circular turquoises, haggling and talking and drinking Tibetan tea and appraising the foreigners that pass like punters eyeing horses in the paddock.

I have made friends with one of the Casanovas. He loves Bob Hope and Paul McCartney; he wants to live in California. "I have heard the girls are very loving and happy" (closing his eyes and moaning gently). He dreams of doing nothing and driving a long red sports car, which he imagines to be the American Way of Life; he says, "I will be your friend forever if you teach me how to do disco"; he is handsome, dark, eighteen, but already he has crow's-feet, and a strained look when he doesn't think he is being watched. "I do not like this country . . . why should I like it? There are no films here, there are no good coffeehouses, there are no girls. What can I do with a Ladakhi girl? I can't even hold her hand. Ladakhi girls are not happy" (the moan again). "I like cities, too, very tall cities . . . What kind of a life is this? I spend all day waiting to cheat some old German woman. Sometimes I wait for two days, three days for the right old German woman to smile at and sell my bells and necklaces to for fifteen times the price I bought them at. I smile a lot. This goes on for three months, and then I have to give the money to my family—to my father who is old, to my mother who is old, to my sister, who is still at school, to my brother, who is in Delhi studying, to my other brother who is in Delhi studying. And I have to spend the winter walking round the villages of Kulu and Spiti—the people are even dirtier than they are here—I have to spend all the winter getting frozen in Kulu trying to cheat the villagers there out of bells and bowls and spoons and turquoise necklaces so I can come and cheat the old German ladies here! No one lives like this in America, do they?"

"The Tibetans were always a tough people," Hans said; "they had to be to survive in their high, cold world; and now, in exile, they continue to survive and adapt. Why shouldn't the boys wear sneakers and want to go to America? It's a sad dream but to them technology still seems miraculous . . . "

He added, "But the old Tibet is still here: it is in some of the monks, some of the families; it is in the children, in the mountains, in the old women ... Ladakh holds fragments of it in its old hand."

⤜●⤛

A MOUNTAIN RETREAT*

Vicki Mackenzie

Tenzin Palmo, with her small band of companions, began to climb the mountain which stood behind Tayul Gompa in the direction in which they had been told the cave lay. They trudged up and up in a steep ascent, leaving the habitations of human beings far behind. Higher and higher they went, across the sweet-smelling grasses which gave off aromatic scents as they brushed by, climbing more than 1,000 feet beyond the Gompa, their chests bursting with the effort and the altitude. This was not a trek for either the faint-hearted or the short-winded. The way was perilously steep and treacherous. There was no path to follow and the drop beside them was sheer. At various points the way was made more hazardous by wide streams of loose scree—boulders and stones that the mountain rising over them habitually shrugged off as though irritated by their presence. They had to be traversed if the cave was to be found, but one false foothold on those slippery stones meant likely death.

Undaunted, they carried on. After two hours of climbing they suddenly came across it. It was so well blended in with the mountain, so camouflaged, that until they were almost upon it they had no idea it was there. It was certainly not the archetypal cave of one's imagination or of Hollywood movies. Here was no deep hollow in the mountainside with a neat round entrance and a smooth dirt floor, offering a cozy, self-contained, if primitive living space. It was less, much less than that. This "cave" was nothing more than an overhang on a natural ledge of the mountain with three sides open to the elements. It had a craggy roof which you had to

* In 1976, Diane Perry (Tenzin Palmo) secluded herself in a cave in Lahoul at a height of 13,200 feet. She spent the next twelve years there seeking enlightenment. This essay describes how she found the cave, and her life as a seeker.

stoop to stand under, a jagged, slanting back wall, and beyond the ledge outside a sheer drop into the steep V of the Lahouli valley. At best it was a flimsy shelter. At worst a mere indentation in a rock. It was also inconceivably small: a space measuring at most ten feet wide by six feet deep. It was a cupboard of a cave. A cell for solitary confinement.

Tenzin Palmo stood on the tiny ledge and surveyed the scene. The view was sensational. How could it be otherwise? In front of her, stretching in a 180-degree arc, was a vast range of mountains. She was almost eye to eye with their peaks. Right now, in summer, only the tops were covered with snow but in the long eight-month winter they would constitute a massive wall of whiteness soaring into the pristine, pollution-free, azure-blue sky above. The light was crystalline, imbuing everything with a shimmering luminosity, the air sparkling and crisp. The silence was profound. Only the rushing gray-green waters of the Bhaga river below, the whistle of the wind and the occasional flap of a bird's wing broke the quietness. To her right was a small juniper forest, which could provide fuel. To her left, about a quarter of a mile away, was a spring, gurgling out from between some rocks, a vital source of fresh, clean water. And behind her was yet more mountain towering over her like a sentinel. For all the awesome power of her surroundings, and the extreme isolation, the cave and its surroundings felt peaceful and benign, as though the mighty mountains offered security by their sheer size and solidity, although this, of course, was an illusion—mountains being as impermanent as everything else made of "compounded phenomena."

She was 13,200 feet above sea level—a dizzying height. At this altitude it was like contemplating living just below the peak of Mount Whitney in the Rockies or not far short of the top of Mont Blanc. In comparison Britain's highest mountain, Ben Nevis, at 4,402 feet, was a pygmy. It would have to be stacked three times on top of itself to approach the spot where Tenzin Palmo now stood. Up here the eye was forced upward and outward, bringing the mind automatically with it, forcing both beyond the confined boundaries of the earthbound mortals below. It was no wonder that the highest peaks had always been the favored haunts of solitary meditators.

Tenzin Palmo took all this in and, in spite of the minute size and condition of the overhang, was sold. "I knew instantly. This is it," she said. It had everything she needed. Here, perched like an eagle on the top of the world, she would most definitely not be bothered by the clamor and clutter of human commerce. She would have the absolute silence she yearned for. The silence that was so necessary to her inner search, for she knew, like all meditators, that it was only in the depth of silence that the voice of the Absolute could be heard. She could bury herself in the confines of her cave to pursue her spiritual practices without interruption. She could go out and look at the mountains and the infinite sky. She would see no one. No one would see her.

There were other attractions. Fortuitously, considering her quest to attain Enlightenment as a woman, she had landed in the midst of a vortex of female spiritual energy. On the summit of the mountain opposite was a curious black rock called by the locals "The Lady of Keylong." Even in the midst of winter the shape remained inexplicably free of snow. On closer inspection one could make out the silhouette of a kneeling woman draped in a mantle with a baby at her breast and one hand stretched feeding a small bird. To the Western eye it bore an uncanny resemblance to the Madonna and child, although to the Lahoulis she was Tara, the female Buddha of Compassion. High on a precipice nearby could be found a faded blue and gold painting of the same goddess. It had apparently appeared there spontaneously several centuries earlier, having moved itself from the opposite side of the valley, its form still clearly visible to the perceptive eye. And down the way, not far from the cave, was a spot said to be inhabited by the powerful Buddhist protectress Palden Lhamo, traditionally depicted riding on a mule. One day several years later Tenzin Palmo was to see footprints of a mule embedded in the snow at this very spot. Strangely there were no other footprints leading to or from it.

All in all it was perfect. Here she could finally devote her entire energy and time to profound and prolonged meditation. She could begin to unravel the secrets of the inner world—the world that was said to contain the vastness and the wonder of the entire universe.

If she was happy at her discovery of the cave, her companions were not. They proceeded to throw at her all the objections and discouragements that had been hurled at women who wanted to engage in serious meditation in total isolation down the ages. Tenzin Palmo deftly fielded each one.

"It's too high! Nobody, let alone a woman, can survive at this altitude. You will die," they chorused.

"But caves are warmer than houses. They are thermostatically controlled. My house in Tayul is freezing in winter and I survive that. This cave will be better," she replied.

"Well, living so far away from any living person you will be a sitting duck for thieves who will break in and rob you," they retorted.

"There are no thieves in Lahoul. You can see for yourself how the Lahouli women walk around wearing all their jewelry quite openly and no one tries to rob them," she argued.

"Men from the army camp will come up and rape you," they tried again.

"By the time they have climbed this high they will be so exhausted all they will want is a cup of tea," she responded.

"What about the ghosts? These places are haunted, don't you know? You will be terrified," they continued.

At this point Tenzin Palmo's Tibetan failed her. Believing they were talking about snakes instead of ghosts (the word being similar in Tibetan), she blithely replied, "Oh I don't mind them at all." This nonchalant declaration impressed her detractors almost to silence, but not quite.

"Well, we're not going to help you move up here because if we do we will only be aiding you in your own death. And we are not going to be party to that." They were adamant.

"If I get permission from my guru, Khamtrul Rinpoche, will you agree and help?" she asked. They finally nodded their heads. A letter was duly dispatched to Tashi Jong, and after asking her several searching questions about the position and condition of the cave Khamtrul Rinpoche gave his permission. The objections were at last quelled.

In that one brief argument Tenzin Palmo overturned centuries of tradition, which decreed that women were not capable of doing extensive retreats in totally isolated places in order to advance themselves to higher spiritual levels. In doing so she also became the first Western woman to follow in the footsteps in the Eastern yogis of old and enter a Himalayan cave to seek Enlightenment.

Before she could begin her great work, however, the cave had to be made habitable. With the help from her Lahouli friends she employed laborers to brick up the front and side of the cave with walls made especially thick to keep out the ferocious cold. A small area inside was partitioned off to use as a storeroom for her supplies of food. It was essential, but reduced her living space still further, to a minuscule area of six feet wide by six feet deep. The floor also had to be scooped out to give her room to stand up, then baked earth was put on top of it, then flagstones, then more earth. They put in a window and a door, which Tshering Dorje insisted open inward—an insight which was to prove invaluable in the drama that was to follow. Then they slapped mud and cow dung on the floor and walls. After that they leveled off the ledge outside, making it into a patio where Tenzin Palmo could sit and bask in that breathtaking view. Finally they constructed a stone wall around the perimeter of the cave to keep the wild animals at bay and to establish a boundary for her retreat area.

Into the cave Tenzin Palmo put her furniture: a small wood-burning stove (a legacy of the Moravian missionaries who had once tried to convert the Lahoulis) with a flue pipe that thrust out of the front wall; a wooden box for a table covered with a flowery tablecloth; a bucket. On the walls she hung pictures of Buddhist deities in their various manifestations. A handy depression in the wall became her bookshelf holding her precious dharma texts, carefully wrapped in yellow cloth to keep the loose pages together, bookbinding never having made it to Tibet. On a natural ledge she placed her ritual implements of dorje and bell, the mystic thunderbolt signifying compassion, the bell Emptiness or wisdom. These were the two "wings" of Tibetan Buddhism which, when realized, were said to fly you all the way to Enlightenment. And against the back wall was her altar, holding the images of her personal meditational deities, a miniature stupa (representing the Buddha Mind), and a text (representing the Dharma). In front of this she set up seven small offering bowls which she filled with water. They represented the seven gifts offered to any distinguished visitor who graced your house with his or her presence: water for drinking, water for washing the feet, flowers, food, perfume, light, and music.

And then there was the most unusual object of all, a traditional meditation box. This was a square wooden structure measuring 2 feet 6 inches by 2 feet 6 inches and raised slightly off the ground to insulate the meditator from rising damp. It was where she would spend the greater part of her life. Over the years she developed a remarkably close attachment to it: "I loved my meditation box. I'd wrap myself in my cloak and be perfectly snug there, out of the way of drafts," she said enthusiastically.

When it was finished the gaping, jagged hole in the mountain had been transformed into a pretty little house with a crooked rocky roof, so quaint it could have come out of the pages of a fairy-tale book. It instantly dispelled any notion of clichéd cave-living.

"It was a very pukka cave," Tenzin Palmo admitted. "The few people who saw it were always very surprised how neat and cosy it was. It was small, certainly. There was no room to dance! Although when I did my long retreat I did do Hatha yoga there. Yoga was great in counteracting all the sitting I did and in helping with the problems with my spine," she said, referring to the back problems which had plagued her since birth. "But the cave was so small I had to do different postures in different parts of the cave, depending on where there was room."

Didi Contractor was one person who witnessed the cave. A large, gray-haired woman now in her late sixties, she had come to India from California many decades earlier and had led a colorful life in an extended family with her Indian husband. She had met Tenzin Palmo during one of her visits to Khamtrul Rinpoche and had stayed in touch. As an interior designer (responsible for such famous landmarks as the Lake Palace in Udaipur), she wanted to throw a professional eye over Tenzin Palmo's unorthodox living arrangements to make sure she was safe: "The climb up was horrific, especially over the loose scree. I looked down on the tiny houses in the valley below and thought, 'If I fall I'm strawberry jam.' Tenzin Palmo, who escorted me, however, bounded up like an antelope. When I finally got there I was reassured. The cave was very secure and safe. The walls were thick—although I did arrange for her to have double glazing put on the windows. Most importantly, it was south-facing, which meant it got the sun for the whole day which was essential in winter. My God, it was tiny though. There was just room for me to lay my sleeping bag down beside her meditation box. That was it," she said, from the mud-brick house which she had built herself just below Dharamsala, home of the Dalai Lama and his government in exile.

With the cave finished, Tenzin Palmo moved in and began her extraordinary way of life. She was thirty-three years old. This was to be her home until she was forty-five.

⌒

Her quest may have been purely spiritual but before she could get down to grappling with the immaterial she first had to conquer the eminently mundane business of simply staying alive. For the bookish, otherworldly, and decidedly unrobust woman, this was a challenge.

"I was never practical. Now I had to learn to do umpteen physical things for myself. In the end I surprised even myself at how well I managed and how self-sufficient I became," she admitted.

The first priority was water.

"Initially I had to get my water from the spring, which was about a quarter of a mile away. In summer I'd have to make several trips, carrying it to my cave in buckets on my back. In the winter, when I couldn't get out, I melted snow. And if you've ever tried to melt snow you would know how difficult that is! A vast amount of snow only gives you a tiny amount of water. Fortunately in the winter you don't need a lot because you're not really washing either yourself or your clothes and so you can be very economical with the water you use. Later, when I did my three-year retreat, and could not venture beyond my boundary, someone paid for a water pipe to be laid right into the cave's compound. It was an enormous help," she explained.

Next was food.

There was of course nothing to eat on that sparse mountainside. No handy bushes bearing berries. No fruit trees. No pastures of rippling golden wheat. Instead she arranged for supplies to be brought up from the village in the summer, but as often as not they would not arrive and Tenzin Palmo would be reduced to running up and down the mountain herself carrying gigantic loads. "It took a lot of time and effort," she said. For the bigger task of stocking up for her three-year retreat Tshering Dorje was put in charge:

"I would hire coolies and donkeys to carry up all that she needed," he recalled. "There would be kerosene, tsampa, rice, lentils, flour, dried vegetables, ghee, cooking oil, salt, soap, milk powder, tea, sugar, apples, and the ingredients for ritual offerings such as sweets and incense. On top of that I employed woodchoppers to cut logs and these were carried up as well."

To supplement these basic provisions with a source of fresh food Tenzin Palmo made a garden. Just below the ledge outside her cave she created two garden beds in which she grew vegetables and flowers. Food to feed her body, flowers to feed her soul. Over the coming years she experimented to see what would survive in that rocky soil. "I tried growing all sorts of vegetables like cabbages and peas but the rodents ate them. The only things they wouldn't touch were turnips and potatoes. Over the years I truly discovered the joy of turnips! I am now ever ready to promote the turnip," she enthused. "I discovered that turnips are a dual-purpose vegetable. You have the wonderful turnip greens, which are in fact the most nutritious of all vegetable greens and absolutely delicious, especially when young," she waxed. "No gourmet meal in the world is comparable to your first mouthful of fresh turnip greens after the long winter. And then you've got the bulb, which is also very good for you. Both of them can be cut up and dried, so that right through the winter you've got these wonderful vegetables. Actually I was waiting for the book *One Hundred Eight Ways to Cook Turnips* but it never showed up," she joked.

She ate once a day at midday, as is the way with Buddhist nuns and monks. Her menu was simple, healthy, and to ordinary palates excruciatingly monotonous. Every day she ate the same meal: rice, dhal (lentils), and vegetables, brewed up together in a pressure cooker. "My pressure cooker was my one luxury. It would have taken me hours to cook lentils at that altitude without it," she said. This meager fare she supplemented with sourdough bread (which she baked) and tsampa. Her only drink was ordinary tea with powdered milk. (Interestingly, the traditional tea made with churned butter and salt was one of the few Tibetan customs she did not like.) For dessert she had a small piece of fruit. Manali was renowned for its apples and Tshering Dorje would deliver a box of them. "I'd eat half an apple a day and sometimes some dried apricot."

For twelve years this was how it was. There was no variation, no culinary treats like cakes, chocolates, ice creams—the foods which most people turn to to relieve monotony, depression, or hard work. She professed she did not mind and as she logically pointed out: "I couldn't pop down to Sainsbury's if I wanted anything anyway. Actually, I got so used to eating small quantities that when I left the cave people would laugh seeing me eat only half an apple, half a slice of toast, half a quantity of jam. Anything more seemed so wasteful and extravagant."

And then there was the cold. That tremendous, unremitting, penetrating cold that went on for month after month on end. In the valley below the temperature would regularly plunge to -35° in winter. Up on that exposed mountain it was even bleaker. There were huge snowdrifts that piled up against her cave and howling winds to contend with too. Once again, Tenzin Palmo made light of it. "Just as I suspected, the cave proved to be much warmer than a house. The water offering bowls in front of my altar never froze over in the cave as they did in my house in Tayul Gompa. Even in my storeroom, which was never heated, the water never froze. The thing about caves is that the colder it is on the outside the warmer it is on the inside, and the warmer it is outside the cooler it is inside. Nobody believed this when I told them, but the yogis had told me and I trusted them," she insisted.

For all her avowed indifference, the cold must have been intense. She lit her stove only once a day at noon and then only to cook lunch. This meant in effect that when the sun went down she was left in her cave without any source of heat at all. Somehow she survived. "Sure I was cold, but so what?" she stated, almost defiantly, before adding in a somewhat conciliatory tone, "When you're doing your practice you can't keep jumping up to light the stove. Besides, if you are really concentrating you get hot anyway." And her comment begged the further question of how far she had got in her ability to raise the mystic heat, like Milarepa had done in his freezing cave all those centuries ago, and the Togdens, who had practiced drying wet sheets on their naked bodies on cold winter nights in Dalhousie. "Tumo wasn't really my practice," was all she would say.

Endurance was one thing, however, and comfort another. The pleasure of a hot bath, a fluffy towel, scented soap, a soft bed, crisp sheets, an easy chair, a clean lavatory—the soft touches that most women appreciate and need—she had none of. This desire for physical ease was said, by men, to be one of the biggest obstacles to women gaining Enlightenment. How could they withstand the rigors of isolated places necessary to spiritual progress, they argued, when by nature they wanted to curl up cat-like in front of a warm fire? In this, as in many things, Tenzin Palmo was to prove them wrong.

Her bath was a bucket. She washed sparingly, especially in winter when water was scarce and temperatures reduced body odors to zero. Her lavatory in summer was the great outdoors—her privacy was guaranteed. "In the winter I'd use a tin and later bury it." None of this bothered her. "To be honest I didn't miss a flushing toilet or a hot shower because I'd already been so long without those things," she said.

Compounding her asceticisms was the total absence of any form of entertainment. Up in that cave she had no TV, no radio, no music, no novel, in fact no book which spoke of anything but religion. "There was no 'luxury' I missed. Life in Dalhousie had prepared me admirably. I had everything I needed," she repeated.

Arguably, the most radical of all her deprivations was the absence of a bed. It was not that the cave was too small, it was simply that Tenzin Palmo did not want one. She intended to follow in the tradition of all serious meditators and train herself to do without sleep. According to the sages, sleep was nothing but a tragic waste of precious time. If we spent eight hours of every day asleep, that amounted to a third of our life which, they calculated, if we lived until we were seventy, added up to some twenty-four years of voluntary unconsciousness. Time which could be spent striving for spiritual betterment in order to help all living beings. Knowing this, the yogis disciplined themselves not to fall asleep but to use the refined levels of consciousness induced by meditation to bring about both mental and physical refreshment. It was agreed that the quietness and solitude of a cave was the perfect place to practice such a feat, for even the best of them would have been hard-put enduring sleeplessness while living in the midst of a busy town. But sitting up all night in their remote hideaways they learnt to see that whatever images arose from the subconscious, be they in the waking, semi-waking, or sleeping state (should they nod off), were nothing but projections, "mere appearances" from their own minds. It was, they said, an invaluable exercise.

In actuality this meant that for as long as Tenzin Palmo was in the cave she never fully lay down. Instead she spent the night, every night, sitting upright in her meditation box. "The idea is that you're meant to stay sitting up in order to meditate. It's good for the awareness," was all she would say on the matter. "If I really felt I had to I would curl up inside my meditation box, or flop my legs over the side."

And at such moments you wondered how much of Tenzin Palmo's capacity to endure these prolonged physical hardships was due to her unadorned childhood in the East End of London, her mother's stoical genes, or some innate predisposition for high-altitude cave dwelling—as the Tashi Jong lamas had recognized.

Not least of all her austerities was the isolation. As she had anticipated, even longed for, she was quite alone. Occasionally during the summer she would see a shepherd or yak herder. Sometimes the nuns from Tayul Gompa or a friend would visit for a day or two. Following the pattern she had established she would ensure that every year she saw Khamtrul Rinpoche for further guidance on her retreat. Very rarely she would leave for a few weeks to attend some teachings. But mostly she was completely by herself for months every year, cut off by the snows, and for the last three years she saw and spoke to literally no one.

Tenzin Palmo more than coped: "I was never lonely, not for a minute. It was nice if someone visited, but I was perfectly happy not seeing anybody. In that cave I felt completely safe. And that's a wonderful feeling for a woman to have. I never used to lock my door or window. There was no need. The cave was on the road to nowhere," she said. Interestingly, however, a male friend she lent the cave to once while she was away on a summer errand did not find the cave experience so easy. He left after two days, spooked by the solitude. "Me, I found it the easiest thing in the world," she said.

If human company was rare, animals were everywhere.

Any woman of fainter heart or flabbier backbone might well have been unnerved at the array of beasts which prowled around and even entered her cave. But Tenzin Palmo was never frightened of any animal and they, in turn, were never afraid of her. It was yet another unusual facet of an already unusual woman. "Animals are drawn to Tenzin Palmo—but what is interesting is that whereas usually, when there is that kind of attraction, the feeling is reciprocal, with Tenzin Palmo she is completely detached," commented Didi Contractor, the friend who had visited her cave when Tenzin Palmo first moved in.

"I like animals and I respect them but I am not St. Francis," Tenzin Palmo said crisply. Nevertheless, her encounters with the animals around her cave bore a strong resemblance to the tales told of the brown-robed friar in his cave in Assisi.

Like St. Francis, she too had her "brother wolves."

At night she could hear them on the roof above her head making their long, mournful sounds. They roamed around the mountains, looking for food, seeking their mate, baying at the moon. Tenzin Palmo, sitting in her cave, knew they were very close and did not stir an inch.

"I love wolves," she said simply. "For a long time I listened to them howling, which was wonderful. In the mornings after it had snowed I used to see their paw marks around the cave, but I never saw them. Then one day I was sitting outside on the patio, soaking up the sun, and five of them came by. They stood very close, just a few yards away. They were beautiful, not mangy or bedraggled as I had imagined. I thought they would look rather like jackals, but they were extremely handsome with those strange yellow eyes and sleek brown coats. They seemed very well fed, though heaven knows what they found up there to live on. They just stayed there and gazed at me very peacefully. I was so happy to see them. I smiled back and sent them lots of love. They stood there for a few minutes more and then left," she reported.

She also came close to encountering the rarest and most beautiful of the wild cats, the snow leopard. When Peter Mathiessen wrote his haunting book *The Snow Leopard* about this near mythic beast only two Westerners were ever thought to have seen one.

"I once saw its prints outside the cave and on the windowsill," Tenzin Palmo said, her voice rising with excitement at the memory. "There were these big pug marks, very strange, with a kind of hole in the middle. I drew it and later showed it to two zoologists and they both immediately said it was snow leopard, which apparently has a distinctive paw." While the elusive snow leopard might well have seen Tenzin Palmo, much to her sorrow she did not ever see it.

More exotic and enticing still was the completely bizarre set of footprints that she found one morning in the snow running along the boundary wall. She looked at them in puzzlement:

"Everyone says there are no bears in Lahoul but the first year that I was there I discovered these huge footprints outside the fence. They were much bigger than a man's but looked similar to a human's with an instep. You could see all the toes but they also had claws. It looked like a human print with claws. And these footprints came all the way down from the mountain and had got to where the boundary was and the creature was obviously very confused. I think this must have been its cave. You could see from the tracks the prints made, it was wandering around and then it went up again."

Could it possibly have been the mythical Yeti? Had Tenzin Palmo inadvertently moved into a Yeti's den?

"I don't know—I never saw the footprints again. But the Tibetans are familiar enough with the creature, whatever it is, to have a name for it, and tell stories about it. Lamas also talk about it so I don't see why it should not exist," she said. Further support for the actual existence of the Yeti came in 1997 when Agence France Press reported that "bigfoot" tracks had been found in Shennonjia National Nature Reserve, in Hubei province, by China's Researchers for Strange and Rare Creatures: "The head of the committee said a research team found hundreds of footprints 2,600 meters above sea level. The biggest footprint is thirty-seven centimeters long, very similar to that of a man but larger than that of a man's, and is different from the footprint of a bear or any other identified animals," the story read.

Much more familiar were the rodents—the same rodents that ate the cabbages and peas Tenzin Palmo attempted to grow in her garden. They came into her storeroom trying to get at her grains and dried vegetables and again Tenzin Palmo adopted a curiously friendly attitude toward these intruders.

"They were mostly mice and hamsters and in the autumn there were an awful lot of them. They were terribly sweet. Sometimes I used to trap them in a cage and then take them outside and let them go. It was very interesting watching them because each one you trapped had a different response," she said, hinting at the Buddhist belief that animals, since they possess minds, are subject to reincarnation like the rest of us. In this respect it was perfectly logical that animals could well be former or future human beings in the endless stream of becoming and unbecoming.

"Some of them were frightened and would cower in the corner of the cage. Others would be very angry and roar and try and rip the cage trying to get out. Others would put their little paws on the bars and push their noses through and look at you and allow you to pet them. They'd be so friendly. Each one had completely different reaction," she went on.

"Then there were the martens, which look a bit like weasels, only prettier. They were gray with a white front, huge eyes, and a big bushy tail. There was one that used to slide open the window, get inside my storeroom, and head for the saucepan which had my bread inside wrapped in a cloth. This marten would take off the saucepan lid, unwrap the cloth, and then eat the bread. It wasn't like a rat, which would just gnaw through the cloth. Then it would proceed to unscrew the plastic lids of the containers holding the fat, pull off the zinc covering, then eat it. It was amazing. Everything I had it would undo. I tried putting food outside for it but this would often get frozen and the marten would look so let down. I read somewhere that if you can catch one when they're young they make excellent pets because they're so intelligent."

Another visitor was the little stoat which she caught sight of in her garden. It was about to run away when it obviously thought better of it and bravely decided to approach Tenzin Palmo instead.

"It came trotting all the way up to me, stood there, and looked up. It was so small and I must have been enormous to it. It just stood there looking at me. Then it suddenly became excited. It ran back to the fence and began swinging on it, hanging upside down and looking at me all the time to see if I was still watching—like a child."

If the animals never frightened her, there was an occasion, just one, when man did. Then it seemed that her breezy optimism that no male would bother to climb that high to harm her was sadly misplaced.

"It was during a summer when a young boy about fifteen or sixteen years old came by with his flock of sheep. He was extremely strange. He would sit on this big boulder near the cave and look down on me. If I smiled at him he would just glare back. One morning I discovered the pole with my prayer flag on it had been thrown down. Another time the stones in my spring had been moved so the water no longer flowed. Then the window to my storeroom was smashed, although nothing had been taken. I was certain it was this boy and worried because he had an infinite amount of time to sit there thinking up mischief. He could do anything he wanted! I felt very vulnerable," she recalled.

She was so worried, in fact, that she called on her old friends the Dakinis, praying to them in her familiar way:

"Look here," she said, "this boy has obviously got a lot of psychological problems, so please do something to change his mind and help him," she prayed.

As usual, the Dakinis took up Tenzin Palmo's challenge.

"A couple of days later I found on my gate a bunch of wildflowers. Then when I went to my spring, not only had it been repaired but it had been put back together so much nicer. After that, when I saw the boy he gave me a nice smile. He was completely transformed. Dakinis are very powerful," she added.

And so Tenzin Palmo, the girl from Bethnal Green, learnt to live in her cave watching the seasons come and go. As the years went by life took on its own rhythms.

"In winter, which lasted from November to May, the blizzards made it particularly difficult. There would be these great big snowdrifts which I had to clear from above the cave with a shovel. That meant I had to walk through them. It was very physical work and not very good for the back. I had to throw the snow over the top of the cave. It took days sometimes. I would just finish and then it would snow again. I would do it over and over again. It had to be done for me to be able to get to my wood pile. The first snow was nice but after months and months of it I'd be saying 'Oh no, not again.'"

"The first signs that spring was on its way were these little rockflowers, very delicate, which would appear usually while it was still snowing. I could spend hours looking at them. Actually, spring was for me the most difficult time. The snow would thaw and come seeping through the cracks of the cave, flooding it. I could actually watch streams of water running down the walls soaking everything. I had sacks to mop it all up, which I would then have to dry and use again. I used to have to lay everything out in the sun to dry out. Even my meditation box, which was above the ground and lined with layers of cloth, would get damp. It was a real nuisance. You'd dry everything out, put it back, and then it would flood again. Outside, everything got really muddy. One of the questions which Khamtrul Rinpoche had asked me when he was vetting the cave was whether it was wet. I said no because I honestly thought it wasn't. If he had known how damp and musty it got he might never have agreed to let me live there," she conceded.

By the end of May Tenzin Palmo could begin to garden, planting her vegetables and flowers—cornflowers, marigolds, calendulas. She enjoyed gardening even though it demanded much fetching and carrying of water. For the last three years of her solitary retreat someone sent her a packet of flower seeds from England and much to her amazement they flourished in that foreign soil, transforming her Lahouli cave into a cottage garden.

"There were dahlias and night-scented stock. So beautiful! But I was the only one to see them," she said. By full summer the entire landscape had turned green—the fields, the valleys, and the willow trees planted by the Moravian missionaries to halt the erosion of the landslides. "Now, you could burn sitting in the sun while the part of you in the shade would still feel chilly," she said.

In summer the birds started coming back: the choughs, a red-legged crow, were regular visitors. She would watch them perform the beautiful aerial dances for which they are famous, and would sometimes cut pieces off a mat to provide nest furnishings for them. Once, one evening when she was coming back from a rare visit to the village, she came across an extraordinary scene.

"As I turned a corner I saw hundreds upon hundreds of vultures sitting in circles. They were grouped on the boulders, on the ground, all around. It was as though they had come together for a meeting. I had to walk through the middle of them! There was nowhere else for me to pass. Now these birds are big, about three feet high, with hooded eyes and strong, curved beaks. I took a deep breath, started saying the OM MANI PADME HUNG mantra, and walked right through them. They didn't even move. They just watched me out of the corner of their eyes. Later I remembered that Milarepa had had a dream in which he was a vulture and that among Tibetans these birds are regarded as extremely auspicious," she recalled.

With autumn the world around her was transformed into a blaze of brilliant color. It was spectacular. "The mountains in front of me turned blood-red crossed with lines of dazzling yellow—the willow trees whose leaves had turned. Above these were the snow mountains soaring into the bright blue sky. This was the time when the villagers would harvest their crops. I could hear them from my cave singing in the valleys below as they worked their yaks."

A letter home to her mother dated May 8, 1985, when she had just begun her long three-year retreat revealed how easily she was managing with her difficult situation, and how, despite her extreme isolation and singular way of life, others were not forgotten:

Dearest Amala [Tibetan for "mother"],

How are you? I hope that you are very well. Did you have a nice stay in Saudi?

No doubt you have written but Tshering Dorje hasn't been up so there has been no mail. He is rather late and I hope that this is only because of being busy with plowing and other field work. He did come up in early March, as the SP [Superintendent of Police] had brought new forms to be filled out for the visa. Fortunately this year there was not too much snow and February was so mild that most of the snow at that time had melted (it snowed again later, of course). However, poor Tshering Dorje has now developed arthritis in both knees and can only hobble around painfully with a stick—so imagine having to come all the way up to the cave through the snow just so I could sign some papers! He should have forged my signature. Anyway I do hope that his bad knees are not the reason for his not coming now. Lahaul is all up and down and also TD earns his living by leading trekking parties in Ladakh and Zanskar so this is really a big problem for him.

Here everything is well. This morning I planted out potatoes and more turnips. The weather is still rather cold and it snows from time to time but my cave is not as wet as usual because there was never a really heavy snowfall at one time. My water supply happily kept running all through the winter though it got covered in a canopy of ice every night. What a joy to have water so close by and not to have to bother with melting snow. This also saved on wood.

So the winter was quiet and pleasant and February so mild and gorgeous that in Keylong they had rain! (The weather made up for it in March and April!)

My hair is getting long and falling out all over the place. A great nuisance—no wonder the yogis just mat it.

Because of being in retreat and Tshering Dorje only coming up twice a year you must not worry if there are long intervals between my letters. I can no longer go down to Keylong to post them. Tell May that I wore her sweater (and yours) all winter and indeed still have them on. They have been very useful, so many thanks. Stay very well, All my love, Tenzin Palmo.

For all the physical hardships she endured, the misgivings of others, and the prejudice against her gender attempting such a feat, the truth remained that Tenzin Palmo in her cave was sublimely happy.

"There was nowhere else I wanted to be, nothing else I wanted be doing. Sometimes I would stand at the edge of my patio and look out across the mountains and think, 'If you could be any place in the whole world, where would you want to be?' And there was nowhere else. Being in the cave was completely satisfying. I had all the conditions I needed to practice. It was a unique opportunity and I was very, very grateful."

MOUNTAINS IN MY BLOOD

Ruskin Bond

It was while I was living in England, in the jostle and drizzle of London, that I remembered the Himalayas at their most vivid. I had grown up amongst those great blue and brown mountains; they had nourished my blood; and though I was separated from them by thousands of miles of ocean, plain, and desert, I could not rid them from my system. It was always the same with mountains. Once you have lived with them for any length of time, you belong to them. There is no escape.

And so, in London in March, the fog became a mountain mist, and the boom of traffic became the boom of the Ganges emerging from the foothills.

I remembered a little mountain path which led my restless feet into a cool, sweet forest of oak and rhododendron, and then on to the wind-swept crest of a naked hilltop. The hill was called Clouds End. It commanded a view of the plains on one side, and of the snow peaks on the other. Little silver rivers twisted across the valley below, where the rice fields formed a patchwork of emerald green. And on the hill itself, the wind made a *hoo-hoo-hoo* in the branches of the tall deodars where it found itself trapped.

During the rains, clouds enveloped the valley but left the hill alone, an island in the sky. Wild sorrel grew amongst the rocks, and there were many flowers—convolvulus, clover, wild begonia, dandelion—sprinkling the hillside.

On a spur of the hill stood the ruins of an old brewery. The roof had long since disappeared, and the rains had beaten the stone floors smooth and yellow. Some enterprising Englishman had spent a lifetime here making beer for his thirsty compatriots in the plains. Now, moss and ferns and maidenhair grew from the walls. In a hollow beneath a flight of worn stone steps, a wildcat had made its home. It was a beautiful gray creature, black-striped, with pale green eyes. Sometimes it watched me from the steps or the wall, but it never came near.

No one lived on the hill, except occasionally a coal burner in a temporary grass-thatched hut. But villagers used the path, grazing their sheep and cattle on the grassy slopes. Each cow or sheep had a bell suspended from its neck, to let the boy know of its whereabouts. The boy could then lie in the sun and eat wild strawberries without fear of losing his animals.

I remembered some of the shepherd boys and girls.

There was a boy who played a flute. Its rough, sweet, straightforward notes traveled clearly across the mountain air. He would greet me with a nod of his head, without taking the flute from his lips. There was a girl who was nearly always cutting grass for fodder. She wore heavy bangles on her feet, and long silver earrings. She did not speak much either, but she always had a wide grin on her face when she met me on the path. She used to sing to herself, or to the sheep, to the grass, or to the sickle in her hand.

And there was the boy who used to carry milk into town (a distance of about five miles), who would often fall into step with me, to hold a long conversation. He had never been away from the hills, or in a large city. He had never been on a train. I told him about the cities, and he told me about his village—how they make bread from maize, how fish were to be caught in the mountain streams, how the bears came to steal his father's pumpkins. Whenever the pumpkins were ripe, he told me, the bears would come and carry them off.

These things I remembered—these, and the smell of pine needles, the silver of oak leaves and the red of maple, the call of the Himalayan cuckoo, and the mist, like a wet facecloth, pressing against the hills.

Odd, how some little incident, some snatch of conversation, comes back to one again and again, in the most unlikely places. Standing in the aisle of a crowded tube train on a Monday morning, my nose tucked into the back page of someone else's newspaper, I suddenly had a vision of a bear making off with a ripe pumpkin.

A bear and a pumpkin—and there, between Goodge Street and Tottenham Court Road stations, all the smells and sounds of the Himalayas came rushing back to me.

LIFE

"What is it like to live with such beautiful mountains?" I once asked Vidhya earnestly.

She looked up, looked back at me, and laughed. "They're just there," she said.

A NIGHT IN A GARHWAL VILLAGE

Ruskin Bond

I wake to what sounds like the din of a factory buzzer, but is in fact the music of a single vociferous cicada in the lime tree near my window.

Through the open window, I focus on a pattern of small, glossy lime leaves; then through them I see the mountains, the Himalayas, striding away into an immensity of sky.

"In a thousand ages of the gods I could not tell thee of the glories of Himachal." So confessed a Sanskrit poet at the dawn of Indian history, and he came closer than anyone else to capturing the spell of the Himalayas. The sea has had Conrad and Stevenson and Masefield, but the mountains continue to defy the written word. We have climbed their highest peaks and crossed their most difficult passes, but still they keep their secrets and their reserve; they remain remote, mysterious, spirit-haunted.

No wonder, then, that the people who live on the mountain slopes in the mist-filled valleys of Garhwal have long since learned humility, patience, and a quiet resignation. Deep in the crouching mist lie their villages, while climbing the mountain slopes are forests of rhododendron, spruce and deodar, soughing in the wind from the ice-bound passes. Pale women plow and laugh at the thunder as their men go down to the plains for work, for little grows on the beautiful mountains in the north wind.

When I think of Manjari village in Garhwal I see a small river, a tributary of the Ganga, rushing along the bottom of a steep, rocky valley. On the banks of the river and on the terraced hills above, there are small fields of corn, barley, mustard, potatoes, and onions. A few fruit trees grow near the village. Some hillsides are rugged and bare, just masses of quartz or granite. On hills exposed to wind, only grass and small shrubs are able to obtain a foothold.

This landscape is typical of Garhwal, one of India's most northerly regions with its massive snow ranges bordering on Tibet. Although thinly populated, it does not provide much of a living for its people. Most Garhwali cultivators are poor—some are very poor. "You have beautiful scenery," I observed after crossing the first range of hills.

"Yes," said my friend, "but we cannot eat the scenery."

And yet these are cheerful people, sturdy and with wonderful powers of endurance. Somehow they manage to wrest a precarious living from the unhelpful, calcinated soil. I am their guest for a few days.

My friend Gajadhar has brought me to his home, to his village above the little Nayar River. We took a train into the foothills and then we took a bus and finally, made dizzy by the hairpin bends devised in the last century by a brilliantly diabolical road engineer, we alighted at the small hill station of Lansdowne, chief recruiting center for the Garhwal Regiment.

Lansdowne is just over 6,000 feet high. From there we walked, covering twenty-five miles between sunrise and sunset, until we came to Manjari village, clinging to the terraced slopes of a very proud, very permanent mountain.

And this is my fourth morning in the village.

Other mornings I was woken by the throaty chuckles of the red-billed blue magpies, as they glided between oak trees and medlars; but today the cicada has drowned all birdsong. It is a little out of season for cicadas but perhaps this sudden warm spell in late September has deceived him into thinking it is mating season again.

Early though it is, I am the last to get up. Gajadhar is exercising in the courtyard, going through an odd combination of Swedish exercises and yoga. He has a fine physique with the sturdy legs that most Garhwalis possess. I am sure he will realize his ambition of joining the Indian Army as a cadet. His younger brother Chakradhar, who is slim and fair with high cheekbones, is milking the family's buffalo. Normally, he would be on his long walk to school, five miles distant; but this is a holiday, so he can stay at home and help with the household chores.

His mother is lighting a fire. She is a handsome woman, even though her ears, weighed down by heavy silver earrings, have lost their natural shape. Garhwali women usually invest their savings in silver ornaments. And at the time of marriage it is the boy's parents who make a gift of land to the parents of an attractive girl—a dowry system in reverse.

There are fewer women than men in the hills and their good looks and sturdy physique give them considerable status among the menfolk.

Chakradhar's father is a corporal in the Indian Army and is away for most of the year.

When Gajadhar marries, his wife will stay in the village to help his mother and younger brother look after the fields, house, goats, and buffalo. Gajadhar will see her only when he comes home on leave. He prefers it that way; he does not think a simple hill girl should be exposed to the sophisticated temptations of the plains.

The village is far above the river and most of the fields depend on rainfall. But water must be fetched for cooking, washing, and drinking. And so, after a breakfast of hot sweet milk and thick chapattis stuffed with minced radish, the brothers and I set off down the rough track to the river.

The sun has climbed the mountains but it has yet to reach the narrow valley. We bathe in the river. Gajadhar and Chakradhar dive off a massive rock; but I wade in circumspectly, unfamiliar with the river's depths and currents. The water, a milky blue, has come from the melting snows; it is very cold. I bathe quickly and then dash for a strip of sand where a little sunshine has spilt down the mountainside in warm, golden pools of light. At the same time the song of the whistling thrush emerges like a dark secret from the wooded shadows.

A little later, buckets filled, we toil up the steep mountain. We must go by a better path this time if we are not to come tumbling down with our buckets of water. As we climb we are mocked by a barbet which sits high up in a spruce calling feverishly in its monotonous mournful way.

"We call it the mewli bird," says Gajadhar. "There is a story about it. People say that the souls of men who have suffered injuries in the law courts of the plains and who have died of their disappointments transmigrate into the mewli birds. That is why the birds are always crying *un-nee-ow*, *un-nee-ow*, which means 'injustice, injustice!'"

The path leads us past a primary school, a small temple, and a single shop in which it is possible to buy salt, soap and a few other necessities. It is also the post office. And today it is serving as a lock-up.

The villagers have apprehended a local thief, who specializes in stealing jewelery from women while they are working in the fields. He is awaiting escort to the Lansdowne police station, and the shop-keeper-cum-postmaster-cum-constable brings him out for us to inspect. He is a mild-looking fellow, clearly shy of the small crowd that has gathered round him. I wonder how he manages to deprive the strong hill women of their jewelery; it could not be by force! In any case, crimes of violence are rare in Garhwal; and robbery too, is uncommon, for the simple reason that there is very little to rob.

The thief is rather glad of my presence, as it distracts attention from him. Strangers seldom come to Manjari. The crowd leaves him, runs to me, eager to catch a glimpse of the stranger in its midst. The children exclaim, point at me with delight, chatter among themselves. I might be a visitor from another planet instead of just an itinerant writer . . .

The postman has yet to arrive. The mail is brought in relays from Lansdowne. The Manjari postman, who has to cover eight miles and delivers letters at several small villages on his route, should arrive around noon. He also serves as a newspaper, bringing the villagers news of the outside world. Over the years he has acquired a reputation for being highly inventive, sometimes creating his own news—so much so that when he told the villagers that men had landed on the moon, no one believed him. There are still a few skeptics.

Gajadhar has been walking out of the village every day, anxious to meet the postman. He is expecting a letter giving the results of his army entrance examination. If he is successful he will be called for an interview. And then, if he is accepted, he will be trained as an officer-cadet. After two years he will become a second lieutenant. His father, after twelve years in the army, is still only a corporal. But his father never went to school. There were no schools in the hills during the father's youth.

The Manjari school is only up to Class 5 and it has about forty pupils. If these children (most of them boys) want to study any further, then, like Chakradhar, they must walk the five miles to the high school in the next big village.

"Don't you get tired walking ten miles every day?" I ask Chakradhar.

"I am used to it," he says. "I like walking."

I know that he has only two meals a day—one at seven in the morning when he leaves home and the other at six or seven in the evening when he returns from school—and I ask him if he does not get hungry on the way.

"There is always the wild fruit," he replies.

It appears that he is an expert on wild fruit: the purple berries of the thorny bilberry bushes ripening in May and June; wild strawberries like drops of blood on the dark green monsoon grass; small sour cherries and tough medlars in the winter months. Chakradhar's strong teeth and probing tongue extract whatever tang or sweetness lies hidden in them. And in March there are the rhododendron flowers. His mother makes them into jam. But Chakradhar likes them as they are: he places the petals on his tongue and chews till the sweet juice trickles down his throat.

He has never been ill.

"But what happens when someone is ill?" I ask, knowing that in Manjari there are no medicines, no dispensary or hospital.

"He goes to bed until he is better," says Gajadhar. "We have a few home remedies. But if someone is very sick, we carry the person to the hospital at Lansdowne." He pauses as though wondering how much he should say, then shrugs and says: "Last year my uncle was very ill. He had a terrible pain in his stomach. For two days he cried out with the pain. So we made a litter and started out for Lansdowne. We had already carried him fifteen miles when he died. And then we had to carry him back again."

Some of the villages have dispensaries managed by compounders but the remoter areas of Garhwal are completely without medical aid. To the outsider, life in the Garhwal hills may seem idyllic and the people simple. But the Garhwali is far from being simple and his life is one long struggle, especially if he happens to be living in a high-altitude village snowbound for four months of the year, with cultivation coming to a standstill and people having to manage with the food gathered and stored during the summer months.

Fortunately, the clear mountain air and the simple diet keep the Garhwalis free from most diseases, and help them recover from the more common ailments. The greatest dangers come from unexpected disasters, such as an accident with an ax or scythe, or an attack by a wild animal. A few years back, several Manjari children and old women were killed by a man-eating leopard. The leopard was finally killed by the villagers who hunted it down with spears and axes. But the leopard that sometimes prowls round the village at night looking for a stray dog or goat slinks away at the approach of a human.

I do not see the leopard but at night I am woken by a rumbling and thumping on the roof. I wake Gajadhar and ask him what is happening.

"It is only a bear," he says.

"Is it trying to get in?"

"No, it's been in the cornfield and now it's after the pumpkins on the roof."

A little later, when we look out of the small window, we see a black bear making off like a thief in the night, a large pumpkin held securely to his chest.

At the approach of winter when snow covers the higher mountains the brown and black Himalayan bears descend to lower altitudes in search of food. Because they are short-sighted and suspicious of anything that moves, they can be dangerous; but, like most wild animals, they will avoid men if they can and are aggressive only when accompanied by their cubs.

Gajadhar advises me to run downhill if chased by a bear. He says that bears find it easier to run uphill than downhill.

I am not interested in being chased by a bear, but the following night Gajadhar and I stay up to try and prevent the bear from depleting his cornfield. We take up our position on a highway promontory of rock, which gives us a clear view of the moonlit field.

A little after midnight, the bear comes down to the edge of the field but he is suspicious and has probably smelt us. He is, however, hungry; and so, after standing up as high as possible on his hind legs and peering about to see if the field is empty, he comes cautiously out of the forest and makes his way toward the corn.

When about halfway, his attention is suddenly attracted by some Buddhist prayer flags which have been strung up recently between two small trees by a band of wandering Tibetans. On spotting the flags the bear gives a little grunt of disapproval and begins to move back into the forest; but the fluttering of the little flags is a puzzle that he feels he must make out (for a bear is one of the most inquisitive animals); so after a few backward steps, he again stops and watches them.

Not satisfied with this, he stands on his hind legs looking at the flags, first at one side and then at the other. Then seeing that they do not attack him and so not appear dangerous, he makes his way right up to the flags taking only two or three steps at a time and having a good look before each advance. Eventually, he moves confidently up to the flags and pulls them all down. Then, after careful examination of the flags, he moves into the field of corn.

But Gajadhar has decided that he is not going to lose any more corn, so he starts shouting, and the rest of the village wakes up and people come out of their houses beating drums and empty kerosene tins.

Deprived of his dinner, the bear makes off in a bad temper. He runs downhill and at a good speed too; and I am glad that I am not in his path just then. Uphill or downhill, an angry bear is best given a very wide berth.

For Gajadhar, impatient to know the result of his army entrance examination, the following day is a trial of his patience.

First, we hear that there has been a landslide and that the postman cannot reach us. Then we hear that although there has been a landslide, the postman has already passed the spot in safety. Another alarming rumor has it that the postman disappeared with the landslide. This is soon denied. The postman is safe. It was only the mailbag that disappeared.

And then, at two in the afternoon, the postman turns up. He tells us that there was indeed a landslide but that it took place on someone else's route. Apparently, a mischievous urchin who passed him on the way was responsible for all the rumors. But we suspect the postman of having something to do with them . . .

Gajadhar has passed his examination and will leave with me in the morning. We have to be up early in order to reach Lansdowne before dark. But Gajadhar's mother insists on celebrating her son's success by feasting her friends and neighbors. There is a partridge (a present from a neighbor who has decided that Gajadhar will make a fine husband for his daughter), and two chickens—rich fare for folk whose normal diet consists mostly of lentils, potatoes, and onions.

After dinner, there are songs, and Gajadhar's mother sings of the homesickness of those who are separated from their loved ones and their home in the hills. It is an old Garhwali folk song:

> Oh, mountain-swift, you are from my father's home;
> Speak, oh speak, in the courtyard of my parents,
> My mother will hear you; she will send my brother to fetch me.
> A grain of rice alone in the cooking pot cries,
> "I wish I could get out!"
> Likewise I wonder: "Will I ever reach my father's house?"

The hookah is passed round and stories are told. Tales of ghosts and demons mingle with legends of ancient kings and heroes. It is almost midnight by the time the last guest has gone. Chakradhar approaches me as I am about to retire for the night.

"Will you come again?" he asks.

"Yes, I'll come again," I reply. "If not next year, then the year after. How many years are left before you finish school?"

"Four."

"Four years. If you walk ten miles a day for four years, how many miles will that make?"

"Four thousand six hundred miles," says Chakradhar after a moment's thought, "but we have two months' holiday each year. That means I'll walk about 12,000 miles in four years."

The moon has not yet risen. Lanterns swing in the dark.

The lanterns flit silently over the hillside and go out one by one. This Garhwali day, which is just like any other day in the hills, slips quietly into the silence of the mountains.

I stretch myself out on my cot. Outside the small window the sky is brilliant with stars. As I close my eyes, someone brushes against the lime tree, brushing its leaves; and the fresh fragrance of limes comes to me on the night air, making the moment memorable for all time.

——◆——

THREE SPRINGS*

Jemima Diki Sherpa

When there are gatherings in our valley, the women sit with the women and the men sit with the men, and the children tear about evading adult arms that reach out to obstruct their fun. The men form a long line on low benches along the front wall of the house, patriarchs sitting at the end closest to the fireplace with the wide-legged weariness of aging masculinity, down through the established householders with their

* This essay, which first appeared on the writer's personal blog, was written after an avalanche in the Khumbu Icefall on Mount Everest killed sixteen local guides and porters.

roars of laughter, past the young fathers bouncing sticky toddlers on their laps, through the self-conscious new and prospective grooms, to the awkward youths who cram together and snicker and mutter and jostle each other.

Everyone wears down jackets.

In such a line as this, a gambler would have good odds that any man, picked at random, has stood atop Everest; chances better still that he has been partway up the mountain a dozen times only to return to Base Camp, collect another load, and head off to cross the treacherous icefall again. What elsewhere is extraordinary—the raw material that can be spun into charitable foundations, movie rights, pub boasts, and motivational speaking tours—is quotidian in the villages of Thame Valley. Even our monks shed their deep-red robes in spring and come back snow-burnt, the marks of sun goggles etched pale across their cheekbones and their lips chapped flaking white with bleeding crimson cracks.

When I finished high school and left Kathmandu for university in New Zealand, I was conditioned for the reactions my last name would elicit. "They ask how many kilos you can carry," says every Sherpa who has ever traveled abroad. But I was caught by a more common response: "Shuuurpa," in the muted antipodean accent, "Seriously? That's AWESOME!"

It is something to behold, the open-hearted enthusiasm that the Sherpa name elicits in the Western mind. It is (as every random company that has capitalized on it well knows) the branding mother lode—stimulating a vague positive association founded on six-odd decades of mountaineering myth-building. I wondered what deep, subconscious connections, what snippets of information, what flashes of imagery were being evoked.

"Awesome" how? I came to ask myself. More importantly, "awesome" for *whom*? Uncharitably, I imagined them imagining themselves as conquering heroes, assisted by a legion of faithful Sherpa ready—and cheerful—to lay down sweat and lives in service for arduous, but ultimately noble and glorious, personal successes. Still, it is undeniable that, in "post"-colonial democracies where ethnic minorities carry the burden of insidious and vicious prejudices at every turn, Sherpas are fortunate. Everyone loves us, everyone trusts us, and everyone wants their own collectable one of us. Internet listsicles call us "badass" and we have a very large, very coveted piece of real estate in our backyard. It is a stereotype, sure, but a *positive* one.

Any vague hopes my new acquaintances may have had of me self-lessly and singlehandedly lugging their furniture upstairs on moving days were swiftly dashed. I lived life some, and then meandered my way home more than half a decade later. Village-born though I was, and po-tato farmers and yak herders though my grandparents may have been, despite the yearly trips to the Khumbu homeland, I am a Kathmandu city girl. Like post-arts degree twenty-somethings the world over, I was adrift. With equal parts defeat, hope, terror, self-congratulation, and wildly under-informed plans and good intentions, I arrived "home" to live in Thame—elevation: 3,550 meters; population: *maybe* fifty people on a good day.

Village life. This should be amusing.

That was spring 2012, on the first of the Nepali year. It seemed a fit-ting day for a new chapter.

Two weeks later, a first cousin died on Everest.

Family circumstances were such that I hadn't seen him since we were both infants. My father and another cousin walked to Tengboche to at-tend the funeral. Grim-faced, they returned. He had a wife and a three-month-old baby, and the then-standard five-lakh (roughly US$5,000) payout for fatalities would not extend far past the death rites.

Morbidly, perhaps, I read a surprisingly long article on his death. His safety harness had not been clipped in, veteran Western (and *only* West-ern) climbers quoted by the half-dozen on the topic of Namgya's death. Overconfidence, the implication was, even though the quote hedged, "I wouldn't say it's because they are overconfident." *Strong Sherpa competi-tive spirit, intra-village rivalries.* "A bit complacent." *Sometimes novices just plain forget.* "These guys just pretty much dance across the ladders."

This was my first adult experience of the endless, repeating nature of death talk during the spring season. So-and-so, from village such-and-such, his cousin—no, married to her sister, my aunt's—it happened like this. He was such a good person. They say he fell into a crevasse. *Om mani padme hum.*

And then: "These boys, they go too fast. They hurry to get more work."

For a lifetime of mountaineering talk, I'd always tuned out. Nuptse and Lhotse get mixed up in my head, and I can never remember the elevations of things, or how many acclimatization nights there are before a summit, and every climbing company has a name that sounds the same—Adventure-something, Mountain-something.

But here was how it connected to life, to the cousin I barely knew, to other relatives I knew better who were still on the mountain. As a young high-altitude expedition worker, the more you carry, the more you are paid. There is a per-kilogram equation for payment, and there is value, both in hard cash and in securing future work, in proving you are good. If you prove you're good, you get hired next season, possibly recruited by one of the better companies, climbing literally up the mountain and figuratively up the ranks. The best way to do all this is to move fast and carry a lot. And the best way to do *that* is to dance, possibly unclipped, across the icefall ladders.

And yet. This one potential factor, this one whisper of motivation, the veteran mountaineers did not make mention of when the article posed the question "Why did Namgya skip a seemingly simple, and potentially life-saving, step?"

So it *must* have been that Sherpa competitive spirit.

Spring finishes. The potatoes have been planted. The summer fog rolls in, and Thamserku disappears into the mist for days on end. Summer finishes. In autumn I prove I am an exceedingly incompetent dilettante potato harvester. I have better luck interviewing people for an academic study; in a Namche coffeeshop, I approach a foreign climbing guide. He pretends to be cagey and worried about his name getting out there. I read him the consent form. Anonymity. You'll really just be a data point, I say curtly, and he looks a bit crushed. He rambles and makes grand pronouncements on how things should be run if anyone was thinking properly. Question 8.1: How satisfied are you in your job? Very satisfied. Question 8.4: Do you have plans besides guiding in the future? Maybe write a book about my experiences, he says. The Nepali guides I've asked speak of the lack of alternatives and the limitations of their bodies and their health: *Khai, tyeti bela nai bichar garnu parcha.* Or *Ke garne, aru bikalpa nai chaina.* Question 8.3: *Ajai kati barsa samma yo guiding kaam garnu huncha hola? Aba jati barsa samma jiu le saath dincha bhanumn na, bahini.*

Autumn finishes, and the winds grow colder. Mid-December we descend to Kathmandu. We aren't the only ones; people have trickled down from all the mountain areas, flowing into a river that swirls and swirls clockwise around Boudha in the winter sun.

Spring again, and a friend from university arrives with her boyfriend. I introduce them to Khukuri rum, and the next day of collecting flight tickets and packing for the mountains aches by for all of us. The air in Lukla is crisp, and we set off, arriving home the next day. I open up the house, and it is eerily undisturbed despite my aunt's visits. They have plenty of time and a trip to the lakes of Gokyo won't fill it all, so for days we sit around and read books and make coffee and listen to Kiwi reggae.

I'm bringing in some laundry when my cell phone rings. It's a friend from Kathmandu who works for an international news bureau—there's been a fight, have you heard, who do you know at Base Camp.

The Internet has gone mad. Links upon links, hundreds of comments, this one said, then he said, then he said, accusations, counter-accusations, updates, debates, threats, tantrums, analysis, They, Us. I read and I read.

Two aunts and a woman I don't know are weeding a field below ours. I go down and sit with them, and they break for tea out of a thermos and a huge pot of boiled potatoes, peeled with grit-stained hands and dipped in salt and chilli powder from a plastic bag. Did you hear about some fight? I ask, and they haven't. But an icefall doctor has died, originally from down in Solu, but married to so-and-so in her village, two daughters, *nyingje* . . .

My friends and I leave for Gokyo. I carry a pack of cards and along the trail I teach them how to play Callbreak, nabbing guides and porters to come and be our fourth player. Only a couple of hands in at a tiny lodge in Dole, the game is somehow taken over by trekking guides and I am left keeping score. It becomes a high-stakes game of champions—expert card counters with perfect dramatics. "On a king of hearts, and my . . . three of spades. *La kha ta.*" Uproar. The round finishes, and as the cards are shuffled some go out to take a leak. I ask—hey, this fight. The foreigners are pissed off apparently, have you heard . . . ? Nothing, but—the icefall doctor, I was in Lukla once and we stayed in the same place for two days, such a nice guy, good experience, but . . .

We reach Gokyo and the lodge owner, an aunt of a cousin, lets me use the Internet for free. The catch is I have to go to the unheated outside room, a maze of satellite phone wiring and solar batteries, where a creaking PC is connected via LAN cable to the router. I can see my breath.

Unread messages, most on the latest in the brawl circus. So-and-so's "expert" opinion that Sherpas are, as a culture, fundamentally incapable of violence; so-and-so's equally "expert" opinion that the jig is up, they've always been spoiled brutes. And then that phrase: The Sherpa Mob. I snort with laughter, and make Sherpa Mobster jokes on Twitter until the cold creeps up to my thighs from the concrete floor and my fingers begin to seize.

I go inside the dining room to warm up. Husband-of-aunt-of-cousin has heard something about an argument but no details, *khai*, someone must have done something to set someone off. But did you hear, Mingma, the icefall doctor . . . Was it two daughters or three?

The next day my friends and I trudge for what seems to be an eternity up the glacier to Gokyo's fifth lake. It's the best view of Everest, the lodge owners have assured us—better than from Kalapatthar. When it finally comes into view, Cho Oyu looms to our left as we face eastward—and there it is. Barren black rock, a rather bland dented triangle compared to the beautiful, dramatic ridges that surround it.

All of this, for that.

I see my friends off, and make my way back to Namche. I'm in a lodge kitchen, eating popcorn and listening to four men I don't know, one with wind and sunburn scabs so bad along his cheeks that they look like reptilian scales. They're fresh down from the climbing season and drinking cans of beer. I think of asking them about the fight, but one begins to talk about how a foreign climber—a woman, not his client—came upon a corpse on the mountain and began wailing and crying and wouldn't move. I had to grab her and shake her, he says, I had to yell at her—if you stop you will die, we'll all die right here, that one's gone already, let it go . . . The conversation moves on.

Spring finishes. The summer fog rolls in, and our elderly neighbors move their livestock up to the high pastures. They come down occasionally, bringing treats of fresh milk or yogurt or soft young cheese. Without their animals to feed our scraps to, I spend a lot of time reading about composting techniques. I have a month's work with a group of foreign students. A young Sherpa academic is with us for the first part of the journey. We stop for the night at her aunt's lodge. Her aunt rents horse rides to tourists. "She's saving any money she gets from that for an iPhone," she tells me, and we laugh. Later, as a moth flutters above the bed, I wonder what Namgyal might have been saving for. An iPhone costs what an iPhone costs, and so does a future for a baby daughter.

The group moves on, often the only foreigners on the trails in the summer mists. In one village we invite the women's savings and credit group to talk to them. A member laughs when she tells me how much they save each week. Their group savings really wouldn't go far up here, where inflation rises steeply every year. "Being in Sherpa culture has become too expensive in Khumbu," she says.

The students leave. I stay on, then later try to fly out from Lukla and get stuck in the fog for eight days before the plane arrives. In Kathmandu, the monsoon rains cease and summer finishes. I return in the autumn.

It is strange, trying to recall the last time you saw someone who lived, with such comforting regularity, at the periphery of your own life. My mind stubbornly insists that on the last day when my father and I were walking down toward Kathmandu for the winter, Au Tshiri called for us to come in for a cup of tea. But I know this may just be a trick of the brain, a composite of every other time he made that same invitation. In my memory, he's spinning a thread of yak wool through a spindle that dangles from his fingers, but again this may just be echoes from every other time I saw him, leaning in a sunny spot somewhere beside his house with the nasturtiums that grow up the front on strings that guide them, calling out to me, "When did you come? Where is your father?"

I try now to remember when in the last two years he began building the extension on his home, a retirement plan—a tea shop and bakery. But when exactly, spring or summer or autumn, it was that we got that sack of rice as a contribution to the build and my aunt went down to help with something—digging a trench for a cable, perhaps? It eludes me. It seemed as long as I could remember there had been the chipping of rocks, the digging of foundations, the laying of stone, the smell of fresh cement as I walked past, observing now a window has gone in, a wall is up, the roof . . . until my father and I stopped in on him one time as we passed—from where? The everyday things you don't make note of—and it was finished, neatly painted, and he was inside making a tray of lamps for an offering. I'll make tea, he said; this can wait—no, no, we replied, we'll come back another time.

It is spring again, and this year I am still in Kathmandu. The heat is stifling; I had forgotten what this time of the year is like here. And then, on Friday, the news comes in, the body counts, four, no six, no ten ... I call my father. I'm OK, he says in his measured, understated way, but things here are not good. Four from our Thame Valley, he says; I heard someone from Khumjung, and two from Pangboche. Au Tshiri went as well.

For a moment, I think I have misunderstood.

On Monday the cremations happen. It was a good day, says my father, very clear and none of the wind or rain that can make a cremation difficult. His sons were both there. The most auspicious spot was on the slope with the waterfall—you know the one. From there we could see the smoke from another cremation happening down-valley in Phurte. I guess another one was happening up-valley too, but not for the one in Yullajhung; they didn't find his body ...

I picture next year, at gatherings around Khumbu, when the women sit with the women and the men sit with the men, when the children dart about and pull faces at each other from behind their parent's backs, and the cups of tea are poured and served first to the patriarchs, then to the householders, down to the young fathers and husbands. In each line there will be gaps, like missing teeth—if remaining teeth could all shuffle forward, the way that the adolescents, now a little less awkward than last year, will move a little closer to the fire to fill the spaces of the ones that are missing.

———◆———

WHITE BEARERS
VIEWS OF THE DHAULADHAR*

Kirin Narayan

Before I ever saw the Himalayas, I knew them from my grandmother's cupboards. In her home in Nasik where my family visited from Bombay

* Snapshots of life in Kangra, Himachal Pradesh, from the 1970s to the early 2000s.

each vacation, Ba had two large cupboards—a wooden one with a mirror on the front, and beside it a gray steel Godrej safe. Neither contained her clothes, which were always folded up in khaki-covered suitcases under her bed. Instead, both cupboards were stocked with memorabilia from her spiritual quests. Ba could not read, but she liked to boast that in her cupboard she had locked up sacred texts: all four Vedas, the Gita, several Puranas too! On the exciting occasions that Ba brandished keys in the presence of grandchildren, her cupboards swung open with a scent of camphor and saffron. Inside there were indeed holy books, some covered in brown wrapping paper. Also there were khaki cloth bags or silver *thalis* containing packets of ashy *vibbooti*, red kumkum, dried flowers, twisted roots, sugar balls, tiny tridents, rudraksha seeds of rare shapes. There was bright cloth that had been offered in temples, then returned: red and green with gold fringes, or gauzy yellow edged in silver. There were postcards and pamphlets, and framed pictures of different deities. The powers of pilgrimage places from Rameshwaram in South India to Badrinath, Kedarnath, and Gangotri in the northern reaches of the mountains were lodged in these cupboards.

White sari pulled over white hair, slim strong arms extending in grand gestures, Ba told of different gods and goddesses she had sought out at these places and the blessings they had granted her. When she spoke of the Himalayas, she told of arduous hikes, ice *lingams*, glaciers feeding sacred rivers. All around her, as she spoke, were framed god posters with strands of tiny electric lights looped around them. I recognized the Himalayas from Ba's cupboards immediately—behind Shiva Bhagavan! The goddesses Lakshmi and Saraswati, seated in their respective lotuses, had lakes and forests stretching around them; the goddess Durga rode her prancing tiger in what seemed to be the stainless sky. Blue-gray Shiva sat cross-legged, lost in meditation. A cobra was wrapped around his neck, a sickle moon beamed from his forehead, and ice-capped peaks rose around him.

In 1975, when I was fifteen years old, my American mother decided to take up a long-standing invitation from family friends who had a summer home in Kangra, Himachal Pradesh. My parents had separated the previous year, and all my elder siblings had gone off to college in America. My mother and I were rootless, having left our home in Bombay; we were glad for the temporary grounding of a summer invitation. We took the long train trip north in April heat. In Pathankot, we hired a cycle rickshaw to carry our luggage into a chaotic bus yard. The bus up to Kangra was jammed. The seats were hard and narrow, the windows so dusty that you had to peer through them to see out. The bus engine strained as we began our ascent, plains dust settling. The air thinned and cooled, green fields and forests opened out, and suddenly, like specters that just might be unusually shaped clouds, there were mountains.

The Dhauladhar or "white-bearing" range of the western Himalayas rises at a northeastern angle above Kangra valley. The mountains are mostly about 15,000 feet, with the highest peaks at 21,000. The valley, lush and patched with fields, follows the base of the mountains for more than twenty miles at roughly 3,500 feet. Looking up from the valley, the mountains are a stunning presence of green slopes rising to granite and ice. In April, before the summer heat and rains, the mountains were still frosted white like a line-up of opulent birthday cakes.

The friends we had come across India to visit were Sardar Gurcharan Singh and his wife Chattar. They usually lived in Delhi, but for the summer they often lived in a Kangra village. They had a home here on account of Norah Richards, an Irish actress and Indian nationalist who had lived in this village for many decades, carving up her enormous estate into land for landless "untouchables," for her old students from Lahore, and for city artists to retreat to. Sardar Gurcharan Singh was one of the few artists who had actually built on the land he had received from Norah.

Like everyone else, my mother and I addressed the Singhs as "Sardar Sahib" and "Mummy." They had known each other since they were teenagers, and even in their old age, they had a sparkle in each other's presence. Sardar Sahib and Mummy lived downstairs, and they gave us their upstairs room. The room had a low ceiling and shuttered windows that opened out over the fields toward the mountains. On the hedges between fields were wild roses, jasmine, and honeysuckle.

Sardar Sahib had studied Japanese art pottery in the 1920s, then had established a pottery outlet in Delhi, and soon his "Delhi Blue" pieces were sought after for upper-class Indian homes. In this village setting, we ate off plates with white and gray glazes, drank coffee or tea from distinctive mugs of different shapes, sizes, and colors, and were served water from a jug of the most vibrant deep blue. Our meals and tea breaks were invariably accompanied by Sardar Sahib's vigorous laugh as he told stories. He told stories of the great Kangra earthquake of 1905 that he had felt tremors from as a child in Lahore; miracles of the Sikh Gurus; the adventures of his grandchildren in England. Soon after we arrived, my mother and I were folded into his stories: attending a local feast, we were ushered into an inner room where women were crowded on a charpoi. My mother sat down too, and the bed crashed to the floor, taking all the women down with it. Sardar Sahib collapsed with laughter whenever he told this tale, throwing back his turbaned head, his bristling long beard rising slightly off his chest. He regularly offered to bring my mother a sample of the milk-sweet purported to be so libidinally energizing it is called *palang-tod*, "bed-smasher." Mummy Singh, who had perfect teeth and a naughty smile, giggled at his side.

I unpacked my books over a makeshift desk raised off the floor upstairs, and began studying each day for the school-leaving exams I would take that December. As the summer progressed, white clouds steamed up above the melting snow on the mountains. Fleshy white gardenias bloomed in the garden. During the day, we spread out our clothes to dry on the gardenia bushes. At night, Sardar Sahib walked back and forth on the pale ribbon of cement path, chanting in the darkness from the Guru Granth Sahib. On a full-moon night, his beard caught the white of the glaciers and the flowers. When there was no moon, the Milky Way clotted the sky, outlined darkly at one side with mountains. Mummy sometimes walked in the night too, chanting under her breath. She wore tight white churidars around her sturdy calves, and white netted dupattas over her shoulders. The irises of her kohl-rimmed eyes shone when they caught the light.

Sardar Sahib took us around to visit various friends, cautioning them all before they offered seats to my mother. Some were locals, like Masterji, a squat schoolteacher who worked long hours amid tin cans of rare flowers in his garden, and spoke English with a wheeze, or Shastriji, the lanky Sanskrit teacher who was renting rooms in Masterji's huge family house, and whose bed my mother had broken. Also, we visited local residents who originally had come from elsewhere.

Norah Richards, the key outsider in transforming the social life of this village, had died several years ago at a grand old age. Her house was still standing, though, a maze of adobe that echoed with stories of her giant hearing aid, her megaphone for summoning servants, her generosity, her politics, her dietary fads. Visiting the abandoned house, I felt a latecomer, shut out from a legendary era.

One of Sardar Sahib's good friends who often spoke of Norah was the painter from Punjab, Sardar Sobha Singh, who lived across the village by the main road. "GROW MORE GOOD," exhorted raised cement lettering on the outer wall of his house. Sobha Singh had flowing white locks, which he wore without a turban. He only wore white kurta pajamas and white shoes, one of which was a platform shoe because of polio. All day he sat painting at an easel set beside his bed. The finished paintings were exhibited in the room beside him, and poster reproductions of a few favorites were sold to visitors or local people who aspired to middle-class sitting-room decor. The gallery included paintings of Sikh gurus, and scenes from Punjabi folklore, like Heer standing at the door before Ranjha, or Soni swooning beside Mehwal. A popular painting was of "Her Majesty the Gaddin," a pretty pastoralist Gaddi woman wearing a headscarf with a lamb in her arms. There was also a painting of Norah Richards herself, looking out in a regal and mildly disapproving way at the bright acrylics featured on the walls around her. For me, her beaked nose and white ringlets conjured up Miss Havisham from the Dickens novel on my desk.

While fuzzy birds in uncannily acrylic colors hopped and twittered in the aviary outside, Sobha Singh beamed, urging us to "take coffee" brought in on a tray with Milkmaid condensed milk. "For toffee," he said, pulling out a five-rupee note occasionally from the pocket of his kurta and handing it to me. Though I did not consider myself a child anymore, it overwhelmed me to be noticed.

Just down the road from Sobha Singh lived Mangat Ram. Mangat Ram also only wore white kurta pajamas. His white hair was cropped close to his head, and he wore thick black-rimmed glasses over a kind face bleached with white patches of leukoderma. In his small house, he had many musical instruments—sitar, tablas, harmonium, tanpura—and he played them all. I sensed that unlike Sobha Singh, who had his own ambassador car and was surrounded by soft luxury, Mangat Ram was struggling financially like my mother and me. He walked everywhere with a white *jhola* over his shoulder. He even walked to the shop one kilometer away to collect the daily paper. In his front room, Mangat Ram would chat with my mother and Sardar Sahib as I looked on restlessly, wishing there were more books on the shelf to eye. Starved for diversion, I was endlessly delighted when kind Mangat Ram once described a Quaker missionary my mother knew as a "Quacker." I repeated this so often that now when I see images of Donald Duck, I think of Quakers.

Everyone was waiting for the Sanyals to arrive from Delhi. They came later in the summer, and their house up the hill near Norah's was opened and aired. B. C. Sanyal was well known for his sculpture, his paintings, his drawings, and his association with the Lalit Kala Akademi for artists. He had frizzy black eyes, curling black brows, a mischievous punning wit, and a gray beard that he parted in the middle with the minute precision of George Bernard Shaw. Mrs. Sanyal, who taught English at a prestigious Delhi school, chewed paan, exchanged Iris Murdoch novels with my mother, and made memorably exquisite dishes. Sanyal Sahib was usually upstairs, painting on an open-air porch that faced the mountains. It seemed a long time before we trooped up to see his oils, watercolors, and pastels of village women clustered together, ironic self-portraits, jeweled green rice fields, and, inevitably, mountains.

For me, being fifteen amid so many old people was a challenge. They had all the dignity, gravity, and sure humor of seasoned lives, while I was a self-conscious adolescent without a stable home, whose thin skin was continually, painfully erupting. Each morning, I methodically reviewed every subject I would be examined on. In the hot, still afternoons, I walked to the main settlement of the village to Shastriji for help with my Hindi grammar, which had been hopelessly tainted by a Bombay upbringing. Shastriji's daughter Vidhya, tall and lanky like him, with close-set dancing eyes, became my friend, the only friend my age. Some evenings we went to the stream to do laundry or sat at the deserted schoolhouse exchanging confidences. Otherwise, if I was bored with studying, I watched swallows swoop under the eaves. I read my way through all the novels on the shelves, including the Mills and Boons that were Mummy Singh's favorites. The shelves also had art books. I feasted my eyes on the reproductions of Kangra miniature paintings from the seventeenth and early eighteenth centuries, with their romantic scenes of beautiful women waiting for their lovers or setting off on a tryst with Krishna. The flowering trees, bushes, open pastures, curving streams, carved doorways, arched windows were uncannily familiar, echoing our surroundings. I found it odd, though, that the paintings never seemed to feature the Dhauladhar mountains. Sardar Sahib laughed, saying that Krishna had lived in Brindavan, where there were just hills.

"What is it like to live with such beautiful mountains?" I once asked Vidhya earnestly.

She looked up, looked back at me and laughed. "They're just there," she said. "We go about all the work we have to do and we don't even notice them."

I was startled by what Vidhya said, gathering up her family's laundry by the stream. Was she joking or could she really mean it? Staring out of the window from my desk, I learned how each mountain in the Dhauladhar range had its own character, its ridges and shades of white. I longed to know the stories of the mountains, to imagine happenings on those high peaks. If faraway Ba could tell stories of such mountains why couldn't people up close do the same? Yet whenever I asked for stories or names, nobody could answer me. The only mountain that seemed to have its own distinctive personality to the people around me was Parvati's peak. Parvati, from *parvat*, mountains: the daughter of the mountains, and Shiva's wife. As the rains came and snow melted, making new patterns of glaciers and rock, it sometimes seemed to me, looking up from my desk, that Parvati's mountain carried the features of a serene, smiling goddess.

In 1976, we returned for another summer and in 1978 my mother arranged to rent a house up the hill from where Sardar Sahib lived. By 1980, when I had encountered anthropology in college, my curiosity about the lives of village people around us began to jostle against my shyness. Vidhya had married, but luckily only one village away, and she remained my emotional mainstay for daily visits and cups of tea. I began to drop in on other homes where my mother had ties, to sometimes write down the songs that women sang. Partly because of my Kangra experience, I became an anthropologist. A decade later as a young faculty member, I returned for a year to work on women's songs and stories.

The dialect spoken in Kangra is termed "Pahari" or "of the mountains" by local people, though linguists would call it Kangri. It is a sweet language full of "u" sounds: "here" is *ithu*, "there" is *thithu*, and "a little cup for a child" a *kappu*. In the songs that women sang, mountains very rarely appeared since the focus was on goings-on in the joint family, rather than on scenery.

Yet wedding songs implored fathers not to give their daughters to the high and distant slopes, and ballads begged husbands not to leave wives alone in such desolate places. Here is one of the earliest songs I wrote down in a careful Devanagari script that could not quite capture the nuances of the dialect, from a young woman called Bubbly.

> The splashing rain scares me.
> On mountain slopes, pine trees reach out to scratch me.
> I don't want to be alone, take me with you,
> The splashing rain scares me.
> How can I cut fodder when insects bite me?
> When I go to fetch water, thorns scratch my feet.
> Just look at the ravine where I draw water, look at the blisters on
>   my feet.
> Take me along with you, my darling.
> I don't want to be alone, take me with you.
> The splashing rain scares me.
> The lightning crackles, teasing me,
> The herdsmen on the mountains see me and laugh,
> Just look at the leaks in the roof, look at the dung I plaster with!
> Take me with you, my darling.
> I don't want to be alone, take me with you.
> The splashing rain scares me.

Back in the Madison library, reading about Gaddi shepherds who travel with their flocks across the northern wall of the Dhauladhar between Kangra and the next valley of Chamba, I once came across another memorable song about mountains. Like the songs I had heard from Kangra village women, this wedding song also described a bride's longing for the home of her parents when she was married off to a man from a distant village.

> O mother Dhauladhar,
> Bend a little,
> O bend a little,
> On this side lies my mother-in-law's place,

On the other side lies my father's home,
Bend a little, O bend a little.
On the marriage day in a palanquin
My brother gave me a farewell
"Bathe in milk. Blossom in sons."
My brother's wife blessed me,
My mother gave me tears,
Bend a little,
So that I may see
My parents' home.*

It was this song that vividly underlined to me that even as we looked
north at the Dhauladhar from Kangra—mountains rising up as though
at the edge of the world—surely there were also other valleys, like
Chamba, where people looked south at the same range.

In 1994, my mother could no longer stand living in her rented house
with dank foundations, no running water, and a hillside's icy shadow in
the winter months. She moved to a sun-drenched space nearer the foot
of the mountains, where her Austrian doctor friend runs a charitable
clinic. In this village, we encountered new sorts of people: settlements
of Nepalis who had settled there after the Gurkha invasion of 1805, and
also Gaddis who no longer herded their huge flocks of sheep on annual
migrations. One Gaddi Brahmin who had previously worked in the
slate mine became my mother's head workman in the building of her
new adobe house. Pritam was a lanky, narrow-faced man in his early
forties, with a gentle, courtly manner. He always wore a Kulu cap tight
over his forehead, and he seemed to know everyone in the village.

Coming to visit my mother in her new home, I missed the mountains as I had known them. Seen up close, from their base, they were
no longer familiar. I missed my friends from the old village, missed the
solitude of the open pasture behind my mother's old house, where one
looked out at a long flank of mountains across the horizon. At the same
time, being realigned in relation to the mountains brought different
angles of insight into people's lives.

From Pritam, I began to learn some of the lore of Gaddis, whose
wanderings take them into steep pastures and over high passes. Of

* V. Verma, *Gaddis of Dhauladhar: A Transhumant Tribe of the Himalayas* (New Delhi:
Indus Publishing Company, 1996), pp. 97–98.

course, the hills and mountains had names, Pritam said, delighted by my question. We were driving in a van back from Chamba, and he began to point out peaks. In fact, didn't I know that the hill on which my mother's house was located was part of the domain of the serpent deity, Pakhalu Nag? Indru Nag, who controlled rain, was over on that other hill; Bhagsu Nag lived farther up beyond Dharamsala, and his maternal uncle protected Dal Lake.

Pritam's family had originally lived in Brahmaur, in Chamba district, which lies across the Dhauladhar range to the north of Kangra. Pritam's forefathers were hereditary mediums for the serpent god, Pakhalu Nag. When Pritam's great-grandfather migrated over the mountains from Chamba, he brought the deity's *sangal*, or iron rods associated with possession, with him. En route, he threw the heavy rods into a river: "If you have energy (*shakti*), carry yourself!" he said. Later, when the family had arrived at their new home in Kangra, he shook his hand, and the iron chains came in.

At first, the temple for Pakhalu Nag was built higher up on a different hill, called Kabrutu. The family lived there and would only come down to live nearer their fields at harvest. Later, they moved down near their fields, and Pritam's father had a dream: "No one looks after me," the serpent god said, "bring me down." Following this dream, Pritam's father took up a collection from the villagers, and a temple was built on the Toral hill. The stone image of the serpent god with the features of a human being was made in the nearby army cantonment town.

Under Pritam's guidance, I once went to worship this serpent god. We ordered new clothes—an orange shirt and a turban—to be stitched for him by the roadside tailor (who, Pritam assured us, knew the measurements of all the local gods). The silversmith down the road made a small silver snake that would be present at the puja and then go home with me. One monsoon morning as mists blew off the higher mountains, and the water in the ravine tumbled and foamed, I sat cross-legged in the company of a village Pandit and Pritam by a fire, making offerings to the snake god inside, as a huddle of local children and a few fidgety goats looked on.

When Ma and I first visited Kangra, electricity was unreliable. In the monsoon, buses would pull up before fast-rushing streams, and one

would have to wade across and walk the rest of the way to one's destination. There was one phone in the village. At night, satellites blinked
their way across the star-clotted sky. Visiting from graduate school in
the 1980s, it was hard to imagine this quiet valley connecting to the
rush of freeways and the barrage of communication that framed the
rest of my life.

As I write in 2001, my mother, in her new village, has just been
hooked up to e-mail, and messages fly in from her most mornings. She
has reliable electricity now, which can be a nuisance when neighbors
across the way crank up their television as they boil morning tea. Old
adobe houses are being abandoned and new cement ones, with satellite dishes like reclining umbrellas, spring up where there were once
open fields. Everywhere there are tall stacks of bricks or of split river
rocks that people intend to use for their flat-roofed pukka homes. With
tourism having declined in Kashmir, there are more ostentatious hotels
built across the valley; planes fly in to an airstrip each week, and Maruti
taxi vans go honking their way along the winding roads. One tourist
place advertises an "Unavailable Bar," which my curious mother could
not resist investigating: it turns out that the bar carried rare imported
liquor. Some of the local people I have known for all these years like all
these changes, saying that now more things are available; others lament
that the wisdom from the past is being forgotten.

The old people have moved onward: Ba, Sardar Sahib, Mummy,
Masterji, Sobha Singh, Mangat Ram, all gone as Norah had gone before them. I imagine them lifting up from the tops of their heads, leaving the pupa of old bodies behind to soar higher than the Dhauladhar
and merge with the sky. Sanyal remains an embodied inspiration: he
just turned a hundred years old in March 2001, and he is still drawing.

On my wall in Madison, I have a precious watercolor of Sanyal's in
which monsoon clouds rise over fields, partially obscuring the Dhauladhar. Just as Vidhya once observed that mountains merged into the
background, I too often do not see the picture in the rush and scramble of my own routines. When I do stop and really notice this painting,
the Himalayas rise up momentarily in Midwestern America. Rugged
snow peaks with idiosyncratic characters, grand white-bearing people
looking out over shifting horizons—both stand tall inside me.

FRIENDS IN PRISON*

Jawaharlal Nehru

For fourteen and a half months I lived in my little cell or room in the Dehra Dun Jail, and I began to feel as if I was almost a part of it. I was familiar with every bit of it; I knew every mark and dent on the whitewashed walls and on the uneven floor and the ceiling with its moth-eaten rafters. In the little yard outside I greeted little tufts of grass and odd bits of stone as old friends. I was not alone in my cell, for several colonies of wasps and hornets lived there, and many lizards found a home behind the rafters, emerging in the evenings in search of prey. If thoughts and emotions leave their traces behind in the physical surroundings, the very air of that cell must be thick with them, and they must cling to every object in that little space.

I had had better cells in other prisons, but in Dehra Dun I had one privilege which was very precious to me. The jail proper was a very small one, and we were kept in an old lock-up outside the jail walls, but within the jail compound. This place was so small that there was no room to walk about in it, and so we were allowed, morning and even-ing, to go out and walk up and down in front of the gate, a distance of about a hundred yards. We remained in the jail compound, but this coming outside the walls gave us a view of the mountains and the fields and a public road at some distance. This was not a special privi-lege for me; it was common for all the A and B Class prisoners kept at Dehra Dun. Within the compound, but outside the jail walls, there was another small building called the European Lock-Up. This had no enclosing wall, and a person inside the cell could have a fine view of the mountains and the life outside. European convicts and others kept here were also allowed to walk in front of the jail gate every morning and evening.

* A poignant excerpt from *Toward Freedom: The Autobiography of Jawaharlal Nehru* (1941).

Only a prisoner who has been confined for long behind high walls can appreciate the extraordinary psychological value of these outside walks and open views. I loved these outings, and I did not give them up even during the monsoon, when the rain came down for days in torrents and I had to walk in ankle-deep water. I would have welcomed the outing in any place, but the sight of the towering Himalayas nearby was an added joy which went a long way to removing the weariness of prison. It was my good fortune that during the long period when I had no interviews, and when for many months I was quite alone, I could gaze at these mountains that I loved. I could not see the mountains from my cell, but my mind was full of them and I was ever conscious of their nearness, and a secret intimacy seemed to grow between us.

> Flocks of birds have flown high and away;
> A solitary drift of cloud, too, has gone, wandering on.
> And I sit alone with Ching-ting Peak, towering beyond;
> We never grow tired of each other, the mountain and I.

I am afraid I cannot say with the poet, Li T'ai Po, that I never grew weary, even of the mountain; but that was a rare experience, and, as a rule, I found great comfort in its proximity. Its solidity and imperturbability looked down upon me with the wisdom of a million years, and mocked at my varying humors and soothed my fevered mind.

Spring was very pleasant in Dehra, and it was a far longer one than in the plains below. The winter had denuded almost all the trees of their leaves, and they stood naked and bare. Even four magnificent peepal trees, which stood in front of the jail gate, much to my surprise, dropped nearly all their leaves. Gaunt and cheerless they stood there, till the spring air warmed them up again and sent a message of life to their innermost cells. Suddenly there was a stir both in the peepals and the other trees, and an air of mystery surrounded them as of secret operations going on behind the scenes; and I would be startled to find little bits of green peeping out all over them. It was a gay and cheering sight. And then, very rapidly, the leaves would come out in their millions and glisten in the sunlight and play about in the breeze. How wonderful is the sudden change from bud to leaf!

I had never noticed before that fresh mango leaves are reddish-brown, russet colored, remarkably like the autumn tints on the Kashmir hills. But they change color soon and become green.

The monsoon rains were always welcome, for they ended the summer heat. But one could have too much of a good thing, and Dehra Dun is one of the favored haunts of the rain god. Within the first five or six weeks of the break of the monsoon we would have about fifty or sixty inches of rain, and it was not pleasant to sit cooped up in a little narrow place trying to avoid the water dripping from the ceiling or rushing in from the windows.

Autumn again was pleasant, and so was the winter, except when it rained. With thunder and rain and piercing cold winds, one longed for a decent habitation and a little warmth and comfort. Occasionally there would be a hailstorm, with hailstones bigger than marbles coming down on the corrugated iron roofs and making a tremendous noise, something like an artillery bombardment.

I remember one day particularly; it was the 24th of December, 1932. There was a thunderstorm and rain all day, and it was bitterly cold. Altogether it was one of the most miserable days, from the bodily point of view, that I have spent in jail. In the evening it cleared up suddenly, and all my misery departed when I saw all the neighboring mountains and hills covered with a thick mantle of snow. The next day—Christmas Day—was lovely and clear, and there was a beautiful view of snow-covered mountains.

Prevented from indulging in normal activities, we became more observant of nature's ways. We watched also the various animals and insects that came our way. As I grew more observant I noticed all manner of insects living in my cell or in the little yard outside. I realized that while I complained of loneliness, that yard, which seemed empty and deserted, was teeming with life. All these creeping or crawling or flying insects lived their life without interfering with me in any way, and I saw no reason why I should interfere with them. But there was continuous war between me and bedbugs, mosquitoes, and, to some extent, flies. Wasps and hornets I tolerated, and there were hundreds of them in my cell. There had been a little tiff between us when, inadvertently I think, a wasp had stung me. In my anger I tried to exterminate the lot, but they put up a brave fight in defense of their temporary home, which probably contained their eggs, and I desisted and decided to leave them in peace if they did not interfere with me anymore. For over a year after that I lived in that cell surrounded by these wasps and hornets, and they never attacked me, and we respected each other.

Bats I did not like, but I had to endure them. They flew soundlessly in the evening dusk, and one could just see them against the darkening sky. Eerie things; I had a horror of them. They seemed to pass within an inch of one's face, and I was always afraid that they might hit me. Higher up in the air passed the big bats, the flying foxes.

I used to watch the ants and the white ants and other insects by the hour. And the lizards as they crept about in the evenings and stalked their prey and chased each other, wagging their tails in a most comic fashion. Ordinarily they avoided wasps, but twice I saw them stalk them with enormous care and seize them from the front. I do not know if this avoidance of the sting was intentional or accidental.

Then there were squirrels, crowds of them if trees were about. They would become very venturesome and come right near us. In Lucknow Jail I used to sit reading almost without moving for considerable periods, and a squirrel would climb up my leg and sit on my knee and have a look around. And then it would look into my eyes and realize that I was not a tree or whatever it had taken me for. Fear would disable it for a moment, and then it would scamper away. Little baby squirrels would sometimes fall down from the trees. The mother would come after them, roll them up into a little ball, and carry them off to safety. Occasionally the baby got lost. One of my companions picked up three of these lost baby squirrels and looked after them. They were so tiny that it was a problem how to feed them. The problem was, however, solved rather ingeniously. A fountain-pen filler, with a little cotton wool attached to it, made an efficient feeding bottle.

Pigeons abounded in all the jails I went to, except in the mountain prison of Almora. There were thousands of them, and in the evenings the sky would be thick with them. Sometimes the jail officials would shoot them down and feed on them. There were mainas, of course; they are to be found everywhere. A pair of them nested over my cell door in Dehra Dun, and I used to feed them. They grew quite tame, and if there was any delay in their morning or evening meal they would sit quite near me and loudly demand their food. It was amusing to watch their signs and listen to their impatient cries.

In Naini there were thousands of parrots, and large numbers of them lived in the crevices of my barrack walls. Their courtship and love-making was always a fascinating sight, and sometimes there were fierce quarrels between two male parrots over a lady parrot, who sat calmly by waiting for the result of the encounter and ready to grant her favors to the winner.

Dehra Dun had a variety of birds, and there was a regular jumble of singing and lively chattering and twittering, and high above it all came the koel's plaintive call. During the monsoon and just before it the brain-fever bird visited us, and I realized soon why it was so named. It was amazing the persistence with which it went on repeating the same notes, in daytime and at night, in sunshine and in pouring rain. We could not see most of these birds; we could only hear them as a rule, as there were no trees in our little yard. But I used to watch the eagles and the kites gliding gracefully high up in the air, sometimes swooping down and then allowing themselves to be carried up by a current of air. Often a horde of wild ducks would fly over our heads.

There was a large colony of monkeys in Bareilly Jail and their antics were always worth watching. One incident impressed me. A baby monkey managed to come down into our barrack enclosure and he could not mount up the wall again. The warder and some convict overseers and other prisoners caught hold of him and tied a bit of string round his neck. The parents (presumably) of the little one saw all this from the top of the high wall, and their anger grew. Suddenly one of them, a huge monkey, jumped down and charged almost right into the crowd which surrounded the baby monkey. It was an extraordinarily brave thing to do, for the warder and COs had sticks and *lathis* and they were brandishing them about, and there was quite a crowd of them. Reckless courage triumphed, and the crowd of humans fled, terrified, leaving their sticks behind them! The little monkey was rescued.

We had often animal visitors that were not welcome. Scorpions were frequently found in our cells, especially after a thunderstorm. It was surprising that I was never stung by one, for I would come across them in the most unlikely places—on my bed, or sitting on a book which I had just lined up. I kept a particularly black and poisonous-looking brute in a bottle for some time, feeding him with flies, etcetera, and then when I tied him up on a wall with a string he managed to escape. I had no desire to meet him loose again, and so I cleaned my cell out and hunted for him everywhere, but he had vanished.

Three or four snakes were also found in my cells or near them. News of one of them got out, and there were headlines in the press. As a matter of fact I welcomed the diversion. Prison life is dull enough, and everything that breaks through the monotony is appreciated. Not that I appreciate or welcome snakes, but they do not fill me with terror as they do some people. I am afraid of their bite, of course, and would protect myself if I saw a snake. But there would be no feeling of repulsion or overwhelming fright. Centipedes horrify me much more; it is not so much fear as instinctive repulsion. In Alipore Jail in Calcutta I woke in the middle of the night and felt something crawling over my foot. I pressed a torch I had and I saw a centipede on the bed. Instinctively and with amazing rapidity I vaulted clear out of that bed and nearly hit the cell wall. I realized fully then what Pavlov's reflexes were.

In Dehra Dun I saw a new animal, or rather an animal which was new to me. I was standing at the jail gate talking to the jailer when we noticed a man outside carrying a strange animal. The jailer sent for him, and I saw something between a lizard and a crocodile, about two feet long with claws and a scaly covering. This uncouth animal, which was very much alive, had been twisted round in a most peculiar way, forming a kind of knot, and its owner had passed a pole through this knot and was merrily carrying it in this fashion. He called it a "Bo." When asked by the jailer what he proposed to do with it, he replied with a broad smile that he would make *bhujji*—a kind of curry—out of it! He was a forest dweller. Subsequently I discovered from reading F. W. Champion's book—*The Jungle in Sunlight and Shadow*—that this animal was the Pangolin.

Prisoners, especially long-term convicts, have to suffer most from emotional starvation. Often they seek some emotional satisfaction by keeping animal pets. The ordinary prisoner cannot keep them, but the convict overseers have a little more freedom and the jail staff usually does not object. The commonest pets were squirrels and, strangely, mongooses. Dogs are not allowed in jails, but cats seem to be encouraged. A little kitten made friends with me once. It belonged to a jail official, and when he was transferred he took it away with him. I missed it. Although dogs are not allowed, I got tied up with some dogs accidentally in Dehra Dun. A jail official had brought a bitch, and then he was transferred, and he deserted her. The poor thing became a home-less wanderer, living under culverts, picking up scraps from the warders, usually starving. As I was being kept in the lock-up outside the jail proper, she used to come to me begging for food. I began to feed her regularly, and she gave birth to a litter of pups under a culvert. Many of these were taken away, but three remained and I fed them. One of the puppies fell ill with a violent distemper, and gave me a great deal of trouble. I nursed her with care, and sometimes I would get up a dozen times in the course of the night to look after her. She survived, and I was happy that my nursing had pulled her round.

I came in contact with animals far more in prison than I had done outside. I had always been fond of dogs, and had kept some, but I could never look after them properly as other matters claimed my attention. In prison I was grateful for their company. Indians do not, as a rule, approve of animals as household pets. It is remarkable that in spite of their general philosophy of non-violence to animals, they are often singularly careless and unkind to them. Even the cow, that favored ani-mal, though looked up to and almost worshipped by many Hindus and often the cause of riots, is not treated kindly. Worship and kindliness do not always go together.

Different countries have adopted different animals as symbols of their ambition or character—the eagle of the United States of America and of Germany, the lion and bulldog of England, the fighting cock of France, the bear of old Russia. How far do these patron animals mold national character? Most of them are aggressive, fighting animals, beasts of prey. It is not surprising that the people who grow up with these examples before them should mold themselves consciously after them and strike up impressive attitudes, and roar, and prey on others. Nor is it surprising that the Hindu should be mild and non-violent, for his patron animal is the cow.

A VACATION IN DALHOUSIE *

Rabindranath Tagore

We stayed about a month in Amritsar, and, toward the middle of April, started for the Dalhousie Hills. The last few days at Amritsar seemed as if they would never pass, the call of the Himalayas was so strong upon me.

The terraced hillsides, as we went up in a *jhampan*, were all aflame with the beauty of the flowering spring crops. Every morning we would make a start after our bread and milk, and before sunset take shelter for the night in the next staging bungalow. My eyes had no rest the livelong day, so great was my fear lest anything should escape them. Wherever, at a turn of the road into a gorge, the great forest trees were found clustering closer, and from underneath their shade a little waterfall trickling out, like a little daughter of the hermitage playing at the feet of hoary sages wrapt in meditation, babbling its way over the black moss-covered rocks, there the *jhampan* bearers would put down their burden, and take a rest. Why, oh why, had we to leave such spots behind, cried my thirsting heart; why could we not stay on there for ever?

This is the great advantage of the first vision: the mind is not then aware that there are many more such to come. When this comes to be known to that calculating organ it promptly tries to make a saving in its expenditure of attention. It is only when it believes something to be rare that the mind ceases to be miserly in assigning values. So in the streets of Calcutta I sometimes imagine myself a foreigner, and only then do I discover how much is to be seen, which is lost so long as its full value in attention is not paid. It is the hunger to really see which drives people to travel to strange places.

My father left his little cashbox in my charge. He had no reason to

* A fond childhood memory, recounted by the poet in his memoirs.

imagine that I was the fittest custodian of the considerable sums he kept in it for use on the way. He would certainly have felt safer with it in the hands of Kishori, his attendant. So I can only suppose he wanted to train me to the responsibility. One day as we reached the staging bungalow, I forgot to make it over to him and left it lying on a table. This earned me a reprimand.

Every time we got down at the end of a stage, my father had chairs placed for us outside the bungalow and there we sat. As dusk came on the stars blazed out wonderfully through the clear mountain atmosphere, and my father showed me the constellations or treated me to an astronomical discourse.

The house we had taken at Bakrota was on the highest hilltop. Though it was nearing May it was still bitterly cold there, so much so that on the shady side of the hill the winter frosts had not yet melted.

My father was not at all nervous about allowing me to wander about freely even here. Some way below our house there stretched a spur thickly wooded with deodars. Into this wilderness I would venture alone with my iron-spiked staff. These lordly forest trees, with their huge shadows, towering there like so many giants—what immense lives had they lived through the centuries! And yet this boy of only the other day was crawling round about their trunks unchallenged. I seemed to feel a presence, the moment I stepped into their shade, as of the solid coolness of some old-world saurian, and the checkered light and shade on the leafy mold seemed like its scales.

My room was at one end of the house. Lying on my bed I could see, through the uncurtained windows, the distant snowy peaks shimmering dimly in the starlight. Sometimes, at what hour I could not make out, I, half awakened, would see my father, wrapped in a red shawl, with a lighted lamp in his hand, softly passing by to the glazed verandah where he sat at his devotions. After one more sleep I would find him at my bedside, rousing me with a push, before the darkness of night had passed. This was my appointed hour for memorizing Sanskrit declensions. What an excruciatingly wintry awakening from the caressing warmth of my blankets!

By the time the sun rose, my father, after his prayers, finished with me our morning milk, and then, I standing at his side, he would once more hold communion with God, chanting the Upanishads.

Then we would go out for a walk. But how should I keep pace with him? Many an older person could not! So, after a while, I would give it up and scramble back home through some shortcut up the mountain side.

After my father's return I had an hour of English lessons. After ten o'clock came the bath in icy-cold water; it was no use asking the servants to temper it with even a jugful of hot water without my father's permission. To give me courage my father would tell of the unbearably freezing baths he had himself been through in his younger days.

Another penance was the drinking of milk. My father was very fond of milk and could take quantities of it. But whether it was a failure to inherit this capacity, or that the unfavorable environment of which I have told proved the stronger, my appetite for milk was grievously wanting. Unfortunately we used to have our milk together. So I had to throw myself on the mercy of the servants; and to their human kindness (or frailty) I was indebted for my goblet being thenceforth more than half full of foam.

After our midday meal, lessons began again. But this was more than flesh and blood could stand. My outraged morning sleep *would* have its revenge and I would be toppling over with uncontrollable drowsiness. Nevertheless, no sooner did my father take pity on my plight and let me off, than my sleepiness was off likewise. Then ho! for the mountains.

Staff in hand, I would often wander away from one peak to another, but my father did not object. To the end of his life, I have observed, he never stood in the way of our independence. Many a time have I said or done things repugnant alike to his taste and his judgment; with a word he could have stopped me, but he preferred to wait till the prompting to refrain came from within. A passive acceptance by us of the correct and the proper did not satisfy him; he wanted us to love truth with our whole hearts; he knew that mere acquiescence without love is empty. He also knew that truth, if strayed from, can be found again, but a forced or blind acceptance of it from the outside effectually bars the way in.

In my early youth I had conceived a fancy to journey along the Grand Trunk Road, right up to Peshawar, in a bullock cart. No one else supported the scheme, and doubtless there was much to be urged against it as a practical proposition. But when I discoursed on it to my father he was sure it was a splendid idea—traveling by railroad was not worth the name! With which observation he proceeded to recount to me his own adventurous wanderings on foot and horseback. Of any chance of discomfort or peril he had not a word to say.

Another time, when I had just been appointed Secretary of the Adi Brahma Samaj, I went over to my father, at his Park Street residence, and informed him that I did not approve of the practice of only Brahmins conducting divine service to the exclusion of other castes. He unhesitatingly gave me permission to correct this if I could. When I got the authority I found I lacked the power. I was able to discover imperfections but could not create perfection! Where were the men? Where was the strength in me to attract the right man? Had I the means to build in the place of what I might break? Till the right man comes any form is better than none—this, I felt, must have been my father's view of the existing order. But he did not for a moment try to discourage me by pointing out the difficulties.

As he allowed me to wander about the mountains at my will, so in the quest for truth he left me free to select my path. He was not deterred by the danger of my making mistakes, he was not alarmed at the prospect of my encountering sorrow. He held up a standard, not a disciplinary rod.

I would often talk to my father of home. Whenever I got a letter from anyone at home I hastened to show it to him. I verily believe I was thus the means of giving him many a picture he could have got from none else. My father also let me read letters to him from my elder brothers. This was his way of teaching me how I ought to write to him; for he by no means underrated the importance of outward forms and ceremonial.

I am reminded of how in one of my second brother's letters he was complaining in somewhat Sanskritized phraseology of being worked to death tied by the neck to his post of duty. My father asked me to explain the sentiment. I did it in my way, but he thought a different explanation would fit better. My overweening conceit made me stick to my guns and argue the point with him at length. Another would have shut me up with a snub, but my father patiently heard me out and took pains to justify his view to me.

My father would sometimes tell me funny stories. He had many an anecdote of the gilded youth of his time. There were some exquisites for whose delicate skins the embroidered borders of even Dacca muslins were too coarse, so that to wear muslins with the border torn off became, for a time, the tip-top thing to do.

I was also highly amused to hear from my father for the first time the story of the milkman who was suspected of watering his milk, and the more men one of his customers detailed to look after his milking, the bluer the fluid became, till, at last, when the customer himself interviewed him and asked for an explanation, the milkman avowed that if more superintendents had to be satisfied it would only make the milk fit to breed fish!

After I had thus spent a few months with him my father sent me back home with his attendant Kishori.

——◆——

THE LOPCHAK CARAVAN TO LHASA*
Abdul Wahid Radhu

[My] first notebook opened with an especially important event in the life of Ladakh, my native land: the departure of the "Lopchak caravan." Every two years this official expedition left Leh, our small capital, to go to Lhasa to deliver gifts to the Dalai Lama. This caravan thus contributed to maintaining good relations between Ladakh and Tibet, two countries which in reality formed one nation, even if the former was politically answerable to Kashmir and, after October 26, 1947, therefore, to independent India, whereas the latter looked for ways of officializing her de facto independence. This event marked my effective entry into the family profession. With the passing of the years, I have realized that it was the beginning of a very long journey which was never to end since it would allow me an almost uninterrupted inner journey from that time on.

In the evening of this memorable day, after having gone a little more than twenty kilometers, we arrived at Matho. Having settled down for the night in one of the village houses, I inaugurated, by candlelight, my diary, the first page of which is transcribed here:

* This essay has been excerpted from *Tibetan Caravans* (1997).

Today, September 19, 1942, the twentieth day of my life as a married man, I left my family, my wife, aunt, and sister. I left for Lhasa to learn the trade of being a merchant, supervised by my Uncle Abdul Aziz, head of the Lopchak caravan. In the seventeenth century the king of Ladakh, Delek Namgyal (1675–1705), signed a treaty with the Lama Mipham Wangpo, representative of the Dalai Lama, at the end of which it was agreed that a *Zhungtshong* (government trade) caravan would go every year from Lhasa to Leh to maintain good relations of friendship and commerce between Ladakh and Tibet. Reciprocally, it was agreed that a *Lopchak* (biannual) caravan would be sent to Lhasa every two years by the *gyalpo* (king) of Ladakh. Both caravans would have the right to freely transport merchandise within the territories of the two countries.

The government of Kashmir had put an end to the treaty a few years previously. At the request of the Tibetan authorities, it was re-established in 1938. This is the caravan that my uncle is now directing. However, no official of the State of Kashmir could give us the least bit of information as to the real objectives of the mission. The authorities concerned seem indifferent to its political and diplomatic implications. Every time my uncle tried to question an official such as the *wazir-i-wazarat* (the first agent of the government) or the local *tehsildar* (administrator of the district), Uncle found that they preferred to avoid talking about the caravan. The authorities in Lhasa, on their part, take a keen interest in these caravans and they wish to see them continue. As for the commercial and political agents of the British government in Lhasa and Leh, they are also favorably disposed toward the caravans.

The head of the preceding Lopchak had written a detailed report of his journey to Tibet and about his contacts in Lhasa. He had sent a copy to the government of Kashmir by intermediary of the *wazir* of Leh and another to the British resident in Srinagar. Whereas the latter immediately testified to the importance he gave to the Lopchak, we learnt at the beginning of the year that the other copy had not even left the *wazir*'s office in Leh!

This morning before the departure, lively activity animated the courtyard of our house. The baggage that our servants had prepared was carried out but we lost time waiting for the *respas* (pack animals). When they finally arrived there weren't enough of them, which forced us to leave six loads and these should reach us tomorrow here at Matho, our first stop.

Upon leaving the courtyard of our house, musicians, singers, beggars, and other bearers of good wishes crowded against both sides of the doorway to greet us. Finally we got underway. And there we were, embarked on a journey which is to last three to four months until we reach Lhasa . . .

The day was very difficult. It was hot. A strong wind was blowing and all sorts of thoughts went through my mind, dominated by the pain of separation.

We arrived in Matho at five o'clock in the afternoon. In spite of the excellent welcome waiting for the caravan from the *gopa* (village chief), the sadness of having left my home didn't loosen its grip on me.

Today, re-reading these notes thirty-eight years later I again see the young man, full of contradictory feelings, who wrote them. Aware of the commercial and political importance of our expedition, I still suffered a good deal for having had to so quickly interrupt the happiness of a marriage which had been celebrated less than three weeks earlier. The profession of caravaneer in Central Asia had certainly not made our elders sentimental, and if I wanted to follow the family vocation I would first of all have to learn to get over many attachments. I was still far from this and my eyes were wet with tears as I put out the candle to forget my sorrow in sleep.

Matho, the terminus of the first lap of our journey, is a typical Ladakhi village with a Buddhist monastery perched like a citadel on a rocky spur with numerous *chortens* or *stupas* rising in layers on the foothills of the Zanskar mountain range. This Himalayan chain closes in the high Indus valley to the south to form Ladakh, properly speaking. To the north, the peaks of the mountain chain called Ladakh rise more than 6,000 meters, passable by an ascending track up to the Khardung La pass above Leh and opening onto the valleys of Shyok and Nubra from where one can see the gigantic peaks of the Karakoram range. To the west, the valley slopes gently down toward Baltistan and Gilgit, today administered by Pakistan. To the east, the valley narrows, rising toward western Tibet where the river has its source.

Forming a slope of the "Roof of the World," Ladakh at this time was one of the most isolated countries of the globe. Srinagar, the capital of Kashmir and the nearest city, was twelve days' journey away on ponyback. The road, or rather the carriageable track which now allows lorries and jeeps to cover the same distance (434 kilometers) in two days, didn't exist and nobody dared land by plane in such a high and lost land (3,400 meters).

Ladakh offers only scanty resources and the inhabitants lead hard lives. At the end of that September of 1942 the scenery was austere. The barley having been harvested and the meadow grass yellowed, almost all the green had disappeared. Only the willows and poplars which grew near the streams still kept their leaves, as well as the apple and apricot trees which surrounded several farms. Snow already powdered the peaks. In two months it would cover even the bottom of the valley but with only a light layer because the climate is relatively dry behind the Himalayan barrier. At that time we would be crossing even higher and more austere lands, through frozen deserts where the mere thought of the Ladakhi homeland would conjure up the sweetness of living.

An important crossroads of the caravan tracks of Central Asia, it was due to its geographical location that Leh became the capital of Ladakh, if the title of capital can be applied to such a modest township. This, then, explains my family's vocation.

However, it was not in order to trade that our ancestor Sheikh Asad Radhu came to settle in Ladakh two centuries ago. This religious man had left the pleasant valley of Kashmir to preach Islam to the inhabitants of this high country whose climate is so harsh. Some people, it seems, were receptive to his words. In any case, his memory is not totally forgotten and a Persian inscription in the Sunni mosque in Leh mentions his name.

His father, Sheikh Muhammad Radhu, had been an eminent religious figure since he had the honor of displaying the reliquary containing a hair of our holy Prophet in the celebrated sanctuary of Hazratbal in Srinigar. This sacred relic is still there. The Radhus were descended from a Hindu-Brahmin family belonging to a sub-caste of "Kashmir pandits" named Trakou, a name that still exists in India. They were converted to Islam at a time difficult to specify.

The first Radhu who settled in Ladakh, Sheikh Asad, had left brothers in Kashmir whose descendents still live in Srinigar. His son, Faruq Radhu, was the first to become a caravaneer merchant. Thanks to this long-distance commerce, our family was to acquire great fame on the tracks of Central Asia.

Faruq Radhu seems to have maintained close relations with the *gyalpos*, the reigning princes of Ladakh. The memory of his name which became Phorokpa (Ladakhis aren't able to pronounce "F") has remained attached to the village of Stok near Leh where a royal castle is located and still inhabited by the rani, a highly respected descendant of the former dynasty. Faruq had received a piece of land there where he had a house built in pure Tibetan style.

The deep, ancient roots of our family thus permit us to affirm our adherence to the country as much as our co-patriots of the Buddhist religion. Although the Muslims remain in the minority in the high valley of the Indus, it is false to claim as certain observers have done that they make up a foreign element in Ladakh. In fact, Muslims have been present there for centuries. An integral part of the population, they have lived in perfect harmony with the tenants of other religions and have even often realized a harmonious symbiosis of the two cultures, Buddhist and Islamic. My grandfather, Haji Muhammad Siddiq, beloved patriarch and respected by everyone, was a particularly remarkable illustration of this typical Ladakhi synthesis: his face, his clothing, his manners, such as the way he had furnished and decorated his home which was always welcoming, and where he always appeared in garments quite similar to Tibetan dress but wearing a white turban.

I can affirm that in Ladakh I never experienced any animosity due to the difference in religions. In the villages Buddhists as well as Muslims called us *Akhon Pa*, a Central Asian expression which originally designated mullas, or religious teachers of Islam. The title of *Khodja*, or *khwaja*, which we normally bear, comes from Kashmir and is used mostly in Leh. Moreover, a fact which seems incredible in Indian society compartmentalized into castes; there even exist alliances amongst families of the two communities.

The Lopchak caravan bore witness to these excellent relations. Directed by a Muslim, it was carrying the official homage to the Dalai Lama from the Ladakhi Buddhists who recognized him as their supreme spiritual authority. In addition, amongst the servants of the caravan appeared two or three youths who were committed to becoming admitted as novices in the monasteries of Tibet.

The day after our departure was already a day of rest and inactivity since we had to wait for the six pack animals which had missed our departure the evening before in Leh. My diary also notes that Khwaja Abdul Aziz received a telegram from the *wazir* of Leh authorizing the caravan to carry a certain quantity of grain for our use. In fact, the government of Kashmir had just decreed the prohibition of exporting cereals to Tibet, a probable consequence of the war which had turned the world upside down but which nobody thought of behind the Himalayan barrier.

September 21, 1942
We took leave of the *gopa* of Matho. Climbing the length of the track to Martselang, we took a last glimpse at Leh. The weather is fine and sunny and we are traveling at a pleasant pace.

We stopped at three in the afternoon at Martselang where we were offered tea, then we left for Upshi, the end of this lap. We arrived at six and the luggage not until nine when we had already had supper. Everyone was tired. We only set up the small tents and the servants slept under the stars.

September 22, 1942
I awoke after a good sleep but it was terribly cold early in the morning. After having shaved, prayed, and had breakfast, I was ready. Our cook left first. With the head of the caravan, the servants, and the mule drivers, we did not leave until eleven o'clock. The day was very hot. At two o'clock we arrived at Miroo and found a warm welcome with the *gopa*. The cook had had time to prepare everything. We had tea and savored all sorts of sweets.

An old family friend came at five o'clock with a teapot and some gifts. What a fine way to greet guests! There is something very admirable about the manners of these people toward each other.

We talked leisurely and spoke of the future. Tibet will not be able to remain a passive spectator. She must change. The old traditions of the fifteenth century, even that which is best of them, must give way to the culture of the twentieth century. I am fortunate to have grown up within the framework of an ancient and beautiful culture. But I was later re-molded by a modern education, with its qualities and defects. At present, I feel it will be difficult to re-adapt myself to this world where nothing seems to change.

At this time, all our family lived in areas which had escaped colonial domination and the impact of modern civilization. The two older sons of Faruq Radhu, Haider Shah and Nasr Shah, had established a flourishing commerce in Ladakh. His third son had settled in Tibet where he had married a Chinese Muslim. Relations remained very close between the cousins of Tibet and Ladakh, and intermarriages were common. My paternal grandfather, son of Haider Shah, had married a Buddhist of Tsethang, a town located several days' walk from Lhasa.

Members of the two older branches had also developed their commercial exchanges beyond Karakoram, in Sinkiang or Chinese Turkestan where some took women and acquired property. Thus did the blood of the principal races and nations of Asia mix in the Radhu veins.

Those who had gone through Western-type schools, as one of my cousins and I had done, remained very rare exceptions. The contact which the others were able to establish with the outside world was still very limited.

Residing initially at Stok, some fifteen kilometers from Leh, after the family became important they built a beautiful house in the little capital very near the royal palace and on the same crag. Still called *Khangpa Nyingpa* (old house), it has remained the property of a cousin. I was born in one of the houses which was built later and located a little farther down.

In Leh, the Radhus held an eminent and envied position. They were wealthy, possessed beautiful property, and large amounts of merchandise passed through their warehouses. Everyone in Ladakh knew them and their reputation spread to neighboring countries, in particular to Tibet where they maintained relations with the best families of the nobility and even the direct entourage of the Dalai Lama.

Several members of preceding generations attained high social positions and were even granted official distinctions. It is thus that Ghulam Muhammad, who was on the best terms with the court of the Maharaja as well as with the British resident at Srinagar, was authorized to add the title of *Khan Sahib* to his name. He was introduced into the leadership circles of Tibet where the English political agent had wanted to make his son, who unfortunately died prematurely, a sort of head of the Muslim community of Lhasa.

As for my great uncle Ghulam Rasul, he had received the title of *Khan Bahadur* from Lord Minto, Viceroy of India, in recognition of services rendered to the Swedish explorer Sven Hedin, who often mentions our family in his work *Trans-Himalaya*. Known for his simplicity, piety, and generosity, out of loyalty to the tradition, he had refused the offer which the famous traveler had made to him to send his son to the West to give him a modern education. It was in the same spirit that my grandfather Haji Muhammad Siddiq had tried in vain to oppose my departure for Srinagar where I was to follow courses in an English-type school.

On this issue, my grandfather disagreed with his cousin Abdullah Shah, who, on good terms with the British administration, had been named *aksakal* which means in Turkoman language "the man with the white beard." This function consisted mainly of overseeing the activities of the Turkmenian merchants of Ladakh. To carry out his duties, he depended on the official called *charas officer*, "charas" meaning hashish, a grass which Chinese Turkistan cultivated in great quantities and which circulated in India. It was an officially controlled traffic and, as *aksakal*, Abdullah Shah was part of this system of control.

A supporter of modern ideas, he was of the opinion that young people should have a Western-type education and this drew the reproaches of my grandfather. "You are going to give these young people over to the *Shaitan*" (devil), he told him.

Haji Muhammad Siddiq, my grandfather, was a patriarch who reigned over a household of some twenty people, members of the family and domestic help. He himself was one of the most eminent and popular persons of Leh where he was happy enough to have been able to preserve the family traditions intact until his death.

His prestige and authority had won him the privilege, sometimes shared with the Buddhist family of the Srangnara, of directing the Lopchak caravan. Every time he led the caravan, he recorded a description of the journey in Urdu or Persian upon his return. These notebooks were veritable guides for Khwaja Abdul Aziz when it was his turn to direct the Lopchak. He accompanied us in 1942 and in the evening of the journey's lap or during the long days of inactivity which the vicissitudes of the expedition imposed upon us, I consulted these notebooks, often beneficially.

> September 23, 1942
> It is around five in the afternoon and I am in Gya where we arrived around one o'clock. Our watches stopped last night in Miroo probably due to the altitude. We reset them according to the projection of the shadows on the ground.
>   Gya is a large and beautiful village. The Lopchak is well received here according to custom. The new gopa belongs to a wealthy family of the area. His welcome is in conformity with the traditions, notably that of the *kalchor*.

This latter term, borrowed from Ladakhi dialect, refers to the welcoming ceremony or of leave-taking celebrated for a guest of note and includes offerings like milk, *chang* (a light beer in countries of Tibetan culture) or even cool water sometimes, dried fruit, rice, or barley flour used to make *tsampa*. It was usually the children and elderly people of their grandparents' generation who brought food and drink on beautiful, brass-wire trays and offered them to the travelers. The latter, in exchange, gave a few coins as symbolic payment. Moreover, the entire *kalchor* ceremony was symbolic since the guests hardly touched the offerings. But at that time I saw in all this mainly a sort of tribute due to the persons responsible for a caravan as important as ours on the part of the villagers.

September 24, 1942
We left Gya with *kalchor* and other traditional greetings of the local people. This is the last village of permanent habitation before the deserts of western Tibet, the immensity of which we have now penetrated, although politically the highlands of the Rupshu, which we shall have to cross these days, are attached to the state of the Maharaja of Jammu and Kashmir.

On this twenty-fourth day of September I reflected a great deal. However, it was the hardest day since our departure from Leh. Normally the day's walk ended at Debrengma, but the Rupshopas (nomads of the region) were not able to receive us. We therefore had to continue to Zara. We are at the foot of the Taklang pass where the track goes through leading to Gartok in Tibet. I found the road terribly difficult. We were walking against a wind of sand that fustigated us. I then recalled the ideas of Rousseau on natural education. He taught that it is by instruction and experience of the natural elements that we become true men. In any case, I feel that nature has just taught me a lesson. Pass after pass, valley after valley, all this walking has made me unbearably tired. And at such an altitude—probably approaching 5,000 meters— we are suffering from altitude sickness. Almost everyone has colic or vomiting. We can barely drink or eat.

I feel worse than last year when I easily climbed the peaks to the west of Toklang whilst taking mountain walks in that same region. Today a few steps takes a great amount of effort. My health must have weakened, undoubtedly because of my prolonged stays in India. Physically I led too easy an existence there and now I am no longer able to live normally as a Tibetan.

We arrived in Zara at about four in the afternoon. We were received according to the Lopchak traditions but the Rupshopas refused to set up our tents. We had to do it ourselves, at the same time feeling the difficult effects of the altitude.

This evening I understand how important it is to have a good tent. Outside the wind is blowing in a rage. Tomorrow is the fifteenth day of the eighth Tibetan month and the night promises us a splendid full moon. The Rupsho *gopa* (chief of the camp) invites us to stay here in Zara tomorrow to watch a horse race. We're obliged to accept because no one will provide us with horses to continue our journey. We can already hear music and drums in the evening.

September 25, 1942
The night was bad and we slept restlessly. Khwaja Abdul Aziz is suffering from a severe migraine and I myself feel dizzy. No one feels well but uncle has experience of these regions and, knowing the cause of these discomforts, is not worried.

The *gopa* came to have a talk with us. He notified us that an officer from the mines sent by the government is in the region because the mountain chain which extends into Tibetan territory is rich in sulfur and borax. In spite of the difficulties in exploiting these minerals, there is a lively competition amongst rival companies, each one attempting to obtain the monopoly.

The music reminds me that the horse race has begun. I can't resist going. Our two servants Lobzong and Rabgyas accompany me.

I've returned from the festival. This magnificent spectacle gave me an impressive glimpse of the life of the Rupshu nomads. What a hard life they have! They appeared to me at once innocent, dirty, and happy.

Now again it is with joy that I recall this gathering of Rupshu nomads and their horses. None of the races which I watched later in Calcutta or Darjeeling gave me as much pleasure. Here at nearly 5,000 meters of altitude in the austere background of the region near the lake which maps generally call Tso Moriri, the race represented an extraordinary performance of sport. The horsemen, young and of a mature age, were soaked in sweat as well as their intrepid little horses which, in the thin air, breathed like bellows and shared in the general excitement. The spectators, many of whom were women, clapped to the rhythm of the drums. Food and drink were served and our servant Rabgyas, who had swallowed large glassfuls of *chang*, the Tibetan beer, had difficulty returning to his tent. But the pleasure of the festival was not merely profane, because rosaries and prayer wheels were seen in many hands and the sacred mantra remained present.

September 26, 1942
The morning was very cold. Uncle seems to feel better, although he slept badly. As nobody was ready, we didn't leave until noon. The lap went as usual. We stopped at Thukje where we had a splendid view of the lake formed by the accumulation of water coming from several valleys. As

we approached we noticed many ducks and other beautiful birds. We arrived at Nganor at five o'clock. The moon rose and is reflected in the lake. A pleasant, light breeze is blowing. There is no one to help us here and we have to depend upon ourselves. Lobzang, Rabgyas, and Qadir have gone to collect wood so that we can heat our tents.

September 27, 1942
This morning a beautiful sun shone on the lake and the surrounding snow-covered peaks. A marvellous spectacle.

Whilst riding I reflected a good deal on the life which was already behind me—on my years of college and university and on the few months I had just spent at home. As for the future, far too divided between the high aspirations of my soul and my material ambitions, I can't envisage it.

I was still absorbed in my thoughts when we arrived at Angano. It was two o'clock. I am writing these notes on a beautiful, sunny afternoon. We are waiting for our baggage to arrive to set up our tents. The Korzogpa have welcomed us warmly but the supplies destined for our caravan are hardly satisfactory. Nevertheless *respa* ponies have come from Korzog with yaks, so we won't have to wait for them tomorrow.

September 28, 1942
Our departure was delayed because the Korzogpa had not sent enough men for the number of animals. Our servants had to go ahead by themselves with the load assisted by several Korzogpa who were present, so we weren't able to leave until the beginning of the afternoon. Passing through Puga, I noticed workers on nearby mountains working at sulfur mining, an abundant mineral in this region.

Today's lap was the longest since our departure and we arrived here at Langsham at 7:30. We were put up in the *kotih* (travelers' rest house) which is nearly acceptable. We have two rooms, one for uncle and me, the other serving as a kitchen and dormitory for the servants. Padma Tsering, another of our servants, left Leh several weeks before us and has joined us here. He went all the way to Gartok (western Tibet) which he left seventeen days ago. He had to delay in Demchog (the first Tibetan town after the Kashmir border) waiting for news of our caravan. He also obtained some information as to the whereabouts of our merchandise expected from Tashigang (in the same region).

In effect, during the preceding Lopchak two years ago, the threat of the Hasakapa raids (a Tibetan term designating the Kazakhs) had forced Khwaja Abdul Aziz to delay considerably his journey to Lhasa and to leave most of his merchandise as well as a hundred horses in Tashigang. Now we had to collect them to take them to their destination. The people who were to assure our transport have made unacceptable demands and are charging double the normal price. This affair is going to oblige us to extend our stay here. While we were waiting, Rab-gyas, Lobzang, Padma, and Rasul charmed us by singing very beautiful traditional songs of Ladakh and Baltistan, called *zhunglu*.

After crossing the Indus at the Choklamsar bridge several kilom-eters from Leh, our route had gone along the left bank of the river and left the river Upshi. From there we headed south. We went farther and farther away from the river until we reached Tso Moriri which my jour-nal calls Nganor Lake. In fact, in these regions which have never been precisely documented, place names are irregular and the few maps at our disposition have considerable differences. Nevertheless, after hav-ing passed near Korzog along the bank of this lake our caravan contin-ued east again and approached the Indus Valley as well as the frontier of Tibet, properly speaking. From then on we were entering the most hazardous phase of the expedition and were to face risks coming from men as well as nature.

First of all, there were the famous Hasakapas or Kazakhs who made the track unsafe. Muslim nomads, they had penetrated into the high plateaus of Tibet, starting from Sinkiang. Usually native of the USSR, they had gone into Chinese territory to escape religious persecution. Small groups had also infiltrated Kashmir but the Maharaja, himself of the Hindu religion, didn't look favorably upon these newcomers who didn't fail to swell the Muslim population that was in the majority in his states. Some Muslim princes of India then agreed to receive them and it is for this reason that ever since then there have been small com-munities of Kazakhs in cities like Hyderabad and Bhopal.

In Tibet, the Hasakapas hadn't come with hostile intentions. They were merely in search of pasture for their herds in the vast area of Changthang (or northern plains). Nevertheless, there were some run-ins with certain Tibetan nomads of a quarrelsome nature who claimed to be the only masters of these deserts. The scuffles degenerated into raids, then into punitive expeditions, and on both sides bellicose in-stincts took over. The result was a general impoverishment of the popu-lation, already much decreased in western Tibet, and for caravaneers, the risk of being pillaged, if not assassinated.

As for nature in the Trans-Himalayan highlands, she could be mer-cilessly rigorous. Our people had already had several bitter experiences such as that of 1932 which turned into a veritable disaster.

Snow fell that year in the Tibetan Changthang desert, the likes of which had never been seen before in living memory. Accompanied by an uncle and three cousins, my father, Khwaja Abdul Karim, had left for Lhasa with a caravan of mules loaded with merchandise. In the region of Kailash they encountered a layer of snow so deep that the animals were immobilized and all perished down to the very last one. By an almost incredible feat they managed to save their own lives and reach Lhasa, but they had lost all their cargo.

I was a child at this time and the image of my grandfather overcome with worry remains in my memory. He only had two daughters, and my father, who had married one of them and for whom he had much affection, was his principal collaborator and successor assigned to head the family commerce.

In the morning and evening it was his habit to take a walk in the streets of Leh, and the people, knowing there was no news of the caravan, shared his anxiety. Finally a telegram arrived which announced that all the men were safe and sound. My grandfather's face brightened, tears came to his eyes, and he immediately withdrew to pray.

He returned saying, "Let us rejoice. They are alive! And let the merchandise stay where it is!"

As for my father, his financial situation was jeopardized since his merchandise had remained under the Changthang snow. He returned to his brother-in-law of course who lived in Lhasa, but it wasn't his relatives whom he turned to in order to obtain the necessary assistance for re-establishing his business. He took a lively interest in the culture and customs of Tibet where he had numerous friends, particularly amongst the Khampas whose dress he often wore. It was the Khampa merchants who lent him enough money to enable him to obtain some fifteen mules as well as servants. I still remember his return to Leh with his new caravan, himself dressed like a Khampa.

Now my father, resolved to persevere in the rectification of his situation, was above all determined to repay the Khampa merchants the money which he owed them. Against the advice of Haji Muhammad Siddiq who, aware of his poor health, would have liked to have kept him for some time in Ladakh, he left for Lhasa with his caravan soon after that. Suffering from a stomach ulcer which he had never taken care of, he was to die en route, in the middle of the desert, soon after crossing the Mayum La pass, which is located between the Indus and Brahmaputra basins.

After burying him, his servants, none of whom were Muslims, began to quarrel amongst themselves over the merchandise of the caravan. One of them, a particularly loyal and faithful Khampa, succeeded in persuading the others that the cargo should be transported intact to Lhasa where the opinion of Haji Muhammad Siddiq would be sought. At Shigatse some of my father's cousins, knowing that his mules were carrying gifts that were destined for them, wanted to take possession of the caravan. The servants were absolutely opposed to this. They responded to the cousins' insistence by threatening to use their weapons and did not allow anyone to touch the merchandise except a representative duly sent by Haji Muhammad Siddiq. The latter, informed of the situation, asked his other son-in-law, Abdul Aziz, who was in Lhasa, to take care of the cargo.

The premature death of my father was one of the causes of the decline of the family. To replace him, Haji Muhammad Siddiq asked Abdul Aziz to leave Lhasa and come settle near him in Leh. Although he was more Tibetan than Ladakhi, my uncle accepted and thus undertook the journey accompanied by his wife and nine-year-old daughter. He had loaded his goods onto my father's mules and took a few of the same servants.

The caravan followed the usual track passing through Shigatse, Lhatse, and the high Brahmaputra. Arrived in Toksum, three days' walk from Mayum La, the travelers heard that Khampa brigands infested the region and had already attacked and pillaged several nomad camps. Khwaja Abdul Aziz was not a man to be stopped by such rumors. He only took the precaution of verifying that his Mauser rifle, which he carefully cleaned, was in good order. And the caravan went on its way.

After the caravan had crossed the Mayum La an episode occurred which has remained famous in the family annals. Abdul Aziz and his companions set up their bivouac on a deserted plateau at a high altitude. As usual, they let the mules graze around the campsite during the night. In the morning the servants had gone to collect them when my uncle noticed a group of horsemen in the distance. At first he thought it was a caravan but when they approached their gait seemed unusual to him and his suspicions were aroused. The strangers came up to the bivouac and whilst conversing amongst themselves, began to attach their mounts to tent pegs. Abdul Aziz noticed that each one was armed with a long flint rifle with a powder keg as well as a sword. One of the two servants who had remained in the bivouac, himself a Khampa, pointed out to them that no one had authorized them to touch the tents, to which they replied with arrogance that they had no authorization to take anything from anyone.

So Khwaja Abdul Aziz, holding his Mauser, approached and sought to drive them away: "You have no business here. Go away. All this is ours."

"Who are you?" asked the bandits.

"I'm going to show you who I am," answered Uncle in a tone expressing not the least fright but rather growing anger.

Then the bandits began to load their rifles. Abdul Aziz, even angrier, cried out to them: "Do you think we came into the desert without better weapons than yours? For us, your rifles are only sticks."

At that moment, the little girl, frightened, began to howl but her mother, who was calmly eating her *tsampa*, ticked her off sharply, "You should be ashamed to cry. Tears have never helped anything!" And, baring her chest she turned toward the marauders, "Just kill us if it pleases you!"

Less courageous, the cook of the caravan, a Ladakhi Muslim, prostrated, terrorized, before the bandits, crying, "Kuch, kuch! Please, please! [spare us]."

Abdul Aziz's indignation reached its peak. He railed at his cook: "You're as crazy as you are cowardly if you think people like this know what mercy is! You're no man!" And he spat in his face. Then, aiming his rifle at the closest bandit, he shouted to them, "If you want to fight, I'm ready. But whatever happens, don't forget that there is law in Tibet and the Government have means of arresting criminals like you and punishing them as they deserve."

The brigands made hesitating movements, looked at each other, and exchanged a few words which the Khampa servant understood. They wondered if they weren't in the presence of a high-ranking official and if it wouldn't be more prudent to let him remain alive. At the same time they noticed the other servant coming back with the mules. So they withdrew, untied their horses, jumped into their saddles, and galloped off.

Abdul Aziz followed them with his eyes and saw them reach a glen where some companions were waiting for them. He remained turned in their direction for a long time, his rifle in his hand, ready to fire at the first one who still dared to approach.

The little girl who was so frightened was later to become my wife. She kept all the details of the episode engraved in her memory.

Nevertheless, the caravan set off again with no further mishap. At the next lap, nomads who already knew what had happened came and prostrated in front of Khwaja Abdul Aziz. It seemed miraculous to them that he had escaped from the bandits when so many of their own people had fallen victim to them. He himself only made this brief comment about the incident.

"If those villains hadn't made me so angry, we would all be dead."

Uncle had, in fact, a strong temperament and he wasn't lacking in pride; perhaps he kept something of the arrogance of certain aristocratic Tibetans with whom he had been in contact for so long in Lhasa. Such a character undoubtedly made him a respected and even feared leader, but did not perfectly suit the occupation which was to be his from then on in the trading company directed by my grandfather Haji Muhammad Siddiq. With his wife and daughter, he moved into the big house in Leh over which the patriarch reigned and with whom he became the principal collaborator in place of my father. It was thus that he was assigned to lead the Lopchak first in 1940 and then in 1942 when I accompanied him.

However, certain indications already made us sense that the days of the trade caravans were approaching their end. My cousin Abdul Haq, who didn't like the precarious existence that these long expeditions into high desert lands forced one to lead, was interested in new means of transport and in the possibility of traveling more rapidly and safely between Leh and Lhasa through India. He had taken the opportunity, which he thought good, of selling the mules and all the caravan supplies that we still owned and the family bitterly reproached him for this. Consequently, at the time of the 1942 Lopchak, we no longer had a caravan which belonged to us. We were entirely dependent on the supplies of the Tibetan administration who put at our disposition 200 to 250 mules whereas on the Indian side, the government of Kashmir advanced us the modest sum of 10,000 rupees.

At the end of that September of 1942 when we went down toward the Indus after having crossed the Rupshu, also called Ladakhi Chang-Tang, and when we approached the border of Tibet, Khwaja Abdul Aziz at least had the satisfaction of telling himself that he was going to cross it as an official. As for myself, I was not easily consolable, having had to be separated from my young wife. All sorts of confused thoughts rushed into my mind. My diary is a witness to this. I also express in it the confused hope of finding light at the end of the way and I wrote:

"Lhasa, perhaps, will give a direction to my life."

—◦—

THE VIEW FROM CHEENA*
Jim Corbett

Naini Tal can best be described as an open valley running east and west, surrounded on three sides by hills, the highest of which, Cheena, rises to a height of 8,569 feet. It is open at the end from which a motor road approaches it. Nestling in the valley is a lake a little more than two miles in circumference, fed at the upper end by a perennial spring and overflowing at the other end where the motor road terminates. At the upper and lower ends of the valley there are bazaars and the surrounding wooded hills are dotted with residential houses, churches, schools, clubs, and hotels. Near the margin of the lake are boat houses, a picturesque Hindu temple, and a very sacred rock shrine presided over by an old Brahmin priest who has been a lifelong friend of mine.

Geologists differ in their opinion as to the origin of the lake, some attributing it to glaciers and landslides, others to volcanic action. Hindu legends, however, give the credit for the lake to three ancient sages, Atri, Pulastya, and Pulaha. The sacred book *Skanda-Puran* tells how, while on a penitential pilgrimage, these three sages arrived at the crest of Cheena and, finding no water to quench their thirst, dug a hole at the foot of the hill and siphoned water into it from Manasarowar, the sacred lake in Tibet. After the departure of the sages the goddess Naini arrived and took up her abode in the waters of the lake. In course of time forests grew on the sides of the excavation and, attracted by the water and the vegetation, birds and animals in great numbers made their home in the

---

* A lyrical, evocative description of one of the many villages in the region of Garhwal where Corbett lived, worked, and hunted.

valley. Within a radius of four miles of the goddess's temple I have, in addition to other animals, seen tigers, leopards, bears, and *sambhar*, and in the same area identified one hundred twenty-eight varieties of birds.

Rumors of the existence of the lake reached the early administrators of this part of India, and as the hill people were unwilling to disclose the position of their sacred lake, one of these administrators, in the year 1839, hit on the ingenious plan of placing a large stone on the head of a hill man, telling him he would have to carry it until he arrived at goddess Naini's lake. After wandering over the hills for many days the man eventually got tired of carrying the stone, and led the party who were following him to the lake. The stone alleged to have been carried by the man was shown to me when I was a small boy, and when I remarked that it was a very big stone for a man to carry—it weighed about six hundred pounds—the hill man who showed it to me said, "Yes, it is a big stone but you must remember that in those days our people were very strong."

Provide yourself now with a good pair of field glasses and accompany me to the top of Cheena. From here you will get a bird's-eye view of the country surrounding Naini Tal. The road is steep, but if you are interested in birds, trees, and flowers you will not mind the three-mile climb and if you arrive at the top thirsty, as the three sages did, I will show you a crystal-clear spring of cold water to quench your thirst. Having rested and eaten your lunch, turn now to the north. Immediately below you is a deep well-wooded valley running down to the Kosi river. Beyond the river are a number of parallel ridges with villages dotted here and there; on one of these ridges is the town of Almora, and on another, the cantonment of Ranikhet. Beyond these again are more ridges, the highest of which, Dungar Buqual, rises to a height of 14,200 feet and is dwarfed into insignificance by the mighty mass of the snow-clad Himalayas. Sixty miles due north of you, as the crow flies, is Trisul, and to the east and to the west of this imposing 23,406-foot peak the snow mountains stretch in an unbroken line for many hundreds of miles. Where the snows fade out of sight to the west of Trisul are first the Gangotri group, then the glaciers and mountains above the sacred shrines of Kedarnath and Badrinath, and then Kamet made famous by Smythe. To the east of Trisul, and set farther back, you can just see the top of Nanda Devi (25,689 feet), the highest mountain in India. To your right front is Nanda Kot, the spotless pillar of the goddess Parvati, and a little farther east are the beautiful peaks of Panch Chuli, the "five cooking places" used by the Pandavas while on their way to Kailas in Tibet. At the first approach of dawn, while Cheena and the intervening hills are still shrouded in the mantle of night, the snowy range changes from indigo blue to rose pink, and as the sun touches the peaks nearest to heaven the pink gradually changes to dazzling white. During the day the mountains show up cold and white, each crest trailing a feather of powdered snow, and in the setting sun the scene may be painted pink, gold, or red according to the fancy of heaven's artist.

Turn your back now on the snows and face south. At the limit of your range of vision you will see three cities: Bareilly, Kashipur, and Moradabad. These three cities—the nearest of which, Kashipur, is some fifty miles as the crow flies—are on the main railway that runs between Calcutta and the Punjab. There are three belts of country between the railway and the foothills: first a cultivated belt some twenty miles wide, then a grass belt ten miles wide known as the Terai, and third a tree belt ten miles wide known as the Bhabar. In the Bhabar belt, which extends right up to the foothills, clearings have been made, and on this rich fertile soil, watered by many streams, villages of varying size have been established.

The nearest group of villages, Kaladhungi, is fifteen miles from Naini Tal by road, and at the upper end of this group you will see our village, Choti Haldwani, surrounded by a three-mile-long stone wall. Only the roof of our cottage, which is at the junction of the road running down from Naini Tal with the road skirting the foothills, is visible in a group of big trees. The foothills in this area are composed almost entirely of iron ore, and it was at Kaladhungi that iron was first smelted in northern India. The fuel used was wood, and as the king of Kumaon, General Sir Henry Ramsay, feared that the furnaces would consume all the forests in the Bhabar, he closed down the foundries. Between Kaladhungi and your seat on Cheena the low hills are densely wooded with sal, the trees which supply our railways with ties, or sleepers, and in the nearest fold of the ridge nestles the little lake of Khurpa Tal, surrounded by fields on which the best potatoes in India are grown. Away in the distance, to the right, you can see the sun glinting on the Ganges, and to the left you can see it glinting on the Sarda; the distance between these two rivers where they leave the foothills is roughly two hundred miles.

Now turn to the east, and before you in the near and middle distance you will see the country described in old gazetteers as "the district of sixty lakes." Many of these lakes have silted up, some in my lifetime, and the only ones of any size that now remain are Naini Tal, Sat Tal, Bhim Tal, and Nakuchia Tal. Beyond Nakuchia Tal is the cone-shaped hill, Choti Kailas. The gods do not favor the killing of bird or beast on this sacred hill, and the last man who disregarded their wishes—a soldier on leave during the war—unaccountably lost his footing after killing a mountain goat and, in full view of his two companions, fell a thousand feet into the valley below. Beyond Choti Kailas is the Kala Agar ridge on which I hunted the Chowgarh man-eating tiger for two years, and beyond this ridge the mountains of Nepal fade out of sight.

Turn now to the west. But first it will be necessary for you to descend a few hundred feet and take up a new position on Deopatta, a rocky peak 7,991 feet high adjoining Cheena. Immediately below you is a deep, wide, and densely wooded valley which starts on the saddle between Cheena and Deopatta and extends through Dachouri to Kaladhungi. It is richer in flora and fauna than any other in the Himalayas, and beyond this beautiful valley the hills extend in an unbroken line up to the Ganges, the waters of which you can see glinting in the sun over a hundred miles away. On the far side of the Ganges is the Siwalik range of hills— hills that were old before the mighty Himalayas were born.

⁊

Come with me now to one of the villages you saw in your bird's-eye view from the top of Cheena . . .

The headman [of the village] is dead now and his daughters have married and left . . . but his wife is alive, and you who are accompanying me to the village, after your bird's-eye view from Cheena, must be prepared to drink the tea, not made with water but with rich fresh milk sweetened with jaggery, which she will brew for us. Our approach down the steep hillside facing the village has been observed and a small square of frayed carpet and two wicker chairs, reinforced with *ghooral* skins, have been set ready for us. Standing near these chairs to welcome us is the wife of the headman; there is no purdah here and she will not be embarrassed if you take a good look at her, and she is worth looking at. Her hair, snow-white now, was raven-black when I first knew her, and her cheeks, which in those far-off days had a bloom on them, are now ivory-white, without a single crease or wrinkle. Daughter of a hundred generations of Brahmins, her blood is as pure as that of the ancestors who founded her line. Pride of pure ancestry is inherent in all men, but nowhere is there greater *respect* for pure ancestry than there is in India. There are several different castes of people in the village this dear old lady administers, but her rule is never questioned and her word is law, not because of the strong arm of retainers, for of these she has none, but because she is a Brahmin, the salt of India's earth. The high prices paid in recent years for field produce have brought prosperity—as it is known in India—to this hill village, and of this prosperity our hostess has had her full share. The string of fluted gold beads that she brought as part of her dowry are still round her neck, but the thin silver necklace has been deposited in the family bank, the hole in the ground under the cooking place, and her neck is now encircled by a solid gold band. In the far-off days her ears were unadorned, but now she has a number of thin gold rings in the upper cartilage, and from her nose hangs a gold ring five inches in diameter, the weight of which is partly carried by a thin gold chain looped over her right ear. Her dress is the same as that worn by all high-caste hill women: a shawl, a tight-fitting bodice of warm material, and a voluminous print skirt. Her feet are bare, for even in these advanced days the wearing of shoes among our hill folk denotes that the wearer is unchaste.

The old lady has now retired to the inner recesses of her house to prepare tea, and while she is engaged on this pleasant task you can turn your attention to the *bania*'s shop on the other side of the narrow road. The *bania*, too, is an old friend. Having greeted us and presented us with a packet of cigarettes, he has gone back to squat cross-legged on the wooden platform on which his wares are exposed. These wares consist of the few articles that the village folk and wayfarers needed in the way of *atta*, rice, *dal*, ghee, salt, stale sweets purchased at a discount in the Naini Tal bazaar, hill potatoes fit for the table of a king, enormous turnips so fierce that when eaten in public they make the onlookers' eyes water, cigarettes and matches, a tin of kerosene oil, and near the platform and within reach of his hand an iron pan in which milk is kept simmering throughout the day.

As the *bania* takes his seat on the platform his few customers gather in front of him. First is a small boy, accompanied by an even smaller sister, who is the proud possessor of one pice, all of which he is anxious to invest in sweets. Taking the pice from the small grubby hand, the *bania* drops it into an open box. Then, waving his hand over the tray to drive away the wasps and files, he picks up a square sweet made of sugar and curds, breaks it in half, and puts a piece into each eager outstretched hand. Next comes a woman of a depressed class who has two annas to spend on her shopping. One anna is invested in *atta*, the coarse ground wheat that is the staple food of our hill folk, and two pice in the coarsest of the three qualities of *dal* exposed on the stall. With the remaining two pice she purchases a little salt and one of the fierce turnips and then, with a respectful *salaam* to the *bania,* for he is a man who commands respect, she hurries off to prepare the midday meal for her family.

While the woman is being served, the shrill whistles and shouts of men herald the approach of a string of pack mules, carrying cloth from the Moradabad handlooms to the markets in the interior of the hills. The sweating mules have had a stiff climb up the road from the foothills, and while they are having a breather the four men in charge have sat down on the bench provided by the *bania* for his customers and are treating themselves to a cigarette and a glass of milk. Milk is the strongest drink that has ever been served at this shop, or at any other of the hundreds of wayside shops throughout the hills, for, except for those few who have come in contact with what is called civilization, our hill men do not drink. Drinking among women, in my India, is unknown. No daily paper has ever found its way into the village, and the only news the inhabitants get of the outside world is from an occasional trip into Naini Tal and from wayfarers, the best-informed of whom are the packmen. On their way into the hills they bring news of the distant plains of India and on their return journey a month or so later they have news from the trading centers where they sell their wares.

The tea the old lady has prepared for us is now ready. You must be careful how you handle the metal cup filled to the brim, for it is hot enough to take the skin off your hands. Interest has now shifted from the packmen to us, and whether or not you like the sweet, hot liquid you must drink every drop of it, for the eyes of the entire village, whose guest you are, are on you; and to leave any dregs in your cup would mean that you did not consider the drink good enough for you. Others have attempted to offer recompense for hospitality but we will not make this mistake, for these simple and hospitable people are intensely proud, and it would be as great an insult to offer to pay the dear old lady for her cup of tea as it would have been to have offered to pay the *bania* for his packet of cigarettes.

So, as we leave this village, which is only one of the many thousands of similar villages scattered over the vast area viewed through your good field glasses from the top of Cheena, where I have spent the best part of my life, you can be assured that the welcome we received on arrival, and the invitation to return soon, are genuine expressions of the affection and goodwill of the people in my India for all who know and understand them.

———◆◇◆———

DEV BHUMI*
Bill Aitken

Many regions of the Himalaya lay claim to the title "abode of the gods" but strictly speaking Uttarakhand is the only genuine claimant. It is true that Kullu at Dasehra is the abode of the gods for they all foregather at the famous annual festival. But this is their temporary abode and the gods thereafter return to their favored sites. Garhwal in the ancient scriptures is also known as Kedarkhand. No one is agreed about the meaning of the word *kedar* which is the place of Shiva's meditation. However at 11,500 feet where a solid stone temple was built in his honor a clue to the word's derivation is found in the marshy meadows that characterize the site. Many small shrines have been built to enclose the numerous tiny springs (*kahi dar*) that bubble up and traditionally the pilgrim is invited to say "Shiva Shambu" to which there is an immediate response in the "bloop-bloop" of bubbling water.

These many springs may have lent a magical aura to this superb site at the base of the vast snow ramparts of the Himalaya. None of the other dhams of Uttarakhand have this scintillating backdrop. Badri, the abode of Vishnu, appears to have been chosen for the hot springs in attendance, as does Yamnotri, the religious source of the Yamuna.

*Wanderings in the "land of the gods." Excerpted from *Footloose in the Himalaya* (2003).

Gangotri has neither a snow panorama nor hot springs but possesses Bhagirath Sheel, the penance stone on which the meditating king influenced Ganga Maharani to flow from Shiva's Kailash down to earth. Could it be that this very ordinary stone once marked the source of the Ganga which has now receded more than nineteen kilometers to Gaumukh? The Gangotri glacier is melting at an alarming rate. When I first went there twenty years ago it was receding at the rate of 30 feet a year; today the ice is retreating at 30 meters a year. By the year 2050 the glacier may not exist.

There is no temple to mark the Gaumukh source of the Ganga because of the changing terrain. The Ganga rises southeast of Gangotri and is blocked from any passage south by the bulk of the Kedarnath massif. Gangotri is remarkable for the broad Bhagirathi river which suddenly narrows near the temple and then after crashing over a spectacularly sculpted waterfall enters a narrow gorge only a meter wide. Instead of seeing some proof of a scientific claim for this being the original source of the river, pilgrim mythology holds that King Bhagirath had built a canal to lead the Ganga round the obstructing Kedarnath.

The Yamnotri and Gangotri temples are both sited under the tree line while Kedar is above it. It is likely Badri once had tree cover that has fallen over the centuries to the demands of pilgrim fuel. At Bhojbhas a few kilometers short of Gaumukh (and higher than Kedar) twenty years ago there were slopes of bhojpatra (birch trees) which have all been cut recently thanks to the increase in pilgrim traffic caused by the building of a motorable bridge to Gangotri. When pilgrims had to walk ten kilometers to the temple fewer came and the environmental toll was bearable.

Now only Yamnotri and Kedarnath require some trekking. The day spent in walking to these shrines and the act of stretching one's legs and lungs makes for a much better mood on arrival. Usually pilgrims who alight at the bus terminals of Badri and Gangotri feel tired, dusty, and bilious. The last thing they need on arrival is the noise and pollution of these seething bus stations with their crowd of porters, hotel touts, and soliciting temple "pandas" (priests). One of the first rules I learnt for visiting pilgrim shrines was from Sri Krishna Prem who had walked from Mirtola to Badrinath in the old days before the roads came: always hire a panda immediately on arrival, for he will keep the others away.

The pandas have their own extremely thorough system of allotting new arrivals, depending on the area they come from. India is divided into districts and a panda's family takes responsibility for catering to the requirements of pilgrims from their allotted area. Your panda will arrange accommodation, food, and darshan in return for an offering. Furthermore he will have kept an accurate register of all in your family who have visited before and to make this more meaningful he will have got the pilgrim to personally write in his register. He will show you the authentic signature of your ancestor and the dates of his stay.

Those who belong to parts not accounted for (say from Pakistan, China, or Peru) have a special panda allotted to them. These arrangements work flawlessly and the stories you hear about the greed of the pandas need to be taken with a pinch of salt. If they were so greedy no one would continue with their services. Whenever Prithwi and I have trekked on the Char Dham circuit the pandas have gone out of their way to show kindness. They have learned the art of good public relations and know that our friends would seek them out by name because of our recommendation.

At the end of May 1980 Prithwi decided to have darshan of Badri Vishal and we set off in her Fiat from Mussoorie taking care to pack a small spade. This was needed to dig out the back wheels from muddy patches found along the little-used road linking Tehri with Srinagar. We spent the first night at Nand Prayag and were lucky to get a room in the forest bungalow since the district forest officer was in residence and gave us permission. The bungalow lay alongside the meeting of the Alakananda and Nandakini rivers and in those days was very peacefully situated. Apart from pilgrim buses, army convoys, and government jeeps, there was no private traffic. The age of nationalized banks and government loans to buy taxis had not yet arrived.

This confluence of rivers marked the traditional site of Shakuntala's ashram in Kalidas's drama. It would be hard for Shakuntala's king to go hunting in these parts nowadays because there are so few trees left. Yet only 150 years ago according to Atkinson's *Gazetteer* tigers abounded in the forests around Karnaprayag.

A new road left Nand Prayag for the interior following the Nandakini as far as Ghat. This was a convenient junction for treks to Rup Kund and the Kuari Pass. Of all the unspoilt sylvan trails in Garhwal the climb to Kuari from Ramni (above Ghat) is amongst my favorites. This bridle path through ancient clumps of mixed forest was known as the Curzon Trail because the viceroy had chosen it for its reputed scenic beauty. However the viceregal party only got as far as the first stage when the trek had to be called off. They were attacked by wild bees, a feature of these hills.

Returning from one of my treks to the source of the Nandakini when I came to the village of Sutol I found not a single male at home. They had all gone to raid the hives of the deadly wild bee. The bees hang their large combs of honey under some inaccessible cliff safe from the wind and rain and beyond the reach of a ladder. But the enterprising villagers lower a man from the top of the cliff and as he dangles in midair he tries to smoke out the bees. Then in a desperate maneuver he breaks off the combs which drop to those waiting at the base of the cliff. Needless to say many are badly stung in this uneven battle and the rewards hardly seem to offset the pains incurred. But the sheer physical courage of the villager lowered almost literally into a hornet's nest is something you cannot but applaud.

Honey enjoys a high religious status in the hills and is believed to be good for every complaint. The theory that it contains the essence of many Himalayan plants is belied by the fact that much of it originates from village sweetshops where due to the paucity of flora the bees are forced to forage. Keeping domesticated bees in the hills is hard work. During the cold weather you have to feed them rather than the other way round. For the rest of the year they require a lot of protection from bears and pine martens. Perhaps their worst enemy is the wasp which comes in several sizes in the hills. The biggest species of hornet runs to two inches in body length. In swatting one of these which was attacking the Mirtola hives I accidentally put my foot on it when it was already dead, but its sting nevertheless penetrated my foot and I had a severe temperature for a week. This variety breeds in combs in the ground and has such strong poison that three stings can be fatal.

After the leafy surroundings of Nand Prayag, Badrinath came as a bit of a letdown. The sprawl of dharmshalas and the crudely painted temple in PWD pink gave the place an air more of a refugee camp than a spiritual destination. The valley hereabouts is very open and we walked up to the village of Mana. Here we experienced some true religion albeit of the local variety. A women was possessed and uttered oracular outbursts which went largely unheard since most of the men were staggering around totally drunk on locally distilled booze.

It is a curiosity of spiritual alchemy that Lord Badri, the most orthodox of Hindu icons and cared for by Namboodri Brahmins, likewise commands the allegiance of these toping Marchas (as the local people were then designated). To prove the point the Rawal of the Badri temple rode up on horseback to bless the bacchanalian ceremonies afoot in Mana.

The word "Badri" is said to derive from the beru (wild fig) on which Lord Vishnu is believed to have survived while doing penance in the valley. The jujube tree is a claimant but does not grow above 6,000 feet. A more likely candidate is *Hippophae salicifolia*, a shrub with an acid fruit that makes a palatable preserve when boiled with sugar. The hill fig—eaten as a vegetable after the latex has been boiled out—grows around Joshimath where Lord Badri descends to spend his winter. In fact Joshimath is famous for possessing what is claimed to be one of the oldest trees in India. This is a fig but of the non-fruiting variety, similar to the tree under which the Buddha sat for enlightenment in Bodh Gaya. Is there a clue here to the origins of the temple?

The insignificance of the structure at Badrinath and the attribute of "vishal" to the deity has led some to argue that the real Badri was higher up on the Tibetan border where there are large, ancient Buddhist stone figures. This would explain the word *vishal* (great). Controversy exists over the belief that Shankaracharya had rescued the image of Badri (said to have been thrown in the river by Buddhist polemical rivals) and reinstated it at the site of the present temple. Another version is that Shankaracharya's followers, after the victory of their guru over the Buddhists in debate, had simply taken over the temple as their legitimate spoils. A similar case has been made for other temples as at Puri, Ayodhya, Kanchipuram, and Srisailem. Chinese travelers before the advent of Shankaracharya describe in detail several Buddhist shrines that mysteriously since then have found their way into Brahminical custodianship. While contemporary Hindu chauvinists list temples destroyed by Muslims, there is silence on Hindu takeovers of Buddhist and Jain sites. Evidence of the likely brahminical takeover of Badrinath lies in the carefully concealed fact that the image worshipped in the temple (invariably obscured by the pujari's floral offerings) is of the Buddha in the lotus posture. Hindus try to evade this awkward fact by claiming that it is as an avatar of Vishnu that Buddha is worshipped in Badri. But why then should Buddhists have thrown the image in the river? And why would Shankaracharya attack an avatar of Hinduism? The truth is many Hindus consider it bad luck to keep an image of the Buddha in their house. Likewise Hindu pilgrims studiously avoid visiting the birthplace of the Buddha and the place where he died.

The next day we walked to Vishnu-paduka to glimpse the lovely vista of Nilkantha framed at the end of the valley. What a superb peak this is and how soiled its reputation became in international mountaineering circles thanks to H. C. Sarin, the president of the Indian Mountaineering Foundation (IMF). The IMF was established to put India on the world mountaineering map and keep up with the Joneses in putting Indians atop Everest. The fact that the IMF was originally housed in the defense ministry compound hints at the early departmentalizing of the infant sport of climbing by the government. Its office was a tiny room in an asbestos barracks where Babu Munshi Ram sat at a desk surrounded on all sides by mounds of yellowing files. A more unmountaineering atmosphere would be hard to imagine but at least Munshi Ram hailed from the hills, which is more than could be said for many of the bureaucratic "experts" who had never set foot in the Himalaya. Sarin's credentials for leading the IMF were based on the fact that as a student he had undertaken a bicycle tour of Norway! But he was defense secretary and effectively controlled the destinies of India's budding mountaineers. This thirst for mountaineering headlines had disastrous repercussions. Nilkantha is a peak as hard to climb as it is beautiful to look upon. The Indian team that claimed to have climbed it did so under extremely adverse conditions. Their leader was invalided back to base with serious frostbite that cost him his toes and the would-be summiters battled with hunger and blizzard conditions to reach what they assumed to be the top. Ignoring the need for cautious appraisal Sarin rushed the news to the press. What followed was a Himalayan pantomime involving a crude cover-up and the unedifying spectacle of climbers wriggling out of previously stated positions.

Jagdish Nanavati of the Himalayan Club, known for his scientific exactitude in recording mountain data, happened to have undertaken a mountaineering course with Sharma, one of the summit claimants. He compared the official version with what Sharma told him. Nanavati plotted on a graph the heights of the various camps and the distances between them assuming they would tally. But there were severe contradictions in the summiters' and official accounts of the time taken to reach camps, a complication being the blizzard conditions. Another crucial factor to be reconciled was the energy levels of the summit party who were out of food and deteriorating rapidly.

Writing a monograph with calculations based on the various versions put out by the expedition Nanavati convincingly demonstrated that an exhausted summit party could not have reached the top but had probably mistaken a lower point as the summit owing to the blizzard. As honorary librarian of the Himalayan Club I discovered Nanavati's monograph in an old trunk. It was addressed to Pandit Nehru but had merited no reply.

Realizing the IMF's reputation was on the line, Sarin appointed a committee to scrutinize the expedition's schedule and detailed a professional surveyor to give his opinion on whether the climbers could have made it to the top in view of Nanavati's reservations. Nanavati was not invited to join the inquiry committee and worse, it was composed of military personnel, all of whom were dependent on Mr. Sarin for their promotions. Aerial photographs were taken and the military surveyor gave his verdict that Nilkantha could have been climbed. Unfazed and using the committee's own findings, Nanavati now drew up a series of photometric angles to prove the top could not have been reached. The military surveyor's narrow interpretation might have been plausible but for the omission of the crucial realities of the weather and the starving condition of the climbers.

From Badri we drove down to Govindghat and set off with our dogs Puja and Chow Chow to visit the gurudwara at Hem Kund. Prithwi had been brought up in the Sikh religion and this was considered a very special pilgrimage. However it was not an old one. In 1930 Sardar Sohan Singh from Tehri, a keen student of the Granth Sahib, had come across a reference that in a former life Guru Govind Singh remembered meditating in a valley surrounded by seven peaks. Like a good pilgrim Sohan Singh checked out many valleys until at last he alighted upon Lokpal (as Hem Kund was formerly known). Immediately he knew his quest had been rewarded by the guru's grace and he now made it his mission to tell other Sikhs about the glories that awaited them if they climbed to Lokpal. When he became too old to climb to the gurudwara his successor Sardar Mohan Singh sat at Govindghat doling out hand-fuls of channa to encourage pilgrims to divert from the trail to Badri.

Some students of modern religion have read Sikh triumphalism into the founding of this gurudwara at Hem Kund since it outtops Tung-nath, traditionally the highest of the shrines on the Hindu spiritual circuit of Uttarakhand. The Hem Kund building is a lavish stadium-like gurudwara funded by overseas Sikhs and took years to complete. Although its design is pleasingly modernistic its size seems out of scale for the small lake on whose shore also sits the tiny and wholly appropri-ate temple of Lokpal (this has also recently been enlarged). The original gurudwara had been a small structure in keeping with the size of the lake. The king-size replacement seemed grandiose and rather pointless. At this altitude pilgrims cannot linger and after a holy dip and wor-ship they descend to Ghangaria the same day. Not even the priest stays overnight because of the lack of oxygen. Such a large building argues an impractical understanding of Himalayan conditions. Hinduism, by contrast, with its centuries of experience in coping with pilgrimage at altitudes, sensibly did not place its main shrines much above the criti-cal 10,000-foot level at which human lungs behave normally. Anything higher and the body faces several serious health risks. The material success of overseas Sikhs not only inspired the inflated design of the Hem Kund gurudwara but contributed to the political agitation for Khalistan, a separate state for Sikhs whose capital would be Amritsar, deemed akin to the Vatican. The more extreme believers funded by for-eign dollars turned to terrorism to try and force the government's hand. To show the government took these triumphalist politics seriously, the district magistrate in Chamoli, on hearing of a Hem Kund devotee's plans to carry building material to Kak Bhusand Tal (to construct a gurudwara), impounded the wooden beams and tin sheets.

Just as Sardar Mohan Singh had read into the surroundings of Hem Kund the interpretation of Guru Govind Singh's memories (the seven peaks are not obvious to any but the most zealous of observers), this new attempt to convert the lake of (Hindu) crows into the site where Guru Govind Singh's hawk nested seemed another instance of spiritual one-upmanship at work. It is noticeable to any who ride a pilgrim bus to the Garhwal shrines that the Sikh pilgrims are far more active in their behavior than Hindu pilgrims. Most of the Hindu pilgrims are peasants from the plains. At road blocks they huddle in their bus and wait apathetically for the debris to be cleared. By contrast Sikh pilgrims will immediately spring from the bus and almost joyfully start rolling boulders down the hill to clear a way. This helps explain why the Hem Kund ascent, in spite of its rigor, is a more vibrant pilgrim experience. All the way Sikhs greet each other with a thunderous "Bole Sone Hal" to which the reply echoing from above is "Sat Sri Akal!" Natural exuberance is probably the real reason for the impressive gurudwara as a climax to the climb.

As a former Sikh maharani conscious of her history, the ascent to Hem Kund was very meaningful for Prithwi. She is a natural devotee with the gift of feeling at home in any situation where true religion is present. Our dogs, being of Tibetan ancestry, felt perfectly at home too in the snow and were allowed into the (unfinished) gurudwara since they had, like the other pilgrims, climbed on their own.

The way to the Valley of Flowers was likewise snowbound at the end of May and when we got there not a flower was in sight. Only a sprinkling of green and pink shoots indicated how the new life would have to sprint to perform its cycle in a brief three months' period. By the middle of August the tiny shoots underfoot would have shot up to become head-high in perfume-laden flowers and then just as quickly they would dry.

Prithwi found the valley disappointing after Smythe's hype and I left her sunning with the dogs while I went to photograph the memorial stone on the grave of the lady botanist from Edinburgh who had slipped while plant-collecting and died here. As I was returning by a lower route I came across in a protected dell the first outburst of flowers in the form of crocuses. The dew on their golden petals glowed like diamonds in the cold sun and I beckoned Prithwi to descend and see how the valley had won its reputation for beauty. She grumbled at having to lose height but once in the magic dell was bewitched by the tenderness of nature's new leaf. In a way this visit was more meaningful than my earlier one during the peak season. The intensity of the beauty in its uncurled potential seemed more wonderful than the even spread of a thousand species in full blossom.

THEY MAKE A DESOLATION AND CALL IT PEACE *

Amitav Ghosh

On the morning of August 24 [1998] I boarded an Indian Air Force plane with [George] Fernandes and his entourage. The plane was a twin-engined AN-32, an elderly and unabashedly functional craft of Soviet manufacture.

We had lunch at a large military base in eastern Kashmir. Fernandes met with a warmly enthusiastic reception: it was clear that he was very popular, among soldiers and officers alike.

At lunch I found myself sharing a table with several major-generals and other senior officers. Some of their names were familiar to me: they were from old soldiering families and I had read about their relatives in books of history. Their fathers and grandfathers had fought for the British Empire in Flanders, North Africa, Italy, and Burma. But their sons and daughters, I was interested to learn, had for the most part broken with these family traditions, choosing to become computer engineers, bankers, lawyers, and the like. Evidently, even among those for whom being a general was a family business, soldiering in the Indian Army no longer held its old appeal.

I was interested to learn of these senior officers' view of the nuclear tests, but I soon discovered that their curiosity on this score far exceeded mine. Did I know who was behind the decision to proceed with the tests? they asked. Who had issued the orders? Who exactly had known in advance?

I could no more enlighten them than they could me; only in India, I thought to myself, could a writer and a tableful of generals ask each

---

* In 1998, after India tested five nuclear devices in Pokaran and Pakistan tested nuclear devices of its own soon after, Amitav Ghosh visited Siachen Glacier, among other places, to understand the motivations behind the tests. This essay, excerpted from *Countdown* (2008), describes his visit to the glacier.

other questions like these. It was confirmation, at any rate, that the armed forces' role in the tests had been minimal at best.

I soon learnt also that the views of military personnel were by no means uniform. Many believe very strongly that India needs a nuclear deterrent; some feel that the tests of May 11 have resulted in certain security benefits for both India and Pakistan by bringing their secret nuclear program into the open—that the two countries would now exercise greater caution in their frequent border confrontations.

But some others expressed private apprehensions. "An escalation of hostilities along the border can happen very easily," a major-general said to me. "It takes just one officer in the field to start off a series of escalations. There's no telling where it will stop."

None of the generals, I was relieved to note, appeared to believe that nuclear weapons were harmless icons of empowerment; in the light of some of my earlier conversations around the country, there was something almost reassuring in this.

After lunch we went by helicopter to Surankote, an army base located on the neck of territory that connects Kashmir to India. Fernandes was to inspect the base and address a gathering.

The base was set in a valley, between steep, verdant hills. The sunlight glowed golden and mellow on the surrounding slopes as we landed. The base was fenced off, and the perimeters of the garrison were manned by guards with machine guns ready at their waists.

We were whisked off the landing pad and taken quickly into the interior of the base. I found myself riding in a vehicle with a young major.

"What's it like here?" I said.

"Bad." He laughed. "Bordering on terrible." He had the coiled alertness of someone whose nerves have been wound to the extreme edge of tautness.

The Pakistani front lines were just a few miles away, he explained. It took just a day to walk over the hills. This camp lay astride the main route used by those who wanted to cross from one side to the other. Nowhere in the state was the tension so great as it was here.

Fernandes had mounted a podium with several other politicians and local dignitaries. A crowd of a few hundred people had gathered to hear them. Behind them were green hills, capped by clouds.

The major pointed at the hills. "While we're standing here talking there are half a dozen operations going on in those hills, right there."

He led me aside. "Let the politicians talk," he said. "I'll show you what's happening here if you want to know." We went into a tent and the major seated himself at a radio set. "This is where we listen to them," he said. He scanned the wavelengths, tuning in to several exchanges.

"Listen," he said, turning up the volume. "They're speaking Punjabi, not Kashmiri. They're mercenaries who've signed up on two-year contracts. They're right there, in those hills." The voices on the radio had a slow, dreamlike quality; they were speaking to each other unhurriedly, calling out cheerful greetings in slow-cadenced rural Punjabi. I had no idea who the voices belonged to.

As we were leaving the tent, the major darted suddenly into a group of people and took some rolls of film from a photographer. "I can't trust them," he said. "I don't know what they've taken pictures of. I can't trust anyone here."

We walked back to the crowd to listen to the speeches. "The politicians talk so well," the major said, his eyes flickering over the crowd. "But what we have here is a war. Does anyone know what's happening here? Does anyone care?"

The crowd was quiet and orderly; the people in it looked as though they had dressed up for the afternoon. After Fernandes had spoken, he was besieged by petitioners, asking for jobs, roads, schools.

Fernandes is very well acquainted with the situation in Kashmir: he knows it better than almost any other Indian politician. During one of his terms as a minister he functioned as a special reporter on Kashmir. He talks often of those days and of how he drove into the Kashmir countryside, all but alone, meeting insurgents informally, militants and local leaders, listening to people's grievances, to their stories of brutalization at the hands of the police and the army. Not the least of the many ironies of Fernandes's present position is that he was once the country's most prominent campaigner against human rights violations by the army. He is on record as having once described an Indian Army operation as "a naked dance of a bunch of sadists and criminals in uniform."

As I watched the petitioners clamoring around Fernandes, I began to wonder what it would be like to try to live an everyday life, the life of schools and jobs, in a village that was sandwiched between that base, with its bristling perimeter fence, and the mountains beyond with their hidden guns and disembodied voices. A line quoted by the Kashmiri poet Agha Shahid Ali kept coming to mind: "*They make a desolation and call it peace.*" But here peace was not even a pretense.

～

The next day we flew to Leh, the principal town in India's northernmost district, Ladakh. As the crow flies, Ladakh is only a few hundred miles from the valley of Kashmir, but it is a world apart, a niche civilization, as it were—a far outpost of Tibetan Buddhist culture that has flourished in a setting even more extreme, in climate, altitude, and topography, than that of Tibet.

Leh's altitude is twelve thousand feet. On landing, we were handed pills to prevent altitude sickness and warned of short-term memory loss. In the afternoon, driving toward the Siachen glacier, we went spiraling over the 18,300-foot Khardung Pass. A painted sign announced this to be the world's highest motorable road. Ahead lay the Karakoram mountains; among the peaks in this range is the 28,000-foot K2, Mount Godwin-Austen, the second-highest mountain in the world.

The landscape was of a lunar desolation, with electric-blue skies and a blinding sun. Great sheets of glaciated rock rose sheer out of narrow valleys; their colors were the unearthly pinks and mauves of planetary rings and stellar moons. The mountains rose to sharp, pyramidal points, their ridges honed to fine, knife-like edges. Their slopes were covered with pulverized rock, as though they had been rained upon by torrents of gravel. Along the valley floors, beside ribbon-like streams, there were trees with whispering leaves and silver bark. On an occasional sandbank, dwarfed by the vastness of the landscape, there were tidy little monasteries and villages, surrounded by fan-tailed green terraces.

Outside the polar snows there is perhaps no terrain on earth that is less hospitable, less tolerant of human claims, than the region around the Karakorams. There are no demarcated borders here. In Kashmir there is a Line of Control that serves as a de facto border. This agreed-upon line stops short of this region, ending at an observation post named NJ 9842.

The Line of Control was a product of the first war between India and Pakistan. In 1948 both countries signed an agreement on this line.

At the time neither India nor Pakistan thought of extending this line into the high Karakorams. "No one had ever imagined," a Pakistani academic said to me in Lahore, "that human beings would ever wish to claim these frozen places."

But it was the very challenge of the terrain that led to the making of these claims. In the late 1970s and early '80s, several international mountaineering expeditions ventured into this region. They came through Pakistan and used Pakistani-controlled areas as their road-heads. This raised suspicions in India. It was discovered that maps were being published in the United States with lines drawn through the region, suggesting delineated borders where none existed. There was talk of "cartographic aggression."

It was these notional lines, on maps used mainly by mountaineers, that were eventually to transform the Siachen glacier into a battleground. It is generally agreed that the glacier has absolutely no strategic, military, or economic value whatsoever. It is merely an immense, slowly moving mass of compacted snow and ice, seventy miles long and over a mile deep.

In 1983, in order to stake India's territorial claims, the Indian Army launched a massive airlifting operation and set up a number of military posts along the glacier. Pakistan responded by putting up a parallel line of posts. There was no agreement on which posts should be where; shoving was the only way to decide.

Since that time, every day, for fifteen years, the Indian and Pakistani armies have been exchanging barrages of artillery fire at heights that range from ten to twenty thousand feet.

We stopped to visit a dimly lit hospital ward. There were some dozen men inside. None of them had been injured by "enemy action"; it was the terrain that was their principal adversary. They were plains-men mainly: in the normal course of things snow would play no part at all in their lives. They were not volunteers: only officers volunteer for service on the glacier. Some of the men were in their twenties, but most were older, some possibly in their late thirties and perhaps even early forties—family men, whose bodies had no doubt begun to slow down a little even before they were sent here. They stared at us mutely and we stared back, trying to think of something cheerful to say. One of them had tears in his eyes.

At some posts on the glacier, temperatures dip sometimes to −40 and −50°C. At these altitudes wind velocities are very high. The soldiers live in tents that are pitched either on the surface of the glacier or on ledges of rock. Shooting at the other side takes up very little of their time. They spend much of their time crammed inside their tents. Such heat as they have comes from small kerosene stoves. These are kept going all night and all day. Kerosene produces a foul-smelling grimy kind of soot. This soot works itself slowly into the soldiers' clothes, their hair, their eyes, their nostrils. When they walk back to their base camps, after their three-month tours of duty, they are enveloped in black grime.

The posts on the glacier are supplied mainly by helicopter. The craft used for this purpose is the Cheetah, a lightweight helicopter, descended from a French prototype, the Alouette. The Cheetah has been in production in India for some thirty years. On the glacier it is frequently required to perform beyond its capabilities. The Cheetah requires a two-man pilot team which means that on some sorties the craft can carry a load of only twenty-five kilograms—about one jerrican of kerosene. High winds and bad weather strictly limit the number of days on which sorties can be flown. In fine weather, the helicopters frequently have to fly under fire.

On the higher reaches of the glacier, the soldiers' dependence on the helicopters is absolute. It sometimes happens, a major-general told me, that the men become besotted with these crafts and begin to pray to them. This is just one of many species of dementia that come to afflict those who live on the glacier.

Supply problems are particularly acute on the Indian side of the glacier, where the military outposts are separated from their roadheads by long stretches of punishing terrain. Helicopter time is too precious to be spent on ferrying men between their bases and their posts. Soldiers make their way across the glacier on foot, hefting loads that are often in excess of those carried by Sherpas on Himalayan expeditions. Because of the glacier's constantly moving surface, each unit must chart its own route. Crevasses appear and disappear in a matter of hours. Some of the posts require a walk of twenty-three days.

"We allow ten extra men per battalion for wastage," an officer told me. Relatively few of the casualties on the glacier are chalked up to hostile fire: the environment imposes a heavier toll on both sides than do the guns of either army. Every year some 1,000 Indian soldiers are believed to sustain injuries on the glacier—about the equivalent of an infantry battalion.

The basic equipment for every Indian soldier on the glacier costs 60,000 rupees—about eleven times what the average Indian can expect to earn in a year. An expert once calculated that every chapati eaten by a Pakistani soldier on the Siachen glacier bears a cost of about 450 rupees (roughly the average monthly wage for the country).

The Siachen glacier, a senior officer told me, costs India the equivalent of about 20 million US dollars per day: this adds up, in the course of a year, to about one billion dollars—about one-tenth of the country's entire defense budget. Pakistan's costs are much lower but still substantial. The total cost of the Siachen conflict is probably of the same order of magnitude as that of the nuclear programs of India and Pakistan combined. If the money spent on the glacier were to be divided up and handed out to the people of India and Pakistan, every household in both countries would be able to go out and buy a new cooking stove or a bicycle.

In 1992, there were signs that both countries had reached an agreement on a simultaneous disengagement from Siachen. It was India reportedly that torpedoed the agreement. The diplomats who had negotiated the settlement were told by top politicians: "A retreat from Siachen will look bad in an election year." The election came and went, leaving the soldiers still at their posts.

We spent a night at a base close to the glacier. In the evening, in the mess, I said to a group of junior officers, "Do you think the glacier serves any purpose for either country?"

One of the officers laughed. "You know," he said, "once, while climbing an ice face, I asked myself exactly the same thing."

Another officer added quickly: "But of course we have to stay."

"Why?"

"National prestige—this is where India, Pakistan and China meet. We have to hang on, at all costs."

I was interested to note that Indian soldiers always spoke of their Pakistani counterparts with detachment and respect. Usually they referred to the other side collectively as "He"; sometimes they used the term *dushman*, "enemy." I never once heard any soldier utter a denigratory epithet of any kind.

"Most of us here are from north India," a bluntly spoken major said to me. "We have more in common with the Pakistanis, if you don't mind my saying so, than we do with South Indians or Bengalis."

One morning, in a Cheetah helicopter, I followed Fernandes through the gorges that lead up to the glacier. It was cloudy and the brilliant colors of the rock faces had the blurred quality of a water-washed print. There was a majesty to the landscape, the like of which I had never seen before.

We dipped and turned through a sand-braided river valley, trying to make our way up to a post on the glacier. The men at the post, the pilot said, were waiting eagerly for Fernandes. Before him, no defense minister had ever thought to pay the glacier a visit.

But the landing was not to be. The cloud cover was too thick. We headed toward the black, moraine-encrusted snout of the glacier.

Under an open hangar a *burra khana* had been arranged in Fernandes's honor—a kind of feast. Fernandes left the officers' table and began to serve the other ranks, taking the dishes out of the hands of the kitchen staff. The men were visibly moved and so was Fernandes. It was clear that in this job—arrived at fortuitously, late in his career—Fernandes had discovered some kind of vocation, a return perhaps to the remembered austerity and brotherhood of his days as a seminarian or his time as a trade unionist.

I was introduced to an officer who had just come off the glacier after a three-month tour of duty. He talked proudly of his men and all they had accomplished: injuries had been kept to a minimum, no one had gone mad, they had erected a number of tents and shelters.

He leaned closer. While on the glacier, he said, he'd thought of a plan for winning the war. He wanted to convey it to the defense minister. Could I help?

And the plan? I asked.

A nuclear explosion, he explained, inside the glacier, a mile deep. The whole thing would melt and the resulting flood would carry Pakistan away and also put an end to the glacier. "We can work wonders."

He'd just come off the glacier, I reminded myself. This was just another kind of altitude sickness.

The next day, sitting in his plane, I talked to Fernandes about Pakistan.

"The soldiers are of the same stock on both sides," he said. "We cannot win against them and they cannot win against us. Their strength may not be evenly matched against India but their motivation is much greater. This is the reality."

"Isn't it possible for both sides to disengage from the glacier?" I asked. "Can't some sort of solution be worked out?"

"Does anyone really want a solution?" he said quietly. In his voice there was the same note of despair I'd heard before. "I don't think anyone wants a solution. Things will just go on, like this."

Not for the first time, I wondered why Fernandes had taken the risk of bringing me with him. Was it perhaps because he wanted the world to know of his despair and its causes, hoping perhaps that that knowledge would somehow help avert whatever it was that he feared most?

Later, in Pakistan, the defense-affairs specialist, Shirin Mazari, said to me: "The feeling about Siachen in Pakistan is that we're bleeding India on that front. So let them stay up there for a while and bleed."

"But Pakistan is bleeding too surely?"

"Not as much as India; they're bleeding more."

I came to be haunted by this metaphor, because of its undeniable appositeness—its evocation of the vendettas of peasant life along with its reference to the hemorrhaging of lives and resources on the glacier: how better to describe this conflict than through an image of two desperately poor protagonists, balancing upon a barren mountaintop, each with a pickax stuck in the other's neck, each propping the other up while waiting for him to bleed to death?

To visit the Siachen glacier is to know that somewhere within the shared collective psyche of India and Pakistan, the torment of an unalterable proximity has given birth to a kind of death wish, an urge that is rising ever more insistently to the surface.

THE WRATH OF MANDAKINI*

Hridayesh Joshi

[Having driven over perilous roads for hours] we reached Tilwara [a village just before Kedarnath] at about 1:30 p.m. But on arriving there, we felt our efforts had not been in vain. We could gather information about what lay ahead and got a better idea of the overall situation. Our biggest achievement was meeting a survivor of the Kedarnath flood, a priest named Ravindra Bhatt, who narrated what he had experienced that fateful day.

I am a pujari at the Kedarnath temple. It was raining since June 13. From the fifteenth, however, the downpour was continuous. On the sixteenth, [what felt like] a huge sheet of water gushed down from the upper reaches and the area around Kedarnath was flooded. People ran helter and skelter trying to save their lives but many got swept away. We were horrified and many of us gathered inside the temple. People were wailing and screaming. It was a very scary situation . . .

Bhaiji, we were face-to-face with death—it was as though Yamraj was actually in our midst. When the water receded, we tried to quiet the crowd down and asked them to remain calm. To those who were more agitated, we said, "Have courage . . . this dark night will end . . . it will be morning soon . . . We will survive this." We slept that night thinking that the worst was over, that things would only get better the next day.

The next morning on June 17, just when we thought the nightmare was behind us, there was a loud crashing sound. Within minutes, Kedarnath was filled with water and dotted with huge boulders. I climbed up a three-story building but soon realized that it was shaking and could collapse at any moment. To save myself, I had to jump into the swirling waters below and was swept away. I was in the water for nearly

---

* The Mandakini river rose catastrophically on June 17, 2013 and killed thousands in Kedarnath. Many among those who perished were pilgrims from the plains. The river also devastated entire communities along its banks. Journalist Hridayesh Joshi and his team were among the first to report from ground zero, a harrowing experience which he chronicles in *Rage of the River* (Vandana R. Singh, trans., 2016).

fifteen minutes. And then, miraculously, the water deposited me on the side and I lay there for a long time. Later—the next day actually—rescue workers found me and brought me to safety.

We recorded this first eyewitness account of the Kedarnath tragedy. Up until now all the stories we had were either based on hearsay or of those who were stranded on the way, but Ravindra Bhatt gave us a peek into the horrors Kedarnath witnessed during the floods. Until now, everyone believed that the water from Vasuki Taal had flooded Kedarnath. But now, through Ravindra Bhatt's narration, aired on national television, we told the world for the first time that Kedarnath was destroyed because Chaurabaari lake had breached the banks.

Guptkashi was still about eighty kilometers away. Our plan was to get there before the light faded, but in the current circumstances, it looked like we would not even make it there by late night. We knew that we had to get there to add facts to our reports and it was only from there that we could even consider the possibility of going to Gaurikund, Rambara, and Kedarnath.

"Don't you have any shame?"

A few kilometers ahead, near Mayali, many cars, buses, and jeeps could be seen coming downhill. They were ferrying pilgrims stranded in Kedarnath to Rudraprayag, Dehradun, and Haridwar. Barring a few government vehicles, most of them were privately owned. There were several people who had rushed here looking for loved ones who were stuck in Kedarnath.

When they spotted our mics and cameras, people realized we were from the media and they began cursing how ineffectual the government was. Some even abused the media. None of them had any idea of the challenges we had faced just to get there. They were angry—and understandably so. One of them said, "You people are coming here now ... when everything is gone ... don't you have any shame?" There was no point talking to the overly agitated, because they would exaggerate what happened. Luckily for us, some people were still composed. Even in these extreme circumstances they kept their cool and we felt that they could give us some authentic information.

As Siddharth and I spoke to more and more people we were told that at least thirty thousand people were affected by the disaster—both by the floods and the subsequent landslides. But we had no way to verify these figures. People had suffered irreversible damage and most of them could not comprehend why they had to go through this trauma. Government support was either not there at all or was too little and too late. While we felt that their anger was completely justified, we felt that the number of casualties had been inflated. At any given point of time, it is not possible for more than fifteen to twenty thousand people to be present between Gaurikund and Kedarnath. However, the accounts left no doubt in our minds about the gravity of the situation.

The road ahead was broken and slushy, and hundreds of vehicles were trying to ply in both directions. There was a traffic jam that stretched to over five kilometers. We were in a hurry to move up the mountain, so we took it upon ourselves to act as traffic policemen and get the vehicles moving. We realized that there were not enough policemen to regulate the traffic on the roads. We saw some personnel from the National Disaster Response Force (NDRF) but they all seemed raw and inexperienced. Some of them were just boys who had no idea about the specific rules with regard to driving in the hills. Some of the NDRF rescuers, going up to bring people back from Guptkashi, were actually driving on the wrong side of the road, adding to the chaos on the jam-packed highway. It took us about three hours to get out of the mess and in the process we even had an altercation with the naive NDRF boys. At about 6:00 a.m. we stopped at a village, Dadoli, just thirty kilometers short of Guptkashi. We filed our first major report of the day. Headline: THOUSANDS OF PILGRIMS STUCK IN KEDARNATH, HUNDREDS FEARED DEAD.

THE GENEROSITY OF THE ORDINARY

On the way to Kedarnath, the town of Agastyamuni serves as an important halt. From Dadoli itself we could see the scale of destruction in this critically located town. Standing atop the mountain, the villagers showed us how the Mandakini, in all its fury, had ravaged the town. Many shops and houses were completely destroyed. The entire market was gone and a huge chunk of the road was swept away. Just a kilometer ahead of Agastyamuni, the road splits into two—one goes to Ukhimath and the other to Guptkashi. Normally, this would have been our route to Kedarnath. From Tilwara, we would have come to Agastyamuni, but that day the road was almost completely destroyed. In some parts, kilometer-long stretches had simply vanished. Standing on the mountain, we could seen there was very little of Agastyamuni left.

If Agastyamuni was dealing with its issues, Dadoli had its own unique tale to tell. A heartening tale of generosity. Only two days previously, thousands of pilgrims had come down here from the upper reaches. There was a huge open ground in the middle of the village and all the pilgrims had collected there. They were in a terrible state—hungry, injured, and mentally and physically exhausted. Some had lost their belongings. Some had family—brother, sister, wife, husband, or children—still stuck somewhere. It wasn't easy for the poor villagers to make arrangements for so many people: their food, stay, recuperation, and so on. The people of Dadoli erected a tent for the men. The women and children were sent to live in houses where the villagers took care of them. A village elder told us,

> We didn't have enough *atta*, rice, or dal. The roads were broken. We didn't know when government aid would arrive. Nevertheless we all decided to feed these people on our own. We collected rice, atta, and dal from each household. Everyone contributed and for two full days we offered shelter and food to everyone who reached our village.

Many villagers also showed us videos and photographs of how these arrangements were made. At a time when ration supply lines were cut off and no one had any idea when help would arrive, the exceptional generosity of the people of Dadoli filled us with admiration and respect.

When we began to write this report for our prime-time show that night we had some horrifying stories to tell. As darkness fell, we met a Gujarati family returning from Kedarnath. They had to leave behind their son's dead body somewhere between Kedarnath and Rambara. We heard of many others who had faced similar tragedies. To leave a loved one behind without being able to even perform the last rites . . . it's difficult to even imagine how painful it would have been for them. We were to hear more unsettling stories over the next few days in Kedarnath. Many women had to leave without their husbands. Many children had returned without their parents, while many parents had no choice but to leave their dead children behind. We now realized that this was going to be one of our longest and most difficult assignments.

It was 9:30 p.m. We had not realized that we had not eaten all day, and suddenly we were famished. Satish Negi, an extremely generous and large-hearted resident of Dadoli, took us home and fed us. Not one or two, he took our entire team of ten people to his house. We bathed and were served warm food with utmost love and affection. If we hadn't been offered a meal that night we would have been forced to go without food all day.

Guptkashi was still some thirty kilometers away. As soon as we finished eating, we set out in that direction. We were really tired. It was midnight when we finally reached Guptkashi, and a deathly silence welcomed us.

TIBETANS FROM PEKING*

Dom Moraes

As usual I woke at five. I woke with a vague thought of hard-boiled eggs and liquor and a feeling that Julian and Del and Ved and I were going for a picnic along the Cherwell. Then I inhaled the fetid air of the bedroom and remembered. I went out on the terrace, shouted for a bucket of water, and splashed for a little. Day had come up over Kanchenjunga and there was a flavor of snow, woodsmoke and herbs in the sunlight. I dressed and sat on the terrace, drinking brandy, watching the bazaar waking up, and reading *The Memoirs of Hadrian*. I knew when Das got up because his typewriter started raiding away and there were sleepy shouts of protest. At seven thirty precisely he came out to me. He carried his cameras and typewriter, and, rather depressingly, his first-aid kit.

"Ready? Good. Let us go."

The jeep had arrived. There was a slight delay while we put in eight gallons of petrol from the shop across the street. Then we drove uphill to the post office, and Das sent his telegrams.

The expedition seemed to have begun. But a hundred yards up from the post office, where the road became steep, the jeep suddenly ceased to

* In the late fifties, poet Dom Moraes traveled to Sikkim—then still a monarchy—with a photographer. This essay is a hilarious recounting of a misadventure, involving liquor and the Chinese military, on the Nathu La pass.

work. It rolled gently backward down the hill and stopped again exactly in front of the post office. The postmaster issued forth in some surprise.

"You want to file another message?"

"No," said Das grimly, then to the driver, "Son of a donkey, what has happened to your jeep?"

"Sahib," said the driver, shamefacedly, "now it will work."

He started the engine and we climbed the hill again. At the top the jeep stalled conclusively. Once more we slid gently down to the post office. The postmaster had now been joined by his entire staff. They were laughing.

"Go back to the bazaar, O fatherless one!" Das said between his teeth.

But the engine had died completely. We coasted back under control of the law of gravity. Once in the bazaar, Das jumped out with murder in his eyes.

"Go to Chiranjilal's shop," he said. "I will settle with this bastard."

Chiranjilal was all concern. "It is five past eight," he said. "You will never get there in time for Chhibar." He began telephoning various people to see if another jeep could be found. It was in vain. At eight-thirty Das returned in a fury.

"This driver has paid me back for the petrol," he said, "and I got our old Landrover. But that driver wants five hundred rupees now."

"I will talk to him," Chiranjilal said.

So we all went out—Das, Chiranjilal, the two shop assistants, and myself, to where the driver straddled the front seat of the Landrover, grinning hugely. A small crowd had gathered, including the Tibetan mother and daughter. Chiranjilal, Das, and the shop assistants all shouted at the driver together.

The driver continued to grin, and occasionally to breathe smoke into the air, ogre-wise. Otherwise he gave no sign.

"These are very important sahibs," Chiranjilal said. "Chhibar sahib wishes particularly to see them. You will gain great honor from the Dewan sahib if you take them."

"My honor has already been taken away by these sahibs," said the driver. "I am being generous when I charge only two hundred rupees extra for it."

"We will give you four hundred," said Das, almost pleadingly.

"Five," said the driver, adamant. I looked at my watch. Quarter to nine. Lost, I thought.

At this point the Tibetan mother, at the fringe of the crowd, lifted her beautiful aquiline head and called: "Shame on you, Sanje, and shame on Sikkim. You should be privileged to do anything for these sahibs. And here you are bargaining for more money to give your unchaste wife for jewelry, and bringing your country nothing but disgrace."

The driver looked at her, then looked back at us, and said sulkily: "Two fifty. Get in."

I shot our preserver a grateful glance. She returned a broad wink. I laughed with relief. I could have kissed her.

We left Gangtok at about nine.

"*Bahadur sahib*," Das said flatteringly, "if you get us to Nathu La by eleven, we will call you Rajkumar, a prince."

"Sanje is sufficient for me," said the driver disagreeably. "Do you think I have wings to fly to Nathu La?"

I offered him a cigarette, and said guilefully, "If you get there by eleven, we will pay three hundred rupees."

"Sahib," said the driver, suddenly tractable, "if you say half past eleven, I can do it."

He sucked tentatively at my cigarette as we climbed out of Gangtok into the Himalayan track.

"It will be raining. There is fog ahead. I will try. Sahib," he said, looking at the cigarette in his fingers, "do you make these yourself?"

"They are made by a great sahib in Bilayat," I said, "called Du Maurier."

"Do you know this sahib?" asked the driver.

"Of course," I said.

"If he comes to Sikkim," said the driver, "recommend me to him. He must be rich. I will take him to Nathu La for a thousand rupees."

Then we passed into the mist.

Out of the mist, every so often, mules blundered like moths against the headlights. Behind them the tall shivering muleteers raised their arms in salute as we passed. As we climbed that spiral funnel toward the sky, the air thinned and rain began to whip tinily in with a knife-cold wind. I pulled the waterproof across the doorway, cutting off the view and saving myself from vertigo, for the track had narrowed to a strip of mud disintegrating in rain. We passed a huddle of shacks outside which cold policemen stood. "Karponang," Das said.

"Twenty-three miles still." I looked at my watch again. It was ten to ten. "Good going."

Das said, "Last time I passed through Karponang there were ten feet of snow. Mist everywhere also, you could not see even. I was coming back from taking medicine to the first Tibetan refugees, just after the flight of the Dalai Lama. My driver was driving with one hand and telling his beads with the other: he was a Buddhist. But I also thought we were going to die that day." He hesitated and said: "One should not bother about dying."

Cigarettes gave one a strange ill feeling so I stopped smoking and squinted ahead through the mist-frosted windscreen. Only one of the wipers was working; it hissed and snicked to and fro; as a child I used to call them "vipers." Presently we passed a gutted building.

"The old fifteen-mile checkpost," Das said. "It burnt down last year. Soon comes the new one."

Ahead the mountainside widened and accommodated a kind of village with a worn wooden gate and a barbed-wire palisade across the road. A policeman came dripping out in a waterproof to inspect our pass. He took down the particulars, and nodded, unspeaking. We drove on. "Nine miles to Chhangu."

For the next half hour we leant slowly, noiselessly, through a cotton-thick mist. Rain fell. It was bitterly cold, and I draped my knees with one of Das's blankets. Then we moved out of the mist, to a cold burning of sunlight, and the unwinding road brought us down to a great lake. The mountains lay wobbling gently under the water; the water was powdery and blue, like an eye, like a pearl, and shivered all over by the risings of fish.

"Chhangu Lake."

We climbed again, till we had left the mountain hollow of the lake behind us. Mule caravans were now very frequent. The landscape was changing noticeably. All the way from Gangtok, the mountains had been humped and rough with trees. Now they seemed to have broken off in the air, jagged and pointed, and furred over with thick gray-green lichen, on which broken fragments of limestone lay. Among this lichen browsed enormous antediluvian animals, hung round with black hair, like woolen blankets walking, with horns splaying massively across their low brows. "Yaks." The driver pointed out a reddish flower coquetting in the wind. "Poison-flowers, sahib. You only find them here. Touch, and you die."

The sunlight burnt on, an icy fever, and wind tacked across the shelved valleys, altering the clouds. We reached another hamlet, another worn gate, more barbed wire. Yaks were browsing between the huts. One raised his great matted head with a deep sleepy bellow.

"Sherathan," Das said. "The last checkpost. Two miles to Nathu La. What's the time?"

"Ten past eleven."

"Not bad. Good. *Shabash*, driver. Three hundred rupees for you. Chhibar also may be late," he explained to me.

Now we were climbing all the way, above the blue sockets of two more lakes, anthology of the tears of all the rocks. The landscape had an undated quality, prelapsarian perhaps, and the yaks, shaggy and gentle because their eyes were hidden under hair, might have floundered to Adam's hand in Eden. Ahead the road became well trained, covered with small slaty flagstones like fish scales. Then coming round a bend we saw it lift, under walls, to where a jeep was parked and three uniformed midgets stood. Das gave a deep sigh of achievement. I looked at my watch. Eleven thirty. "That is Nathu La."

We pulled in at a small shelf cut into the mountaintop, a lichen-rusted hummock rising beyond. The shelf had for ornament a small stone boundary post, inscribed "Sikkim-Tibet Border." Pools of water lay about, memorials of the morning's weather. A police officer and two constables greeted us with a request for our passes.

Then Das and I climbed the hummock, to look into Tibet. The sun had come out brilliantly and coldly, and the sky over Tibet was an icy blue. From where we stood the mountain slipped steeply down, dry and boulder-strewn, into the Chumbi Valley, a succession of folds in the ground, thickly forested, rippling to a narrow V. At the point of the V, across the valley, rose a range of forested hills. Beyond them the horizon was like a picture postcard, two scarred snow peaks vivid in the frosty sky, and a glimpse of plains between and beyond. The police officer came silently up behind us, pointing out the higher of the snow peaks.

"That is Chumbiladi."

"Where does Tibet start?" I asked.

"My dear gentleman," said Das, "we are in Tibet. It starts from the boundary post down there."

"Where are the Chinese?" I inquired naively.

The policeman handed me his field glasses. I followed his finger as it swept the Chumbi Valley. Where the valley turned into hills, at the point of the V, I made out a small concrete building among the trees.

"That is their checkpost, at Chumbithan. But who can tell where those rapers of their sisters are? They hide here and there in the jungle and watch us through field glasses. But I can tell you, sahib, there must be a hundred or two between here and Chumbithan, and that is two miles."

"*Chinia aye the aj, kya?*" Das asked. "Have they come here today?"

"*Ji nahin.* No, sir. They will not come till Chhibar sahib has passed. This is their diplomacy."

I turned and looked about. Huge cairns of stones littered the hummock, ominous and druidical. Above them hundreds of improvised prayer flags, made of tattered garments, tautened in the whipping wind out of Tibet.

"What is all that?"

"When these Tibetan folk come back from Kalimpong or Gangtok they throw a stone at the border, to drive away the evil spirits from abroad. Also they put up those flags for good luck."

Clouds swept over the sky, and suddenly mist rose everywhere, and Tibet was blotted out of sight as completely as if it had never been there. I could understand, suddenly, why the Tibetans believe that evil spirits live in these high passes. The cairns loomed gloomily; the prayer flags hung limp, then whiffled in the wind. I found myself strangely exhilarated. "It's the air," I thought, then, as the wind sang over the pass, shivered, helpless with cold.

Das, drinking the wind like a tonic, rushed sharply about, posing the policemen, the drivers, and myself in various places, against the cairns and flags, drooping over the boundary post, etcetera. He had given me his movie camera to hold, and that hand had turned completely numb. I tried to talk to the police officer, but it was difficult to move my lips.

However, "What do you think?" I said. "Will the Chinese attack?"

"Sahib, that is what their officers tell everybody. The yak drivers and the muleteers say that the Chinese promise to be in Sikkim before next summer."

"What will you do then?"

"Fight, sahib. What else? Only the *Sarkar* must give us material for us to fight with. Our radio transmitter here works only three hours a day. If the Chinia should come while it is not working, how can we let them know at Sherathan, so that our boys can be ready there?"

"Well, they can see Nathu La," I said, "through field glasses."

The police officer laughed.

"Sahib," he said, "the garrison at Sherathan has no field glasses. They have asked for some, but the *Sarkar* does not send. If there is fighting at Nathu La, our men at Sherathan will not see it till the Chinia are on their heads."

The mist was thinning. He swept the Chumbi Valley with his field glasses. Then he said, "Someone is coming."

I shouted to Das, who returned from his photography at a trot. He peered through the field glasses, then passed them to me. Four or five men on muleback were snailing up one side of the valley.

"It doesn't *look* like a diplomatic party," I said.

"It may be some traders," said the policeman. "Let us wait." I remembered the brandy. We squatted, all of us, under a cairn, which afforded some protection from the wind, and passed the bottle from hand to hand. Mist went over in little puffs. The brandy had a strange, fiery effect, fifteen thousand feet up: my ears sang and I felt sick.

As the mist lifted again for a minute, we saw the mule riders plodding up from the foot of the hummock toward us. Das jumped up and shouted for his movie camera. He began to work it as the first rider reached us. Three others drifted after him. They were definitely Indian traders: small, heavily muffled men, with nervous rolling eyes, like apprehensive ponies. The first one dismounted, and Das was at him like a terrier.

"Welcome. Where are you from? Yatung, hah? *Kya hal chal hai Yatung me?*"

"*Bahuth mushkil he Yatung me, sahib.* Much trouble. Yesterday the Chinia killed an Indian trader there. Their people stabbed him and looted his shop. Therefore this morning we left there, closing our shops. There are only three Indian shops open in Yatung today, where once there were fifteen."

The police officer interrupted. "Have you seen Chhibar sahib?"

"He was leaving Yatung an hour after we left, Inspector sahib. We thought, if we came before, we would be safe; if we came after, the Chinia would eat our lives."

"So," said Das thoughtfully. "He will still be one hour." He glanced into the misted valley. "Are there any Chinia down there?"

"Many, many Chinia," one of the other traders said. "They are in the forest, three furlongs down the valley."

"Why don't we go down and look at them?" I suggested.

"That is what I also was thinking," Das said.

Brandy and the thin air had brought on euphoria. I heard myself laughing and saying rather stagily, "Two minds with but a single thought."

"*Arre,* don't try these mad tricks," said the inspector in alarm. "If the Chinia see you they will shoot you first and then ask who you are."

"Sahib," said one of the traders. "On my mother's life, it is a mad thing to do."

"Driver," shouted Das, "bring my movie camera." He cast the kind of glance a professional spy might have cast into the valley. "While the mist gives us cover, we shall start. Lend us your field glasses, Inspector sahib."

"Sir," said the policeman, "on my mother's and grandmother's lives, I should forbid you. What will come to me if you are killed or taken prisoner? I will lose my job!"

"Come on, Dom," Das said to me.

So I took a final drink from the bottle, borrowed the inspector's field glasses, turned my coat collar up against the wind, and followed Das into the valley.

The slope was strewn with rocks, which afforded precarious handholds. We had to let ourselves down backward, like mountaineers, and I felt acutely conscious of the wind flapping my jacket, the field glasses dangling round my neck, and the unseen Chinese probably even now gloating over us through their field glasses, like uniformed Fu Manchus.

I reached the bottom of the slope a minute after Das. He did not hesitate, but set off at a brisk walk down the valley. The ground was rough and tussocky, the mist had thickened, and it was impossibly cold. My limbs were like stalactites: lifting one became a creaking, breathless effort. Conversation was out of the question. I simply followed Das, and we were suddenly among trees.

Here there was a clean acid stench of wet earth and herbs. A bird or two shrieked upward through the leaves, but otherwise everything was grave-silent. Our feet scuffing through the undergrowth sounded like a forest fire.

We walked for about twenty minutes, twice passing clearings where ashes remained in ersatz fireplaces made of heaped stones. Then Das stopped. We were both breathless. We sat down and I lit a cigarette. We talked in whispers.

"There don't seem to be any Chinese hereabouts."

"Certainly we are not seeing any. But we must have come the best part of a mile. If we push on, we will be near the checkpost. If I can get a film of some troops without their seeing me, we shall have scooped the world."

I no longer felt any apprehension. It seemed to me reasonable that Das should want to scoop the world. Apart from the difficulty of breathing properly in this rarefied air, I felt quite willing to go on.

"Those fireplaces, do you think they were made by the Chinese?" I was beginning to feel toward the Chinese now as I might toward the inhabitants of Troizen or Zimbabwe.

"Perhaps by the Chinese, perhaps by some muleteers. Let us get on."

We stumbled through the trees. In the forest the mist seemed to be filtered away by the leaves, but overhead the sky was still clogged with gray. This unrewarding sky was our only window to the rest of the world for another twenty minutes, till we stumbled out of the forest onto a bare ridge, littered with chalky rock fragments, between two hillocks. Here we sat down again. I looked round through the field glasses. We were a good way into the valley: the two great snow peaks looked closer and the barren hummock of Nathu La surprisingly far. I put down the glasses and lit another cigarette. Das drummed his fingers on his knee.

"If we pushed on a little farther, we would get close enough to Chumbithan to take a film of the checkpost. Do you think that is a foolhardy plan?"

The clouds rifted: suddenly and fugitively the sun glared from a waste of blue. Idly I picked up the glasses and looked round. The sun caught them, and reflected light flashed on one of the neighboring hillocks.

A moment later, there was an answering flash on the ridge where we sat. Das looked up in surprise. The flash was repeated. I looked through the glasses in the direction from which it came.

On the neighboring hillock, clustered together, was a group of Chinese.

There were about twenty, stocky and tough-looking. Two were in a drab gray-green military uniform with peaked caps. These two were looking at us through field glasses. The rest stood behind, Sten guns and ammunition belts hung over their shoulders. They pointed at us, and were apparently discussing us among themselves.

I told Das. He said very coolly, "Let us get back into the trees in case they open fire. I will take a film." We moved back to the fringe of the forest. Das fitted the telelens on his camera. He knelt down, swiveling it for focus. I was unnerved, but not unpleasantly. I tried to analyze what I was feeling. I hoped to God that they wouldn't think Das's camera was a Sten gun and open fire. I could feel my own heart beating very fast, and I kept on swallowing. But after the initial shock had worn off, I was able to calculate a few things. First, they could not be less than half a mile away. If our information about their weapons had been right, we were out of range. Second, we were going to have to hurry back, for they would certainly send men after us. Das's camera had begun to hum by my side. I put the glasses back on the Chinese. Half a dozen men and one of the officers were already moving downhill. The remaining officer continued to study us through his glasses.

Das's camera ceased to hum. He stood up and turned to me.

"A scoop. You noticed those men coming down the hill, hah? They are coming to get us. Therefore I think we will have to run."

He nodded toward Nathu La.

"Run straight back. We must not stop for anything. Mind the field glasses; they belong to the inspector. Come on."

Of the next half hour I remember very little. I am not a good runner anyway and in the thin clear air of the plateau I was worse than usual. The initial stumbling gallop through the forest rendered me breathless; then my ears filled with a buzzing that shut out all other sound; finally I developed a burning stitch in my left side. That is the physical memory, and there is one visual image: when we came to a small pebbled brook in the forest, I collapsed beside it and lay on my stomach watching the weeds waver slowly in the flow of the current, two long-legged water flies, and a minnow; the moss was cool against my cheek. When I looked up Nathu La seemed far and unreachable. I was willing to stay where I was. Das's voice, breathless but imperative, brought me to a kind of reality.

"Come on. We are nearly there. Quickly!"

So flight began again. I reached Nathu La in a daze, a small iron needle in my side. We scrambled back up the slope and sat down heavily amongst a solicitous group of policeman, traders, and drivers.

"We were beginning to worry," said the inspector.

"We also," said Das, and managed a smile.

The mist had come on again, and there was no sign of the Chinese.

We lay on foam rubber–textured lichen, getting our breath, and in my case helping it along with the remains of the brandy. One of the traders came and squatted beside us.

Das, sighing, heaved himself indefatigably up and reached for his notebook. "This Indian who was killed. Tell me about him."

"It was done by the Tibetans," the trader said. "They came to his shop in the afternoon, and stabbed him five times. Then they looted the shop, took the money from the cashbox, and left."

"Tibetans?" Das said with professional disappointment. "I thought you said Chinese."

"The Chinese say they themselves are Tibetans who have come from Peking. But these real Tibetans were hired by the Chinia, sahib," said the trader. "They did it in the daytime and the bazaar was full of Chinia policemen, but they did not interfere, though he shouted for help."

"Ha!" said Das, and scribbled enthusiastically. "How do they treat you, these Chinese?"

"Sahib, in the daytime we cannot move more than two hundred yards from our houses without a permit. After nine o'clock we cannot leave our houses also. It is jail life. Also they have taken the custom from our shops, and anything they buy they buy on credit, and never pay."

"Why don't you complain to the Indian trade agent at Yatung? He is there to help you."

"Sahib, what can he do? They pay no attention. And if we leave Tibet, they confiscate all our goods. Now we, today, were only allowed to bring our clothes and ten rupees from Yatung. They have only contempt for us Indians. Every Saturday in Yatung they have a clown show with four clowns, and one is Nehru."

"Good, good!" said Das, scribbling a little more. "Who are the other three?"

"Eisenhower sahib, Churchill sahib, and Khrushchev sahib."

"Why Khrushchev?"

"They are very angry that Russia has not supported them over the border dispute."

"What do they say about the border?"

"Sahib, the officers say one day soon they will be coming. At the checkpost at Chumbithan they told us to say that in Sikkim."

"It may not be as easy as they think," said the police officer dourly.

"The Chinia are strong," the trader said.

"How do they treat the Tibetans?" I asked.

"Sahib, all the rich men they have put to building a military road from Shigatse. Also in Yatung two weeks ago they took all the young girls away. They do this to keep the men from running away; also the girls are useful in North Tibet, because they are settling many Chinia civilians there, and they have no women."

"What about the rebels, the Khambas? Is there still any fighting?"

"With them also, they took their families and put them in jail, until the husbands surrendered. Them they shot or put to work on the Shigatse road."

He sat by us, sighing, gathering a little dust in his hand and sifting it away with the slow movements of a tired man. I noticed how jumpy all the traders were. They had lines under their eyes, and all of them had nervous twitchy gestures of the hand.

We sat there, thinking, drinking, and then the inspector said: "Chhibar sahib is coming."

Through the field glasses a file of mules appeared ambling up the valley toward Nathu La. It was a relief. We squatted on the hummock watching them all the way up the valley till they had reached us.

Chhibar came first. He was a large man, rosy and powerful, wearing a fur hat and leather jacket. As his mule crested the ridge, we all shouted, rather raggedly, "Welcome!" He smiled and waved a hand.

After him came his wife, a most beautiful woman in a ballooning quilted jacket that made her look like a little tent, and three Tibetan nurses, each with one of the Chhibar offspring in her arms. They were followed by a baggage train, the muleteers prodding the mules with goads and shouting the Tibetan version of Gittup: "*To to to to to to to,*" on a rising scale. "Very picturesque," said Das, going happily to work with his movie camera. When he had finished, the Chhibar family dismounted, and Das handed his camera to the driver and fished for his notebook.

"How was your trip, Major Chhibar?"

"Fine, fine," said Chhibar, smiling gently.

"What are these reports of your being hindered by Chinese troops on your journey?"

"Untrue," Chhibar sighed.

"The Chinese were helpful?"

"To me, yes," emphasizing the *me.*

"And to other Indians? Say, the traders?"

"Less helpful."

"Would it be true to say that the traders are in fear of their lives?"

"Perhaps." So large, so gentle, so like a wall blocking off undiplomatic questions.

"How many troops would you say there were in Tibet?"

"I can't say. It is a difficult question."

"In Lhasa, then?"

"It is a difficult question. Ten thousand—fifteen thousand."

"And between Lhasa and Nathu La?"

"It is a difficult question. Perhaps the same number again."

"So there are between twenty and thirty thousand Chinese in the area between Lhasa and Nathu La?"

"I would say so, yes."

"Hah!" said Das, but at this point Mrs. Chhibar came up to introduce the children, and I became occupied in teaching one of the little girls how to whistle, and missed the rest.

Then the Chhibars left in the waiting jeep, and Nathu La was desolate again.

I went up to the hummock to get a last look at Tibet. All I saw was mist.

GYALTSEN HAS A VIDEO*

Manjushree Thapa

I

Lo changed my impression of Mustang as a land of deprivation.

We crossed a cairn on a rock-and-dust hilltop and suddenly found ourselves above a vibrant expanse of red and ocher crags, pink buckwheat fields, and a sparkling blue-green river. In the middle of this valley was a settlement of neat white houses that had enamel, colored windows to herald the arrival of another, more Tibetan world. Eagles circled the vast blue sky.

The first village we went to, Ghemi, had wide cobbled lanes that led up to an earth-red *chorten*. It was mid-morning, and we could hear only the sounds of the wind. The wheat fields rustled, the sand shifted, and voices drifted from far away. Then, from the other side of the *chorten* came a clip-clop of hooves, and a pale, stately man in slacks and a striped Oxford shirt rode into view on a chestnut horse. He smiled handsomely and galloped on, then disappeared into the silence: a princely apparition.

The man who opened the door of the house we went to eat at was just as fanciful. He had taut Tibetan features and pale, soft skin that signaled privilege. His hair was braided around his head. He wore a turquoise on one ear. But his clothes came from another place: straight-leg jeans, brown spurred boots, and a blue cashmere pullover. A carved silver knife hung from his leather belt. Instead of greeting us or asking us questions or inviting us in, as others had, this man folded his hands and stared at us silently, with composure. For the first time, I felt embarrassed about my dirty clothes and my wild, dusty hair.

Lo surprised me again and again; its ancient land—blood-red hills made of demons' lungs and *mani* walls of their entrails—was speckled

* An account of travels in Mustang, formerly the Kingdom of Lo, a remote Himalayan region on the Nepal-Tibet border. Excerpted from *Mustang Bhot in Fragments* (2008).

with savvy, self-possessed United Colors of Benetton characters. Of them, the women, who were more traditional, wore *bukkhoos* of spotless silks and satins and variegated rayons. But the men had Hindu names like Rajendra, Gyanendra, Surendra, or—because cultural reclamation coexisted with cultural imperialism—sometimes not. And they wore designer clothes like windbreakers, boots, Ray Bans, maybe even Stetsons, but if not, certainly baseball caps.

♈

These multicultural people were the nobles of Lo, members of the elite Kudak class and relatives of the Raja of Mustang. They equated themselves with Nepal's ruling Thakuri clan and adopted the Hindu name Bista.

Bistas numbered only a few families in each village, but Lo seemed made for them. Theirs was a bustling world of possibilities, with horses to travel through Mustang, plane tickets to take them beyond, land to oversee, villages to direct, festivals to organize and preside over, relatives to visit, connections to maintain and build on. They upheld the mythic grandeur of the old kingdom.

The other Lobas led more common lives. They were divided into Padungu and Rigiri sub-castes. Like the Bhotias of Baragaon, most of them now called themselves Gurung, the name of the ethnic group from south of the Annapurna, partly because identifying themselves as members of a less marginal ethnic group facilitated their dealings with the government.

Our interactions with the women of Lo revealed some class differences among the Loba. Bista women were surrounded by so much high-class propriety that we didn't even meet many. Our status, after all, was only slightly higher than that of a *karmachari*; Bikas was an *engineer* from a *company*, and I was what? Just traveling. The second year, when I was also from a *company,* I became more acceptable—still, few Bista women bothered with us.

Gurung women had none of the waxen preciousness of Bista women. We met them in *bhattis* or on the road as they headed home from a day in the fields, or from a month of farm work at a *ne-tshang*'s farm, or from a trip to Jomosom for timber. Most had dusty, dark robes hitched up to their calves, and they wore polyester or flannel shirts and

LIFE 277

well-worn sneakers. Their faces were red and brown from the sun and their lips were so cracked they looked like dead, dried skin.

Once Gurung women got over their hesitation to use unfamiliar Nepali words, they asked us for cigarettes and swapped views and gossip. "Electricity's too costly," one woman told us, and another said, "Our men all marry Rongbas nowadays." One woman said, pointedly, "Gyaltsen has a *bhirdi-yo*," meaning television.

⌒

Gyaltsen was a Bista. He was the brother-in-law of the Raja of Mustang, off-and-on village head of Tsarang, a big man who moved slowly, with dignity. His house, which stood prominently in the middle of the village, had a courtyard filled not with goats and cows, but with well-groomed horses. The house walls were decorated with Buddhist landscapes, conch shells, and lotuses. Precious wood logs from far south were stacked on the roof, underneath a layer of commonplace twigs.

Because Bikas had official connections to Gyaltsen Bista's family we were allowed to stay at his house. From the day we arrived, Bikas started to examine the surprisingly crude powerhouses of Tsarang and Marang. I watched him work and listened in on his conversations with local powerhouse operators, and learnt something about small hydropower plants.

Tsarang was the first electrified village in the restricted area. The villagers had helped build the plant and pay for some of its cost. The electricity was generated in a shack below the village canal. The houses were wired by a man who came up, now and then, on contract. While he was here, he also did small repair jobs on the lines. The powerhouse operator, a local man, turned the machines on and off every day and oversaw the repair of broken parts in return for a monthly salary.

The simplicity of the setup was impressive. I became sympathetic to Bikas' work. Anything that helped cushion against the land's severity seemed a valuable contribution.

I spent the rest of my time soaking in the small comforts of Gyaltsen Bista's house. The clean earthen rooms were decorated with colorful rugs and strips of cut linoleum. The walls had bright enamel paint and posters of Swiss chalets. A cheerful red cloth stretched over the ceiling and protected us from bits of wood and mud that fell when people walked on the balcony above. In this house, fragments from all over the world appeared out of the blue: Chinese biscuits, Rara Noodles, board games, an electrical cooker, an indoor toilet (with a hole in the floor that opened onto a manure room underneath), pressure cookers, cupboards stacked with cups and extra flasks, and of course, electricity.

I glanced around furtively for signs of Gyaltsen's *bhirdi-yo*, but couldn't find any. We were relegated to the guest room that was sectioned off from the rest of the house by a tin wall. Since there was no space for probing or prying, I saw only what took place in that room and in the kitchen. The abbot of Tsarang's *gomba* came to chant one evening. Favored *karmachari* came to play cards another night. Once, Bistas from Ghemi stopped by for a session of mah-jongg. I saw no signs of a television.

But people were talking. When Bikas and I continued our walk to Lo Monthang, we heard sudden, sharp words in the middle of humdrum prattle. Gurungs said that the Bistas had untold wealth, and Bistas said that the Gurungs were crass. Both camps called the other "they." "They don't know any better," said a Bista, and a Gurung said, "They don't have to walk because they have horses." Another Gurung said, "Chandra's a Bista, but he acts like one of us."

Clearly, the richest Bista families lived well in comparison to most Gurung families. Gyaltsen Bista's daughter exuded the self-confidence that came from economic security. She was educated, and she took care of family affairs as well as public responsibilities like the administration of the electrical scheme. She was the only woman I saw in Lo who wore a *kurta-sural*. Her brother divided his time between Kathmandu and Mustang. He was also educated, and suave and self-assured; he cut a dashing figure when he galloped up the dusty hills on a horse, overseeing family responsibilities. The two of them were always impeccably turned out during religious festivals.

This was what it meant to be well off in Mustang: having modern amenities—electricity, health care, and education, maybe even television—to ease harsh rural conditions, and having tradition to mask this modernity.

It was not an extravagant life, but it felt that way in context.

The walled city of Lo Monthang jutted out of a green valley that was surrounded by a horizon of barren hills. The "city" looked dismally tiny from a distance, but as we approached it I saw that it was teeming with life. Two hundred-odd houses, their inhabitants, and their inhabitants' animals were tightly packed into an enclosure small enough to walk through in fifteen minutes. The wall that encased the settlement was punctuated, in places, by the windows and doors of the houses on the other side.

There were two lodges in Lo Monthang. One was near the post office, opposite the Raja's palace. The room where guests slept was painted sky-blue after the modern style in the cities. An artfully painted *trompe-l'oeil* curtain lined the top of the walls. The beds had clean foam mattresses and wool carpets. On a cupboard were photos of the lodge owner—a Bista—in front of Lo Monthang's wall, and a Grateful Dead sticker. Across the room lay burlap sacks filled with Rara Instant Noodles, Pashupati Biscuits and Yak cigarettes, and jerricans full of kerosene.

We stayed there the first year and found it comfortable but isolated. Family members spent most of their time in the kitchen, and no one dropped by to talk.

The lodge we stayed in the second year was entirely different. It was run single-handedly by a woman named Dolma Gurung, and even the Bistas came there to relax, chat, gamble, drink themselves silly, and maybe pass out for the night.

◇

The guys—Mustang-elite, Kathmandu-exposed, world-weary Rabindra, Jamyang, and Krishna Bista—sat in a circle and played a dice game which made them whoop, cry, shout, curse, hiss, and smack each other on the knee. Each player chose a number and yelled it out loud as he slapped the dice onto a leather pad. Then the player lifted his hands and everyone screamed and yelled about the result. The room thundered with excitement.

Jamyang turned to us every so often to make a wry remark.

"Development?" he said, and he raised an eyebrow. "With people like this, there's no fear of that in Mustang."

The other men roared with laughter, but Jamyang kept a straight face.

"Keep a dog's tail in a bamboo pipe," Krishna said, from across the room. "Keep it there for twelve years, and still, at the end, it'll be curly. These people are like that." He smirked and let his hair fall over his eyes. But only a few people laughed. Krishna lacked Gyaltsen's finesse; he was too young, too cocksure. He said, "Even Indra's father Chandra couldn't develop this place." He repeated the popular Nepali saying, "Indra's father Chandra."

"Indra's father Dawa couldn't," someone said. Krishna sneered. Others hooted. Jamyang said nothing. He pulled on a cigarette and squinted at the dice. Then he muttered "Shug-shug-shug-shug!" and yelled murderously as he slapped down the dice. The men pulled forward to see what he had rolled. Then they groaned and yelled.

Rabindra sat apart from them. He was older, around thirty-eight he said, though he looked twenty. His eyes were quick, he was more observant, and he was quieter.

He said to us, "I've arranged horses for you to go to the *border* tomorrow. You have to leave early, otherwise the river'll be too high to cross when you return in the afternoon. I'll come at six to wake you."

"Six? Aaack!" Krishna said. "Six!" He shivered with mock horror and looked around for support.

Jamyang grinned. "We," he said, "we Bhotias don't wake up until nine."

Bikas said, "I saw you early this morning on a small horse, with your feet dangling all the way to the floor. Remember?"

He shrugged. "Yeah. I had to let the animals out. But then I went back to sleep." He left the others and came to sit with us.

"The thing about elections," he said, settling in beside Bikas, "the thing was, the election symbols were stupid. Tree, sun, plow." This was part of a several-day-long conversation we had carried on about the last parliamentary elections. Gyaltsen was a supporter of the Nepali Congress Party, whose election symbol was a tree. Krishna, a supporter of the partyless Panchayat regime, had joined the party established by those who had been in power during the Panchayat era, which in the elections ran under the symbol of a plow. Rabindra was decidedly neutral. He wanted out, to go work abroad, he said, "Maybe in Japan or Australia." The candidate of the Communist Party of Nepal (Unified

Marxist-Leninist), whose election symbol was a sun, had won the seat from Mustang.

"They say our MP has four daughters," Krishna said. He shook the hair out of his eyes.

"Maybe you should ask to marry one," a man said. Someone whistled. Krishna sniggered.

Jamyang leant back on the mud bench until his whole body was flat, and only his head was propped up on a pillow.

"You know," he said to us, ignoring the others, "you know what? The reason Congress lost in Mustang is because of that stupid tree symbol. Think about it. The sun gets too hot, trees die. Someone comes and digs them up with a plow, they die. Now"—he held up an instructive finger—"if they'd chosen a more practical symbol like a pressure cooker or a thermos . . ."

The other men roared with laughter, but glib Jamyang was already elsewhere. "Dolma, are you going to let die of thirst?" he yelled, scowling at the door.

Dolma came in, pale and petite and solemn, with a flask in one hand. She filled Jamyang's empty tumbler with *chhaang*. Then she scratched her hair and checked everyone else's glasses. Rabindra said something to her, and she filled up Bikas's glass.

"And who did you vote for, Dolma?" Krishna shouted, swaggering somehow, though he was seated.

Dolma indulged him with a smile and walked toward the kitchen.

"Dolma voted for tree," Jamyang said. "Didn't you, Dolma?"

"I forget," she said. She turned back and flashed a gold-toothed smile.

"Then why do you have a poster of the Congress candidate on your door?"

"There's a poster of Om Bikas Gauchan on the other door," she said, and shrugged. "It doesn't mean a thing."

Krishna said, "Dolma voted for plow."

She laughed, then looked at me knowingly. "They say you shouldn't tell."

The guys shouted: "Congress!" "Communist!" as she left the room.

Jamyang turned back to us.

"Have you heard the one about the Bhotia who sold his goat for only twenty-five rupees?"

He sat up. "There was once a very rich Newar merchant who wanted to show off his new gold ring. He spotted a Bhotia selling goats, so he pointed to one goat with his ring finger and said, 'How much?' The Bhotia got really annoyed. So you know what he did? He decided to show off his gold tooth. He said, 'The goat's worth *pachees*.'" Jamyang stretched his mouth wide to pronounce *pachees*, the Nepali word for twenty-five, and pointed to the tooth that should have been gold, according to Bhotia custom. His, of course, was not; he was too urbane for that. "*Pachees*," he screeched, "Hee, hee. What an idiot. *Pachee-e-e-e*-s."

Dolma walked into the room and said something loudly in Tibetan. The gamblers groaned and stood up slowly and straggled out. Jamyang gulped down the last of his *chhaang* and left with the other men without bothering to say goodnight.

"I told them there was a woman among my guests, and that they should leave," Dolma said to me when the room was empty, and suddenly quiet. "Otherwise they'd play all night."

⌒

Dolma's lodge was tucked into an alley behind the palace. Its guest room looked out on the gate of the walled city. Early in the morning women gathered at the two taps in front of the wall to fill their jerricans—*jerkin*—with water. Then they went home to cook a meal. In a while the men led the cows and goats to grazing lands outside the city wall. The women headed to the fields with empty baskets on their backs and the day's rations—*tsampa* and a flask of tea—in their hands. The alley in front of the city gate bustled with traffic then, and rang with cries and laughter. During the day, when everyone was away, everything was quiet again. A few aged men and women with thick eyeglasses and dark, heavy clothes shuffled by with prayer wheels or beads in their hands. Some children played in the dirt. One or two Rongba—school teachers, border guards, health-post attendants—passed by on the way to work, and monks shuttled from *gomba* to *gomba*. At dusk, men gathered by the gate and gossiped, some working their spindles to make wool, others rocking toddlers on their laps. There was a sudden commotion when the children swarmed out of school, and again when the women came back from the fields with the animals. The kids ran in motley groups that fought and tussled each other. Teenagers gathered in boys' and girls' groups, eyed each other, and launched sudden, fierce attacks to push and shove and flirt. The women exchanged jokes and reproaches with the men as the cows, still hungry after a full day of grazing, nipped viciously at the greenery in their baskets.

⁓

The Raja's palace stood directly in front of the city gate, a four-story whitewashed clay structure with prayer flags on top, endless dusty glass-paned windows, and a dismal wood-carved entrance.

I had a chance to go inside only on the second trip, when I came with an assignment to investigate the possibility of repairing two of the *gomba* of Lo Monthang. A rickety wood staircase led to a dark landing that was decorated with a stuffed Tibetan mastiff. A live one was also tied up there. Farther up the stairs was an outdoor landing where a retinue of servants cooked rice at a wood-fire stove. Up another stairway was a verandah lined with prayer wheels and painted with Buddhist landscapes. Some of the rooms along the verandah were empty and unused. The inhabited ones were closed. The toilet in the palace (I had access to that, but not to the legendary shrine) was like others in Lo, with a hole in the middle of the room, except that the room underneath, where excreta was collected for fertilizer, was a giddy three stories down instead of the customary one.

The room the Raja met visitors in had a linoleum floor, a striped linen ceding, and carved wood furniture mixed with folding metal chairs. A cabinet to the side displayed rows of china and thermos flasks. On the mud benches on the other side sat a row of stately Bista men, Rabindra and Gyaltsen among them. Both men smiled at us in acknowledgment, but they didn't break rank to talk to us. The Raja and Rani sat across from their relatives.

The Raja was a graceful, stout man with unhurried movements and carefully chosen words. He wore a beige jacket over a woolen sweater. His legs were covered by a woolen blanket. He talked to us in Tibetan and let his secretary, a Thakali man dressed in spotless Western clothes, translate for him. Sometimes the Raja spoke a breathy, broken word or two in Nepali. The Rani, a frail-looking woman with watchful eyes, knitted in demure silence.

During our conversation about electricity and *gomba* repair, a relative taking leave from town placed a *khata* on a table beside the Raja. Then he took out a ten-rupee note from his *chuba* and placed it beside the *khata*. He poured butter tea from a flask into the Raja's silver tea bowl. The Raja lifted the bowl and sipped from it without so much as a glance at the man. When he returned the bowl to its stand, the relative filled the cup again. He moved toward the Rani and repeated the same gesture. Then he walked backward out of the room, scratching his head in reverence.

The Raja's informal authority extended to only a few villages other than Lo Monthang, but even that was shrinking. With more and more people exposed to the Nepali government's regulations, and to leftist and populist rhetoric from the political parties, quite a few traditional customs were becoming anomalous. One such custom required villagers to harvest the Raja's crops before their own.

I found out later, from Dolma, that only relatives and those with a vested interest in expressing servitude observed the elaborate protocol followed by the man we had seen. The electrical powerhouse operator of Chhonhup, for instance, also offered a *khata* and money when he arrived to talk about the plant. His job depended on the Raja's goodwill.

When other Lobas had an audience with the Raja they listened silently, scratched their head in humility, and occasionally assented with, "*Kanou, kanou.*"

And if they passed him on the streets of Lo Monthang? I asked Dolma. They didn't have to, but if they wanted to they could scratch their heads and smile at him and respond politely if he addressed them.

"Don't you have to stick your tongue out?"

Dolma looked at me with wide, shocked eyes. "Nowadays only villagers do that," she said gravely. "Those of us from the city just scratch our heads."

If you weren't a Loba, you could do anything; the hierarchy observed by insiders wasn't expected of others. For Rongba like us, a "*Namaste,*" and the superlative form of address, "*Hajoor,*" sufficed.

∽

The walled city of Lo Monthang had three *gomba*: Thugchen, Jamba, and Chhoedhe. Of these, only Chhoedhe had a monastic community, and it belonged entirely to the village's monks. Thugchen and Jamba Lakhang were built by the Raja's ancestors, and they were jointly cared for by monks and laypersons. Keys to these *gomba* rotated from one family to another. For the duration of a month, the family with the keys looked after the *gomba*, secured butter to keep the lamps lit, and opened the door for worshippers.

Because of the poverty of the caretakers, the *gomba* had fallen into dismal, irrevocable disrepair. Moisture and water leaks from the ceiling and walls had destroyed many wall paintings and much of the woodwork on the ceilings. The community undertook heartfelt but inadequate protective measures, like shoveling the snow off the roofs in the winter and cleaning the *gomba* grounds once a year. In Thugchen Lakhang, the villagers had added layers of mud to the ceiling to prevent snow leaks, but the weight of the new mud had bent the beams instead. So the villagers had moved the entire north wall by tearing it down first—and destroying its fresco of eight Buddhas in the process—and rebuilding it closer in. This had helped a little, but moisture seeped in through other walls and continued to wear away the remaining paintings.

Many years ago, the Gomba Repair Committee of the Remote Areas Development Department of the Ministry of Local Development had allocated some funds for the repair of Thugchen and Jamba Lakhang. The villagers spent that money on a few beams and posts from Jomosom which helped hold up the sagging ceilings.

ॐ

On our second trip, a festival was taking place at Thugchen Lakhang. In a mud clearing outside the *gomba*, monks stirred great vats of rice to feed all the worshippers—that is, the entire village. Inside, the immense, smoky interior of Thugchen rumbled with chanted prayers. Worshippers sat cross-legged on mats on the floor, dwarfed by the enormous pastel-shade Buddhas on the walls. Some worshippers swayed in prayer with their eyes closed and their hands clasped around prayer wheels. Others read from texts or prostrated themselves before the deities at the far end of the hall. A few distracted children eyed us as they mumbled prayers.

Tashi Dawa Bista, the village head for the year, sat with the other

Bistas at the base of the statue of Avalokitesvara, the Compassionate One, who towered above the room. The warm yellow light of scores of butter lamps flickered on his face.

"If you've come with good intentions," Tashi Dawa rasped after we made our introductions, "then I welcome you as family." He swayed drunkenly, and his eyes narrowed. "But if you've come with bad intentions I can even—kill you." His eyes shot open, his lips pursed, and his face puffed red.

We met him again later, and found out that he wasn't really as daunting as he liked to appear. On other days he was the bumbling village head, a man who prided his ability to paint, and who had a knack for strolling in front of my camera viewfinder. When he showed me sections of Thugchen Lakhang that needed repair, his creative side took over. "We could put glass on the skylight," he said. "We could repaint some of these Buddhas." He pointed at a wall that had been destroyed by water leaks. "And then we could paint the pillars red with shiny enamel paint that will last a long, long time."

♾

Jamba Lakhang, near Thugchen, had a narrow clay front washed in red earth, and it towered above the flat city houses. Originally, it had four stories: a dark underbelly passage in the bottom, a shrine in the middle, a room on top, and a balcony above. The villagers had walled up the door to the bottom to keep children out. Because I had the approval of the village to investigate repair needs, I was able to go in. The paintings on the walls were dusty and neglected. The floor was covered with rubble. The stairs to the top floor and balcony were broken. I went there using a ladder, and saw, on the top floor, amazingly intricate gold- and silver-touched frescoes. From the balcony I saw a central, breathtaking view of Lo Monthang's lush fields and I realized that Lo Monthang did live up to its name, "Plain of Aspiration."

The middle portion of Jamba Lakhang was in remarkable condition for being five centuries old. In the center of the gallery was a gleaming golden figure of Maitreya, the future Buddha, which towered two stories high. The figure dated back to the fourteenth century. In time, other forms showed up from the dark: rich red-and-green mandala on the wall, gold-speckled thangka, and carved woodwork on the ceiling.

Then, slowly, patches of wall washed away by water leaks, rotting wood on the ceiling, and broken deities and statuettes stashed in a corner.

࿇

During both my stays in Lo Monthang, monks were conducting prayers at one *gomba* or another, and almost the whole village participated. Every time I entered a *gomba* I saw worshippers.

One day, when I was examining the frescoes of Thugchen Lakhang, a young man burst into the hall and strode up to the base of the Avalokitesvara. He muttered something under his breath, then flung himself on the ground with such ardor I thought he might hurt himself. He remained prostrate for a long time. I looked away, suddenly embarrassed by my own stubborn atheism. I couldn't help looking over again. The man had stood up, folded his hands, and he was chanting. Then he flung himself down again, and stood up, and repeated this motion again and again.

Another day, in Thugchen Lakhang, Bikas and I found ourselves surrounded by a mass of teenage girls. They were all dressed identically in black *bukkhoos* and formal black shawls, with their hair done up in braids. Among them was one who was taller than the rest, who stood out because her dress was like a Chinese doll's, with an iridescent, puff-sleeved pink shirt and a billowing satin skirt. She wore coral on her ears and neck. Her hair was done in two buns at the back. She had white, milky skin, flashing black eyes, and rouged cheeks.

She moved toward us slowly and displayed none of the childish inquisitiveness of the other girls. Softly, but with authority, she asked us where we came from. She nodded at our reply and seemed to want to ask more, but she held back in dignity. Then she offered to take us to the *gomba* she was visiting next. "There's a prayer going on there," she said with a gracious smile. We declined politely. Her eyes lingered on us. But perhaps it would have been improper to say much more, she gathered the other girls and led them away. I found out later that she was the daughter of an important lama.

The deep religiosity of the entire community was apparent. When I spoke to the villagers about the possibility of repairing Thugchen and Jamba Lakhang, they all responded warmly. Even those youths whose leftist politics made them skeptical to outside intervention raised no voice of protest. "That will be dharma," one elderly man said, and the others murmured in agreement.

∽

The Chhoedhe Gomba was relatively new in comparison to Jamba and Thugchen Lakhang, particularly the recent additions to it, which included a festively ultra-modern hall called the Naya Gomba. The *gomba* was maintained by the sixty-odd monks of Lo Monthang, whose abbot was Khenpo Tashi Tenzing.

I went to see it on a whim while Bikas surveyed a possible site for a powerhouse. Some young monks showed me the new section of the *gomba*, which consisted of a breezy, well-lit hall with glass windows on the roof, machine-cut wood planks on the floor, and identical photocopy reproductions of the Buddha plastered all over the walls. At the altar, there were two paintings of terrible, dancing Herukas whose bodies flailed about and whose mouths twisted into hideous grins. One of these paintings was ancient and crumbling, with lush, deep colors. The other was a newer replica with bright, flat colors. A young monk pointed out his own broad, acrylic-paint strokes on the newer painting. "I also added these pictures of God," he said, and his face lit up with the pride of accomplishment. He pointed at two photocopies of the Buddha which were glued to the bottom of the painting.

The old section of the Chhoedhe Gomba remained intact, except for a few cracks in the richly colored wall paintings. Beyond the *gomba*, along the northwest corner of the walled city, were the monks' living quarters: handcrafted adobe huts with one room each, which the monks wanted to level and replace with an L-shaped structure, "like school buildings in the south."

∽

By the time I visited the Chhoedhe Gomba, word had gotten around that some Rongba woman was in Lo Monthang to give money for the repair of Thugchen and Jamba Lakhang. For that reason I was treated with an embarrassing amount of respect; after they showed me around, the monks insisted I have some tea.

The monks' mess was a smoky earthen room with an open roof.

Novice monks—little boys who pulled impatiently at their robes—kindled a fire at the hearth. Through the smoke, I saw some older monks on the mud benches across the room. They motioned for me to sit on the tallest bench. I hesitated because that seat was reserved for the most powerful. But they insisted, and when I still showed reluctance one monk almost pushed me down on the bench. The young monks who had guided me brought me a cup of butter tea and a cup of sweet tea, and plates full of biscuits and Chinese candy. I wished I could leave.

A pimply-faced monk with a flashy silver watch translated for the older monks, who had apparently been waiting to talk to me.

"We've got a *bikas*,"—tree plantations were called *bikas*, or development, because the idea was introduced by a foreign development agency—"and we've got fields down by the river. But what we have is hardly enough to feed us all. That's why Lama Tashi Tenzing must go to Tibet to hold prayers. They give him offerings of butter, which he brings back here. He's there right now on the invitation of a *gomba*."

The older monks smiled. One pushed the plate of biscuits toward me. Then he stood up and poured more butter tea into my cup. As soon as I sipped it he refilled the cup.

"Have the biscuits. They're Chinese," the young monk translated for him. "Drink your tea. It'll get cold. Why aren't you drinking your sugar tea? It's not as good as the tea down south, but please do have some."

∽

The day after I visited Chhoedhe Gomba, a revered Sakya Rinpoche, who was also the Rani's uncle, flew off to Kathmandu in a chartered helicopter paid for by some Japanese Buddhists in Kathmandu.

When the helicopter arrived in the morning, the entire village poured out of the city gate and watched it land in a cloud of dust on a plateau outside the walls. Its blades slowed down and the dust settled. The pilot stepped out in a glitter of dark glasses and neon windbreaker. The co-pilot had plainer clothes but he sported the same movie-star moustache. The local children stared at the men in awe and stole behind the helicopter to finger the sleek machine. Men, women, monks, and Rongba employees milled around, peeked inside the helicopter, and commented on the pilots. The neon pilot responded by striding to the edge of the plateau, where he lit an imported cigarette and took in the vista. The other, who agreed to take a message to my family in Kathmandu, spoke only English with me. Rabindra Bista and a schoolteacher asked me to take a snap of themselves in front of the helicopter. Gyaltsen crept up behind them and hammed a sporting smile.

From the Chhoedhe Gomba, there was a low blare of horns. Then a crowd of Bistas dressed in traditional and modern fineries came through the city gates. The old Sakya Rinpoche, dressed in orange robes and a ceremonial yellow hat, sat on top of a slow-moving horse. He dismounted near the helicopter, and the Raja escorted him to his seat. The Bistas crowded around the helicopter to offer the rinpoche *khata* and *chhurpi*—hard cheese—and colorful Chinese candy. Some people pushed and shoved to get near the Rinpoche while others chanted and prayed from afar.

Then the pilots stepped into the clear glass front of the helicopter. The doors closed, the blades swished, and the crowd scattered with laughter and shrieks. The neon pilot, smug and otherworldly with earphones clamped to his head, steered the helicopter away in a storm of dust.

~

Lo Monthang was like that: in the middle of hardship appeared a spark of stunning wealth; in the middle of tradition, change. The society was ruptured by objects and values from all over the world. I couldn't understand everything, but I could see the evidence of change. I read what I saw like a book in a language I only partially understood; I deciphered familiar signs in a jumble of others:

A woman wore glass bracelets like a Hindu woman. A trader wore a Swatch. A man wore a baseball cap with the English word "Friend" stitched on it. A woman weeding her buckwheat field heard I had visited Kaar Gomba in Marang, and presumed I was an infertile pilgrim. So she offered me her son for adoption. "Take, take," she said, pushing the toddler toward me. "You can bring him back when he's educated."

An eight-year-old girl from Tsarang walked alone half a day to fetch a letter.

When speaking Nepali, monks called themselves "lama," though in Tibetan a lama was not a monk, but a priest.

A young monk hesitated to walk with me outside the *gomba* grounds. "You know how it is," he said apologetically. "People talk."

A man said he believed in the Dalai Lama as a religious leader, though not as a king.

A boy said he had seen a cinema in Pokhara.

A woman blushed when I asked her about the custom of polyandry, in which one woman marries several men, usually brothers. She said it wasn't as prevalent as it used to be. "Nowadays our men all want a wife of their own."

Another woman, whose father had two wives, told me I should make speeches at every village telling women to be more assertive. She said, "I'd kill any man who has two wives."

There were six batteries on a window ledge.

Women in the fields hummed songs from Indian movies.

A young man mistook me for a foreigner and said hello to me with the overly virile lilt of an Indian film star.

In keeping with custom, the second sons of most families became monks and the second daughters, nuns. Other customs that were observed: the Kudak—now Bista—still married Tibetan nobility; travelers threw stones on top of cairns and shouted "*Lha gyal lo!*"; people paid up to eight hundred rupees to cap their teeth in gold.

An old man told us incorrectly that the two-story statue in Jamba Lakhang was made in Kathmandu.

A man from Chhosher said the displaced families in his village had asked the government to resettle them south of the Himalaya.

A man said he voted for the communist party because even a nomad in Tibet had more yaks than the Raja of Mustang.

A new school was built in the southern style, with stone for the walls and tin for the roof. The children inside recited Nepali poems by Bhanubhakta Acharya, a nineteenth-century Nepali poet credited for having founded Nepali poetry.

A girl named Chimi Dokka's Hindu name was Rajani.

Mustang's Raja's son was named Ashok Kumar, though his Bhotia name was Jigme Singi.

A woman said she earned forty thousand rupees each winter in India selling acrylic sweaters.

Two women stopped on their journey to Lo Monthang, pulled out packets of Rara Noodles from the folds of their shirt, and snacked on the pre-cooked noodles.

A lama wanted to use his battery-powered loudspeaker at the prayers, but it was broken.

Some women wore Chinese Army–issue shoes.

I saw, from these disjunctions, that the policy of restriction had not kept upper Mustang beyond the reach of the modern world. Instead it had forced people out. No new sources of income had entered the area, nor had traditional occupations found means to grow. The history-book economic cycle—of farming in the spring, tending to the animals in the summer, and trading in the winter—had remained the same for centuries; it had stagnated.

So seasonal migration, the only lucrative option left, had become more of a necessity than a choice. Almost every able-bodied person went south in the winter—either to the mid-hills of Nepal or to cities like Pokhara and Kathmandu, or to India, and some on to Hong Kong or Taiwan. In southern Nepal they sold *jimbu*, an herb used for cooking, and wool and Chinese consumer goods to Rongba. They also sold *little somethings*—trinkets and crafts—to tourists, and operated restaurants along well-traveled routes. In India, they bought and sold acrylic sweaters. Those who journeyed to the Far East traded in radios, televisions, kitchen appliances, ready-made clothes.

People had gone the way of money, and whether that Hinduized them or Westernized them or Nepalized them didn't matter much. Their exposure brought back into the restricted area fragments of the world: transistor radios, smokeless stoves, electricity, running shoes, windbreakers, and new languages—Nepali, Hindi, some English. And through these imports, even those who remained in Mustang all year long took leave of their impossible, traditional way of life.

I understood this impulse to venture out. This was the path all of Nepal took in the 1950s: the one leading out, to prosperity. This was the path my own family took, generations ago.

☙

Back at the lodge after the Sakya Rinpoche's departure, Dolma, Bikas, and I shared Chinese Army rations of preserved whole oranges that came from across the border in an unmarked aluminium can. Bikas had bought it for fifty-five rupees along with a twenty-rupee jar of Chinese Butterfly Cream.

"He's a very important lama," Dolma said, feeding her baby an orange. The girl was wrapped in a smart pink wool suit from Hong Kong. "I asked for his blessing. I don't know when I'll be in Kathmandu to see him again."

"Is he going to live there?" I asked.

Dolma said, "He spends most of his time in the Raja's *gomba* in Lumbini. I saw him there once. But from now on he'll stay at the Raja's *gomba* in Kathmandu. I don't know when I'll be there, though."

"Where will you be this winter?"

"Kalimpong. My older daughter's studying there. I want to visit her."

3

I went to the Nepal-Tibet border the second year with the friend from Kathmandu who had accompanied Bikas and me. A local man acted as our guide. We set out on horses at dawn so that we could return before late afternoon, when the rivers would be too high to cross.

Around Lo Monthang, on the same flat plain, were other peaks with ruins of fortresses that belonged to a time before Lo. West of the city was Namgyal, a nestled hillside with a large hilltop *gomba*. Beyond was Thingkar, where the Raja had his house and all his animals. Thingkar, along with Fuwa and Kimling, was electrified by a common scheme in Chhonhup. To the northeast was Chhoser, a settlement with a hillside dotted with caves that housed people, and a bed of rocks where the river had swept away the fields. The Nepali customs checkpost beyond, near Nhenyol, was a square building that stood alone on a plain, a timid reminder of government presence.

We forded the ice-cold Mustang River, rode beyond all the villages, and climbed up a steady slope. When we reached the top, the Tibetan plateau unfolded in front of us as a thin strip of land that extended over hundreds of miles to a mountain range on the low horizon. The domed sky was crisscrossed by white whirling clouds. A cold wind swept away our words. The Himalaya was visible to the distant south.

The border pillar no. 32 was a cement block with "Nepal" written in the Devanagari script on the Nepali side and Chinese characters on the Tibetan side. It stood absurdly alone in the middle of the wilderness. The Chinese checkpost—where, I had been told, Chinese border guards used diesel-generated electricity to watch TV on the largest television set in the world—was just a speck in the distance, as were the hundreds of yaks grazing on the scant grass of the plateau.

We rode around aimlessly. Every now and then we passed a black tent that belonged to *drogpa*, nomadic herdsmen. The one we made the mistake of approaching was guarded by two Tibetan mastiffs so fierce that they leapt and lunged toward us even though their front legs were strapped to their chest. Two girls—maybe of ten or twelve—peeked out of the tent and told our guide, in Tibetan, that their parents were with the yaks way over there—where those black dots moved.

We passed other *drogpa* who were walking through the plains. One man with a horse and a mastiff, another with five yaks. Three women, who had intricately looped and braided hair, were walking to their tents far away. None of them spoke Nepali, none looked a bit Nepali, but they were.

NOTES ON THE CONTRIBUTORS

BILL AITKEN is an Indian travel writer and mountain lover. His books include *The Nanda Devi Affair*, *The Seven Sacred Rivers*, *Divining the Deccan*, and *Exploring Indian Railways*. He lives in Mussoorie and Delhi.

DHARAMVIR BHARATI was a poet, author, playwright, social thinker, and one of the tallest figures in Hindi literature. His works include *Gunaho ka Devta*, *Andha Yug*, *Suraj ka Satwan Ghoda*, *Kanupriya*, and *Thele Par Himalaya*. He was chief editor of the popular Hindi magazine *Dharmayug* for close to three decades. Dharamvir Bharati received the Sangeet Natak Akademi Award in 1988 and the Padma Shri in 1972.

RUSKIN BOND is the author of numerous novellas, short-story collections, and non-fiction books, many of them classics and several of them set in the villages and towns of the Himalayan region. Among his books are *The Room on the Roof*, *A Flight of Pigeons*, *The Night Train at Deoli*, *Time Stops at Shamli*, *Rain in the Mountains*, *A Book of Simple Living*, and *Friends in Wild Places*. He received the Sahitya Akademi Award in 1993, the Padma Shri in 1999, and the Padma Bhushan in 2014. He lives in Landour, Mussoorie, with his extended family.

JIM CORBETT was an Anglo-Indian hunter and tracker-turned-conservationist, author, and naturalist. After giving up hunting, Corbett played a key role in protecting India's wildlife, especially the endangered

Bengal tiger, and used his influence in the provincial government to establish a national reserve for wildlife. In 1957, the reserve was renamed Jim Corbett National Park in his honor. His books, perennial bestsellers, include *Man-Eaters of Kumaon*, *The Man-Eating Leopard of Rudraprayag*, *Jungle Lore*, and *The Temple Tiger and More Man-Eaters of Kumaon*.

ALEISTER CROWLEY, poet, painter, novelist, mountaineer, ceremonial magician, occultist, and founder of the philosophy and religion of Thelema, was author of several books, including *The Book of Lies*, *Clouds without Water*, *The Confessions of Aleister Crowley: An Autohagiography*, and *Diary of a Drug Fiend*.

SARAT CHANDRA DAS went on two clandestine explorations of Tibet in 1879 and 1881 at a time when the country was out of bounds to outsiders. He returned with numerous Sanskrit and Tibetan texts, based on which he became a formidable scholar on the country and its religion and culture. In 1884 he returned to Tibet as a spy for the British.

FA-HIEN, a Chinese Buddhist monk, traveled from China to India, Sri Lanka, and back between 399 and 412 C.E. His travels have been chronicled in the *Travels of Fa-Hsien, or, Record of the Buddhistic Kingdoms*, translated by the scholar H. A. Giles and published in 1923.

AMITAV GHOSH was born in Calcutta and grew up in India, Bangladesh, and Sri Lanka. He is the author of *The Circle of Reason*, *The Shadow Lines*, *In an Antique Land*, *Dancing in Cambodia*, *The Calcutta Chromosome*, *The Glass Palace*, *The Hungry Tide* and *The Ibis Trilogy* (*Sea of Poppies*, *River of Smoke*, and *Flood of Fire*).

His books have received wide commercial and critical acclaim and many awards, including the Sahitya Akademi Award, the Ananda Puraskar, the Arthur C. Clarke Award, and the International e-Book Award at the Frankfurt Book Fair. *Sea of Poppies* was shortlisted for the Man Booker Prize in 2008 and was awarded the Crossword Book Prize and the India Plaza Golden Quill Award.

In January 2007 Ghosh was awarded the Padma Shri, one of India's highest honors, by the president of India. In 2010, he was awarded honorary doctorates by Queens College in New York and the Sorbonne in Paris. Along with Margaret Atwood, he was also a joint winner of a Dan David Award for 2010. In 2011 he was awarded the International Grand Prix of the Blue Metropolis Festival in Montreal.

ANDREW HARVEY is the founding director of the Institute of Sacred Activism, an international organization focused on inviting concerned people to take up the challenge of our contemporary global crises by becoming inspired, effective, and practical agents of institutional and systemic change, in order to create peace and sustainability. Some of his best-known works include *The Way of Passion*, *The Celebration of Rumi*, and *Perfume of the Desert*.

SVEN HEDIN, geographer, explorer, photographer, and travel writer, was instrumental in making the Trans-Himalayan region known to the West. He also located the sources of the Indus, Sutlej, and Brahmaputra rivers.

EDMUND HILLARY was born in New Zealand, and served in the New Zealand Air Force in the Second World War. He was a participant in the 1951 and 1952 Everest expeditions, and on May 29, 1953, he and Tenzing Norgay became the first men to reach the summit of Mount Everest. After being knighted following the ascent, he achieved many more adventuring firsts in surroundings as varied as the Antarctic and the Ganges. He established the Himalayan Trust, an organization devoted to improving the lives of the Himalayan people, which has built schools, hospitals, and infrastructure for the isolated mountain communities.

JAHANGIR was the fourth emperor of the Mughal Empire who reigned from 1605 to 1627. His life and times are recorded in the *Tuzuk-i-Jahangiri*, known more popularly as the *Jahangirnama*.

JINASENA was a Digambara Acharya in the eighth century. He is credited with writing several seminal texts of the Jain faith, including the *Harivamsa Purana* and the *Mahapurana*.

HRIDAYESH JOSHI is Senior Editor, National Affairs, with NDTV India. He was one of the first journalists to report on the calamity in Uttarakhand. He reports often on natural disasters and environmental issues and has also extensively covered war-torn Bastar in Chhattisgarh.

VICKI MACKENZIE is an author and journalist. After a long stint at various newspapers, in 1976, her focus shifted to Buddhist philosophy and to finding ways to make it accessible to the wider world. Her books include *Reborn in the West: The Reincarnation Masters, Why Buddhism?: Westerners in Search of Wisdom*, and *Reincarnation: The Boy Lama*.

PETER MATTHIESSEN is the author of more than thirty books and the only writer to win the National Book Award for both non-fiction (*The Snow Leopard*, in two categories, in 1979 and 1980) and fiction (*Shadow Country*, in 2008). Matthiessen was also a co-founder of *The Paris Review* and a world-renowned naturalist, explorer, and activist.

DOM MORAES was one of the foundational figures of modern Anglophone poetry in India. His first book of poems, *A Beginning*, was published when he was nineteen; it won him the prestigious Hawthornden Prize. He published ten more collections of poems over a period of nearly five decades, including the highly praised volumes *John Nobody* and *Serendip*, and culminating in the posthumous *Collected Poems 1954–2004*.

KIRIN NARAYAN is a professor in the School of Culture, History, and Language at the ANU College of Asia and the Pacific. Her books include *Storytellers, Saints and Scoundrels: Folk Narrative in Hindu Religious Teaching*; a novel, *Love, Stars, and All That*; *My Family and Other Saints*; and *Alive in the Writing: Crafting Ethnography in the Company of Chekhov*. Since 2001, Narayan has served as an editor for the Contemporary Ethnography series published by the University of Pennsylvania Press. She currently serves on the Committee of Selection for the John Simon Guggenheim Memorial Foundation.

JAWAHARLAL NEHRU was born in Allahabad and educated in England. He played a central role in India's independence movement and was the first prime minister of the country, holding office for seventeen years. A world statesman and leader, Nehru was one of the most important visionaries of modern India. His best-known works are *An Autobiography*, *Glimpses of World History*, and *The Discovery of India*.

ABDUL WAHID RADHU was born into a prominent Muslim merchant family in Ladakh that subscribed to the Sufi Chishti order. He studied in Srinagar and at the Aligarh Muslim University. He later joined the family business, traveling between Srinagar, Kalimpong, and Lhasa.

RAHUL SANKRITYAYAN, a lifelong traveler and writer, visited many cities all over India and the world. A polymath and a polyglot, Sankrityayan is the author of multiple volumes, including *Volga se Ganga Tak*, *Kinnar Desh Mein*, *Tibbat Mein Sava Varsha*, and *Asia Ke Durgam Bhukhandon Mein*.

JEMIMA DIKI SHERPA is a freelance writer and community organizer. She is originally from the Thame Valley in Solukhumbu, Nepal.

FRANK S. SMYTHE was a British mountaineer, botanist, and adventurer. In 1936, Smythe led the expedition which successfully ascended Mount Kamet, then the highest peak ever to have been climbed. Subsequently, in the 1930s, Smythe was thrice part of teams which attempted to climb Mount Everest. An accomplished photographer and a prolific writer, Smythe wrote twenty-seven books in all, the best known among which are *The Kangchenjunga Adventure*, *Kamet Conquered*, and *Adventures of a Mountaineer*.

ARUNDHATHI SUBRAMANIAM is a poet and a seeker—though not always in that order. She has worked over the years as critic, poetry editor and curator. She is the author of four books of poetry, most recently *When God Is a Traveler*. Her prose works include the bestselling biography of a contemporary mystic and yogi, *Sadhguru: More Than a Life*, as well as *The Book of Buddha*. As editor, her books include *Pilgrim's India*, a book on sacred journeys; *Another Country*, an anthology of contemporary Indian poetry in English; and *Confronting Love*, a co-edited volume of Indian love poems.

RABINDRANATH TAGORE, Gurudev, was a polymath who changed the contours of Bengali literature, art, and music, and reshaped them all in a mold distinctly his own. Among his greatest works are the collections of poetry *Gitanjali* and *Sonar Tari*; *Raktakaravi*, a drama; the novels *Ghare Baire* and *Gora*; and his memoir, *Jivansmriti*.

MANJUSHREE THAPA is the author of three novels, *All of Us in Our Own Lives*, *Seasons of Flight*, and *The Tutor of History*; a collection of short stories, *Tilled Earth*; and three books of non-fiction, *A Boy from Siklis: The Life and Times of Chandra Gurung, Forget Kathmandu: An Elegy for Democracy*, and *Mustang Bhot in Fragments*. She has also compiled and translated *The Country Is Yours*, a collection of stories and poems by forty-nine Nepali writers.

MARK TWAIN, hailed by William Faulkner as the "father of American literature," is one of the most celebrated humorists of all time. His books include the timeless classics *The Adventures of Tom Sawyer, The Adventures of Huckleberry Finn*, and *A Connecticut Yankee in King Arthur's Court*.

VIVEKANANDA was a monk, a mystic, and a disciple of Ramakrishna Paramhansa. Credited with introducing the philosophies of Vedanta and Yoga to the Western world, Vivekananda was a key figure in raising interfaith awareness and in establishing Hinduism as a major world religion. Vivekananda also founded the Ramakrishna Math and the Ramakrishna Mission.

ANIL YADAV is a peripatetic author and journalist. His books include a collection of short stories—*Nagar Vadhuyen Akhbar Nahi Padhtin*—and the acclaimed travelogue *Woh Bhi Koi Des Hai Maharaj!*

FRANCIS YOUNGHUSBAND was an officer of the British Army, an explorer, and a writer. In 1903–1904 he led the British invasion of Tibet. After experiencing an epiphany on the retreat from Tibet, Younghusband turned to spirituality. His works include *The Heart of a Continent, The Gleam, The Epic of Mount Everest*, and *Life in the Stars*.

COPYRIGHT ACKNOWLEDGMENTS

The publishers thank the following for permission to reprint copyright material:

Peter Hillary and the Hillary family (www.edhillary.com) for "The Summit"; Anil Yadav for "To Namdapha and Tawang"; Arundhathi Subramaniam for "Just a Strand in Shiva's Hair: Face-to-Face with the Axis of the World"; the Random House Group for "In Search of the Snow Leopard" from *The Snow Leopard* by Peter Matthiessen, published by Chatto & Windus; Andrew Harvey for "Ladakh Sojourn"; Bloomsbury Publishing Plc for "A Mountain Retreat" from *Cave in the Snow: A Western Woman's Quest for Enlightenment*, © Vicki Mackenzie, 1998; Ruskin Bond for "Mountains in My Blood" and "A Night in a Garhwal Village"; Jemima Diki Sherpa for "Three Springs"; Kirin Narayan for "White Bearers: Views of the Dhauladhar"; Siddiq Wahid for "The Lopchak Caravan to Lhasa"; Permanent Black for "Dev Bhumi" from *Footloose in the Himalaya*, © Bill Aitken, 2003; Amitav Ghosh for "They Make a Desolation and Call It Peace"; Penguin Books India for "The Wrath of the Mandakini" from *Rage of the River: The Untold Story of the Kedarnath Disaster*, © Hridayesh Joshi, 2016; Sarayu Ahuja for "Tibetans from Peking" from *Gone Away: An Indian Journal*, © Dom Moraes; and Manjushree Thapa for "Gyaltsen Has a Video."